Indiana Barn Quilt
Coloring Book One
John H. Lettau

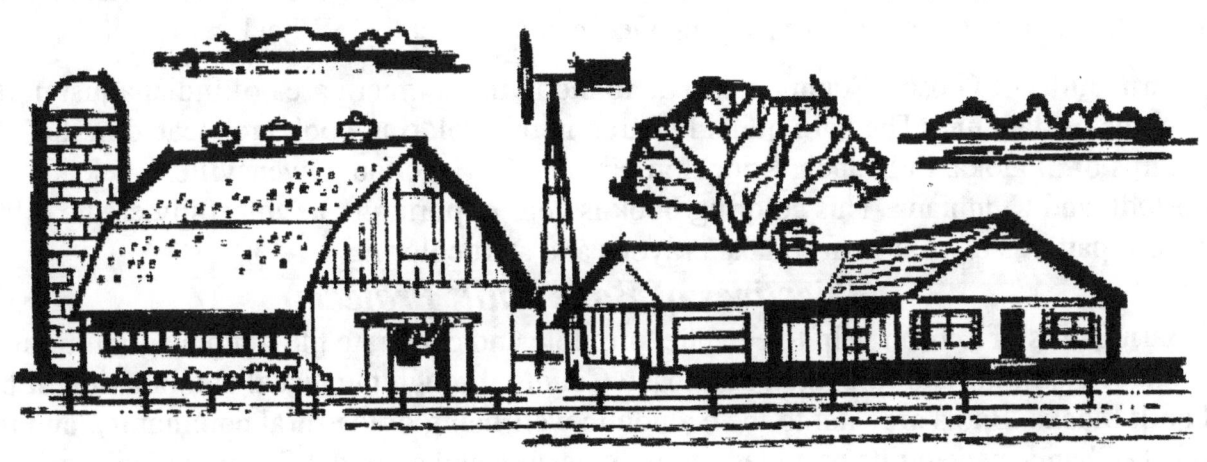

Barn Quilts of Gibson County, Indiana

Cover Barn Quilts

Wheel of Fortune
Star Burst
Bob's Pinwheel
Summer Dayz

Gibson County Indiana Barn Quilt Coloring Book One

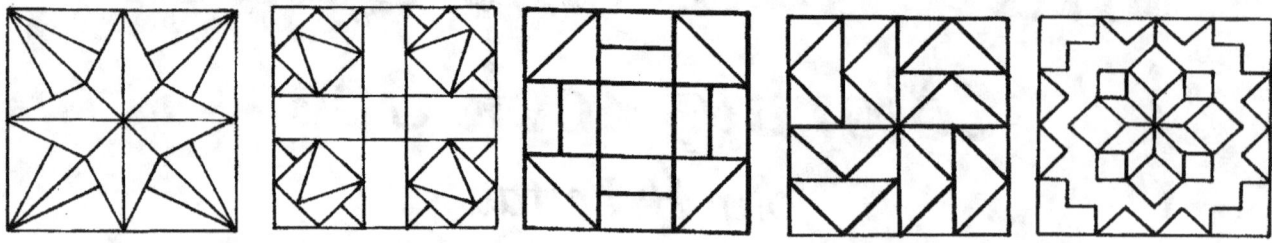

A drive through Gibson County, Indiana is very colorful today because many brilliant "quilt blocks," called barn quilts, are displayed on barns and other buildings throughout the rural area. Five sample barns quilt patterns located in Gibson County are pictured above...Excited Star, Ladies Choice, Lincoln's Platform, Flying Geese and Carpenter's Wheel.

The Barn Quilts of Gibson County are to be found in the southern area of Indiana just north of the Kentucky state line. The barn quilts featured in this coloring book are located in the townships of...Patoka, Ft Branch, Princeton, Francisco, Hazelton, Owensville, Buckskin, Haubstadt, and Cynthiana. This coloring book is your opportunity to colorfully create different barn quilt patterns of your own so take crayons and start coloring.

Objectives of Barn Quilt Projects

The Barn Quilts of Gibson help to educate, promote and celebrate the unique agricultural heritage of the farms and rural area of Gibson County through the visual combination of barns and quilt blocks. Barns are vital to the economic well-being of the rural community, and the comfort of hand-made quilts provided warmth, beauty, and an outlet for individual artistic expression.

Making a barn quilt allows individuals and volunteer groups the opportunity to create and paint their own quilt block, The design that is chosen may represent a family patterrn from a loved family quilt or perhaps a new pattern meaningful to the individual creator(s).

What is a Barn Quilt?

A barn quilt is made by painting a barn quilt pattern on two 4' by 8' sheets of ¾ inch plywood then mounting them on barn to form an eight foot square. Two coats of primer are applied to both sides of the boards and the edges. After the pattern is drawn out Frog (painter's) tape is applied. Three coats of each color are applied, with each coat being allowed to dry overnight. After the quilt is finished, it is allowed to dry for at least two weeks before it is put upon a barn.

Barn Quilts of Gibson County Information

Gibson County Visitors & Tourism Bureau
702 West Broadway Princeton, Indiana 47670
888-390-5825   812-385-0999   Fax 812-385-0545
www.giboncounty.org

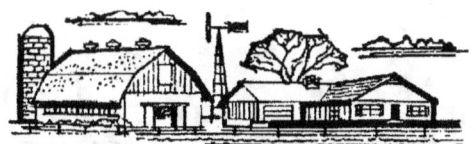

Barn Quilts of Gibson County Indiana Book One

Lincoln's Platform	E 390 N	Francisco
Variable Star	N 200 W	Patoka
Stepping Stones	N 650 E	Patoka
Sunny Paths	E Carithers Rd	Princeton
Union Square	W SR 65	Hazelton
Eight Point Star	N 275 W	Princeton
Spring Star	E 50 S	Princeton
Flying Geese	W SR 68	Haubstadt
Carpenter's Wheel	N 100 W	Princeton
Double Aster	S 150 E	Haubstadt
Star of Bethlehem	Lake Inwood Dr	Princeton
Beans & Corn	W Broadway	Princeton
Excited Star	E McRoberts Rd	Patoka
X-Block	S Church St	Ft. Branch
Dewey's Victory	S Hart St	Princeton
Clay's Choice	S Hudson Rd	Patoka
Jacob's Ladder	E 175 S	Francisco
Ladies' Choice	N Main St	Patoka
Granny Square	W 1000 S	Owensville
Weather Vane	S. W. Mill St	Patoka
Card Trick	W 525 S	Ft Branch
Air Castle	Bradley Dr	Haubstadt
Buttercup	S 450 W	Ownesville
Blazing Star	Tretter Park Dr	Ft. Branch
Country Farm	E 1025 S	Haubstadt
December Days	W 1000 S	Haubstadt
Gathering Stars	Brownlee Ave	Princeton
Cat Paw	W Gibson St	Haubstadt
Bisected Star	W Broadway	Princeton
Crossings	W Broadway	Princeton
Janie's Star	W Glendale	Princeton
Jacob's Ladder	N Main St	Owensville
Log Cabin	N 650 E	Francisco
Coffin Star	N 100 W	Princeton
Bear Paws	S US Hwy 41	Ft. Branch
Family Star	E Broadway	Princeton
Missouri Star	N Old Hwy 41	Princeton
Girl's Favorite	S 525 W	Owensville
Mexican Cross	N 275 W	Princeton
Mexican Star	N 575 E	Francisco
Crown of Thorns	S 100 W	Princeton
Wyoming Valley	N 100 W	Princeton
Mayflower	E 350 S	Princeton
Flying Geese	Spring St	Patoka
Flying Kite	W 225 N	Patoka
Patriotic Ohio Star	E 200 N	Princeton
Harvest Star	W 1000 S	Haubstadt
LeMoyne Star	S 350 W	Owensville

Barn Quilt Lincoln's Platform

Gibson County Indiana Barn Quilt

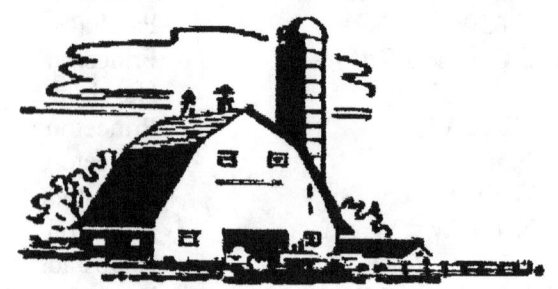

*Barn Location
E 390 N
Francisco, Indiana*

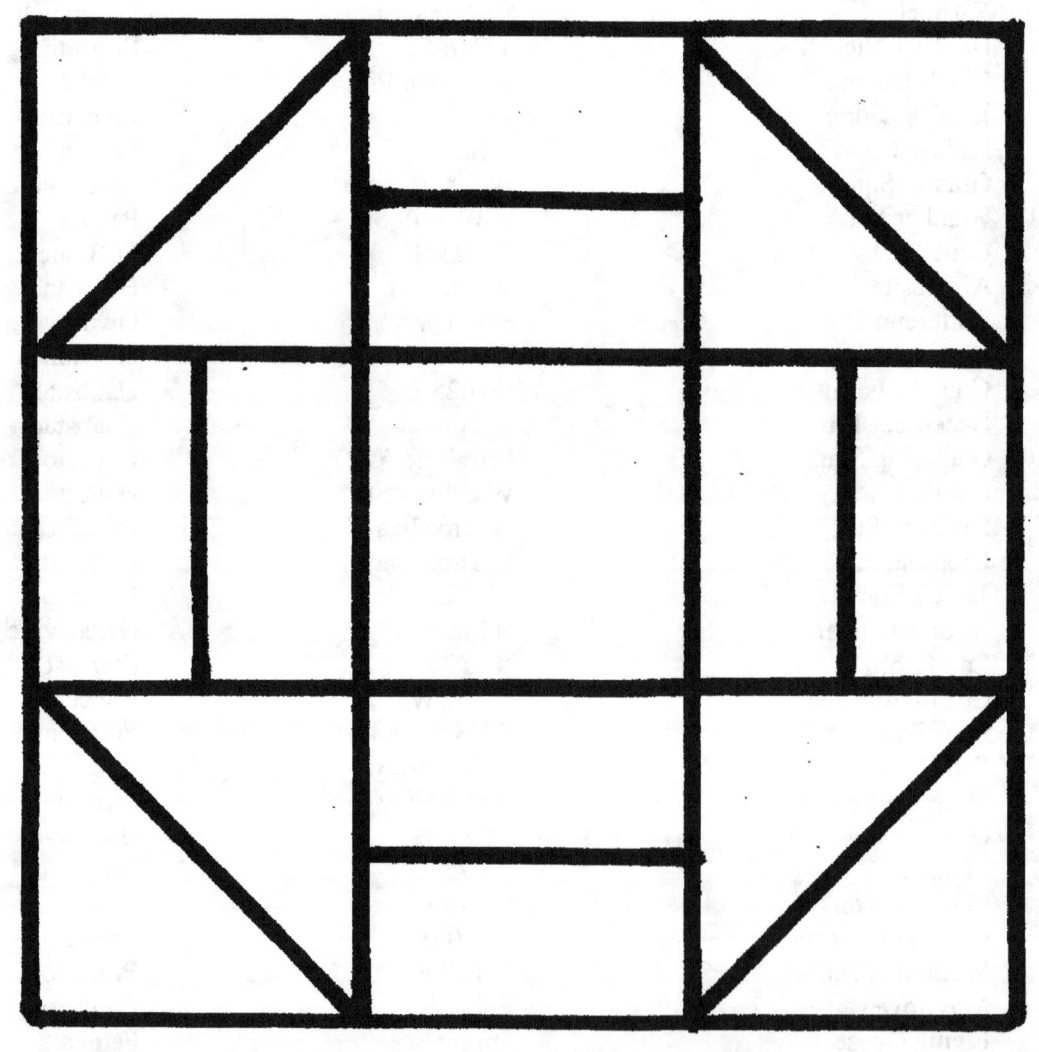

Gibson County Barn Quilt Lincoln's Platform

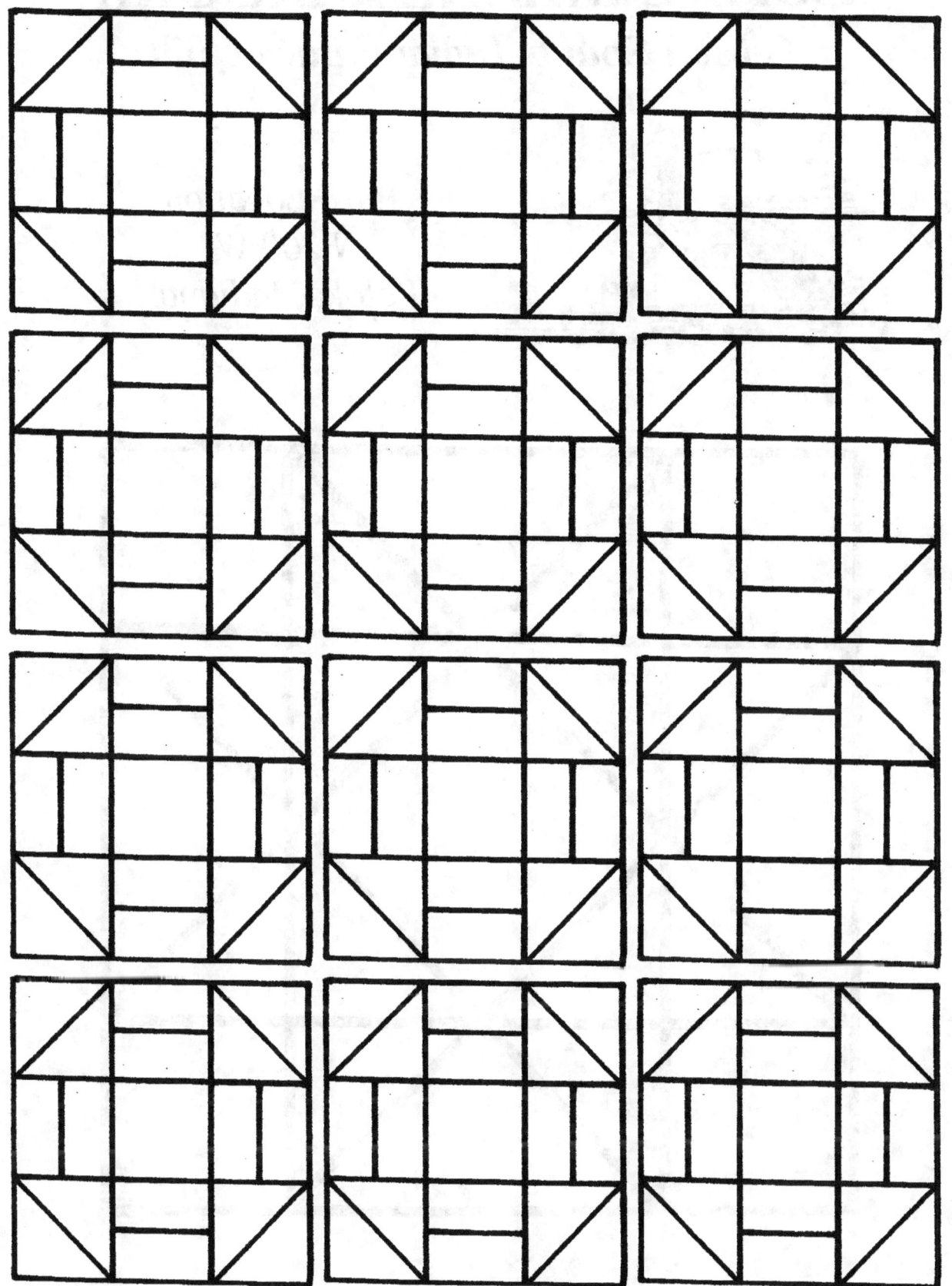

Barn Quilt Variable Star
Gibson County Indiana Barn Quilt

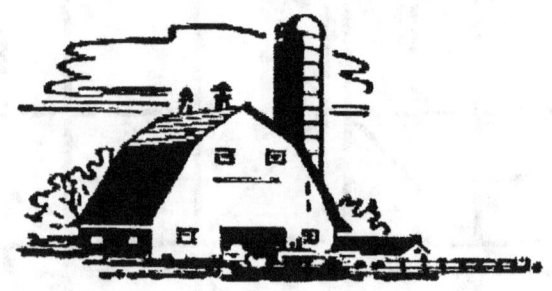

Barn Location
N 200 W
Patoka, Indiana

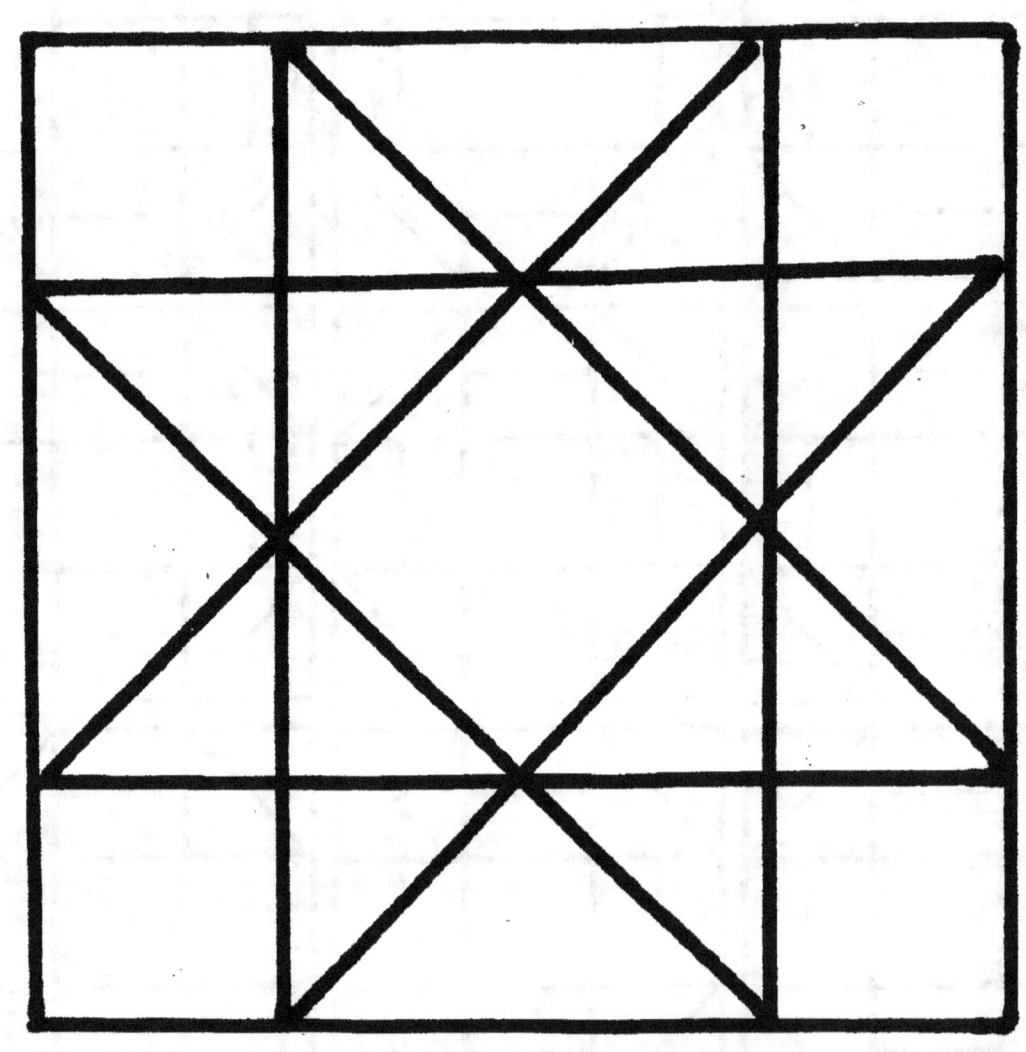

Gibson County Barn Quilt Variable Star

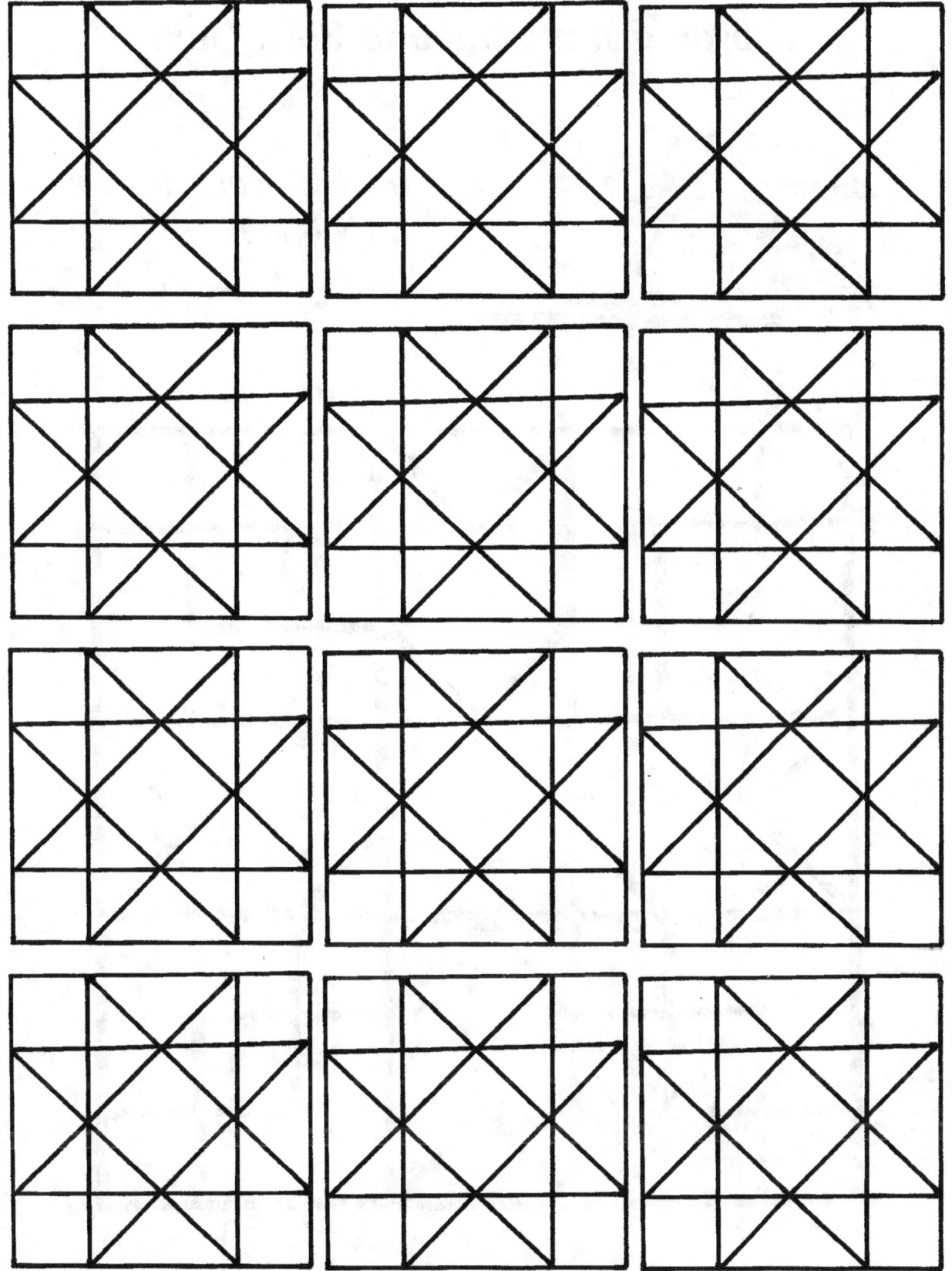

Barn Quilt Stepping Stones
Gibson County Indiana Barn Quilt

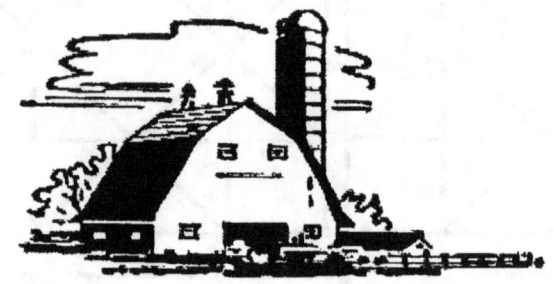

Barn Location
N 650 E
Patoka, Indiana

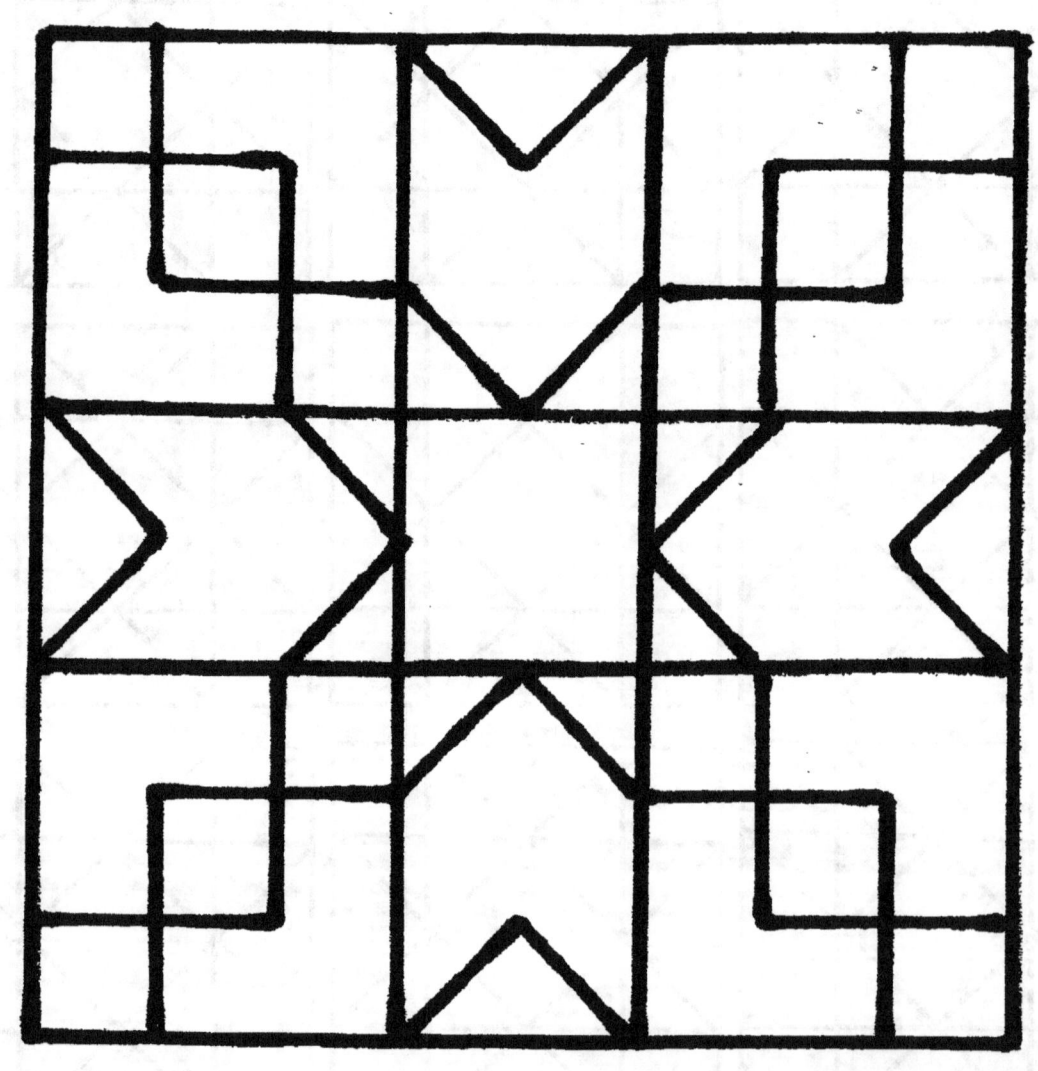

Gibson County Barn Quilt Stepping Stones

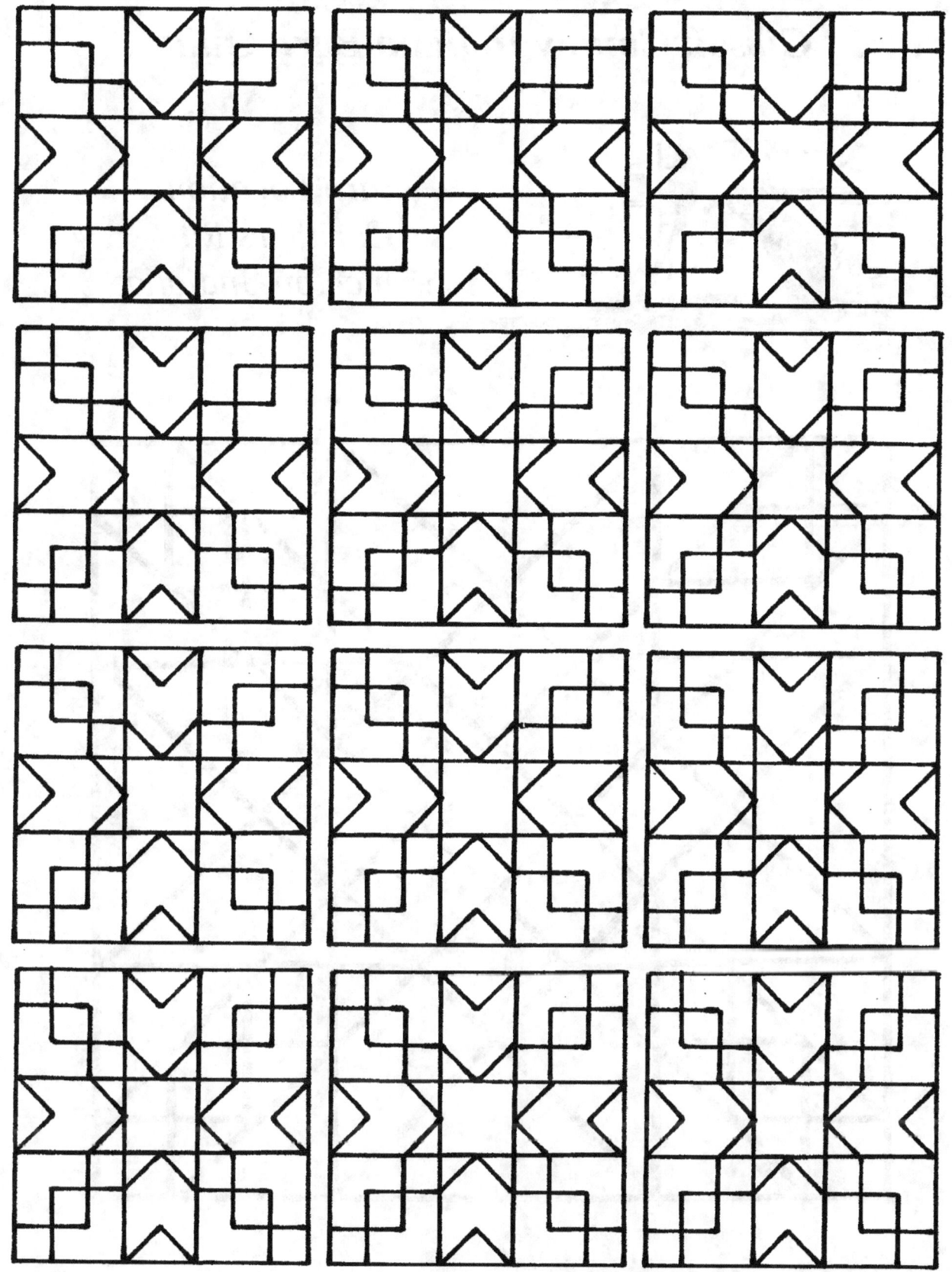

Barn Quilt Sunny Paths
Gibson County Indiana Barn Quilt

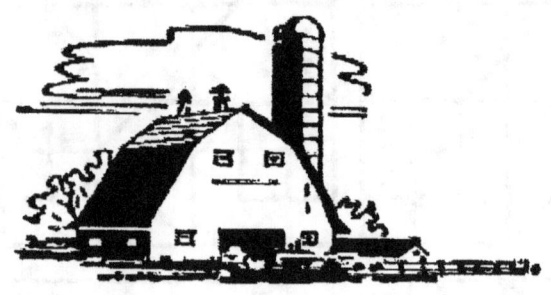

*Barn Location
Carithers Rd
Princeton, Indiana*

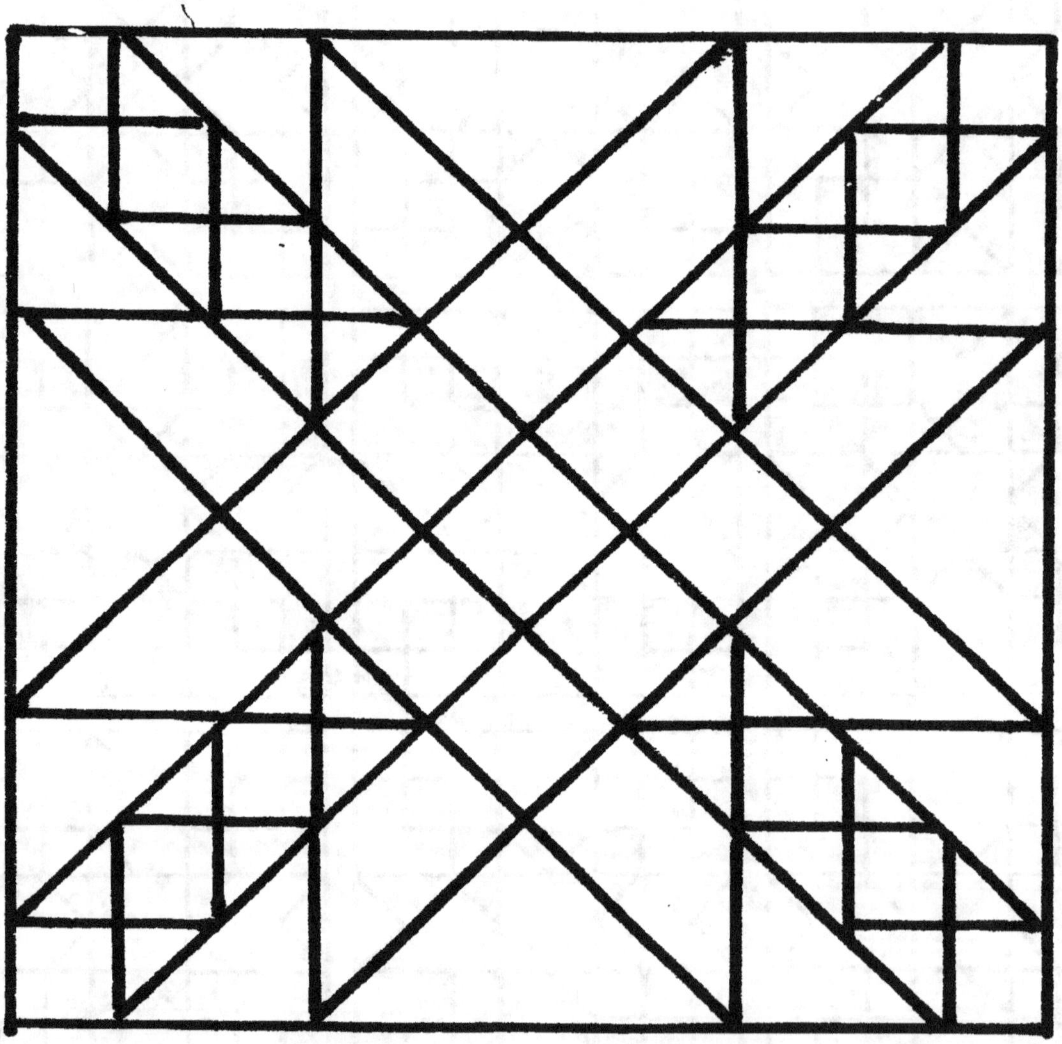

Gibson County Barn Quilt Sunny Paths

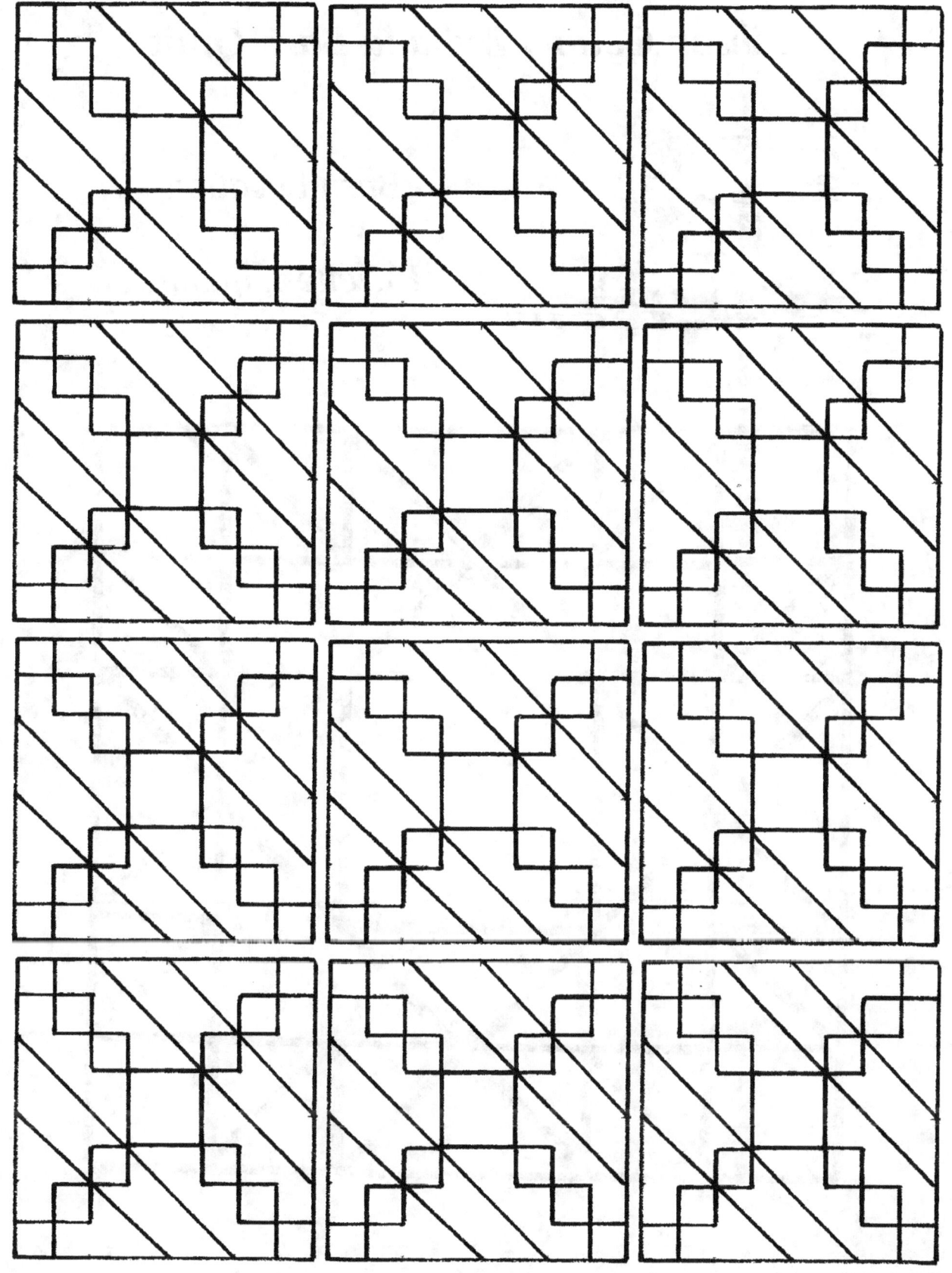

Barn Quilt Union Star

Gibson County Indiana Barn Quilt

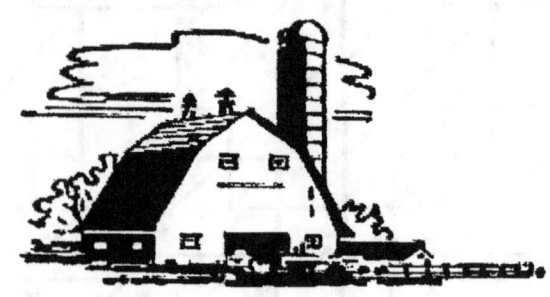

Barn Location
W SR 65
Hazelton, Indiana

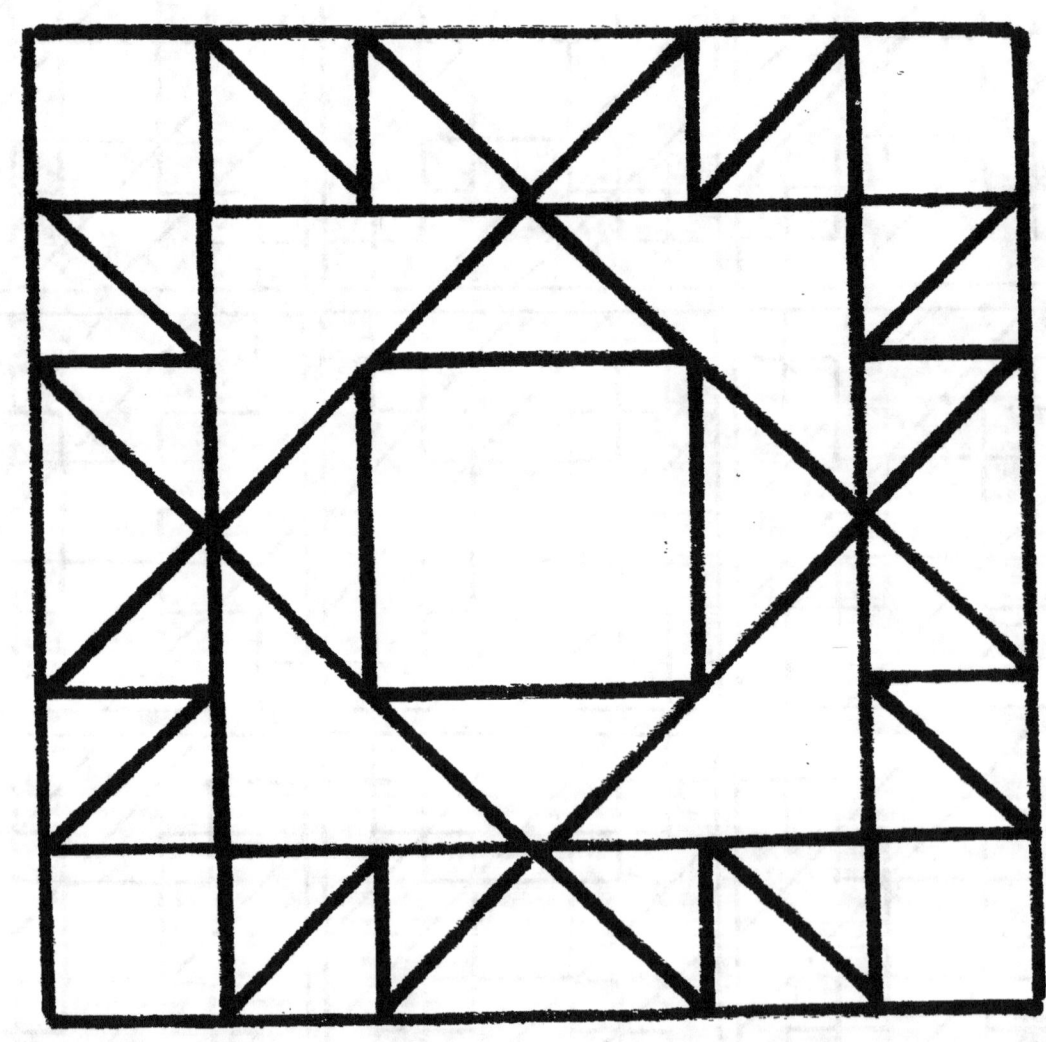

Gibson County Barn Quilt Union Star

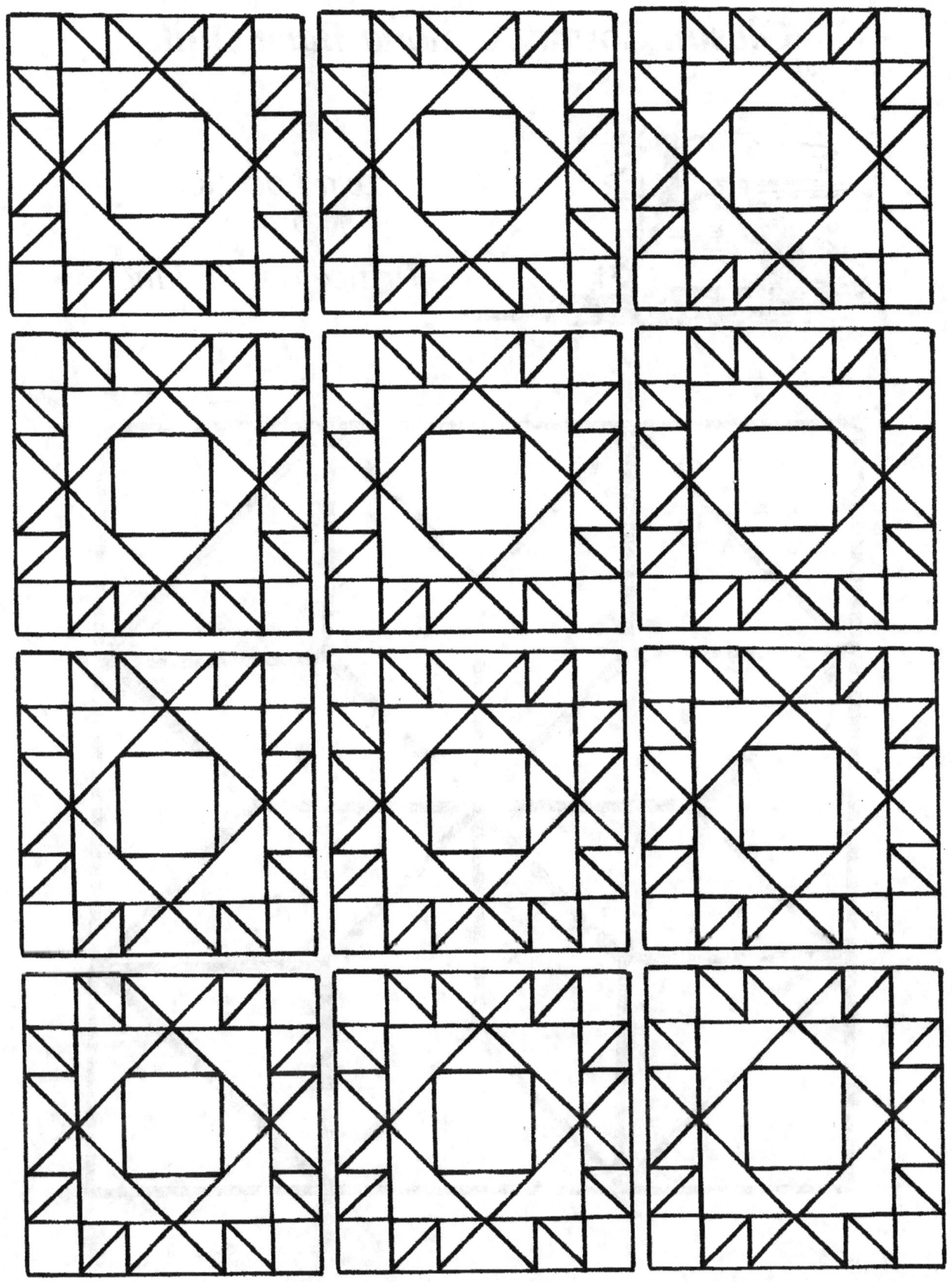

Barn Quilt Eight Point Star
Gibson County Indiana Barn Quilt

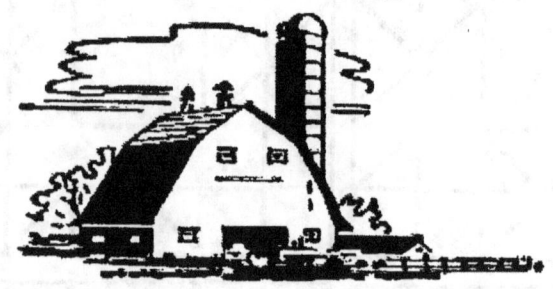

Barn Location
N 275
Princeton, Indiana

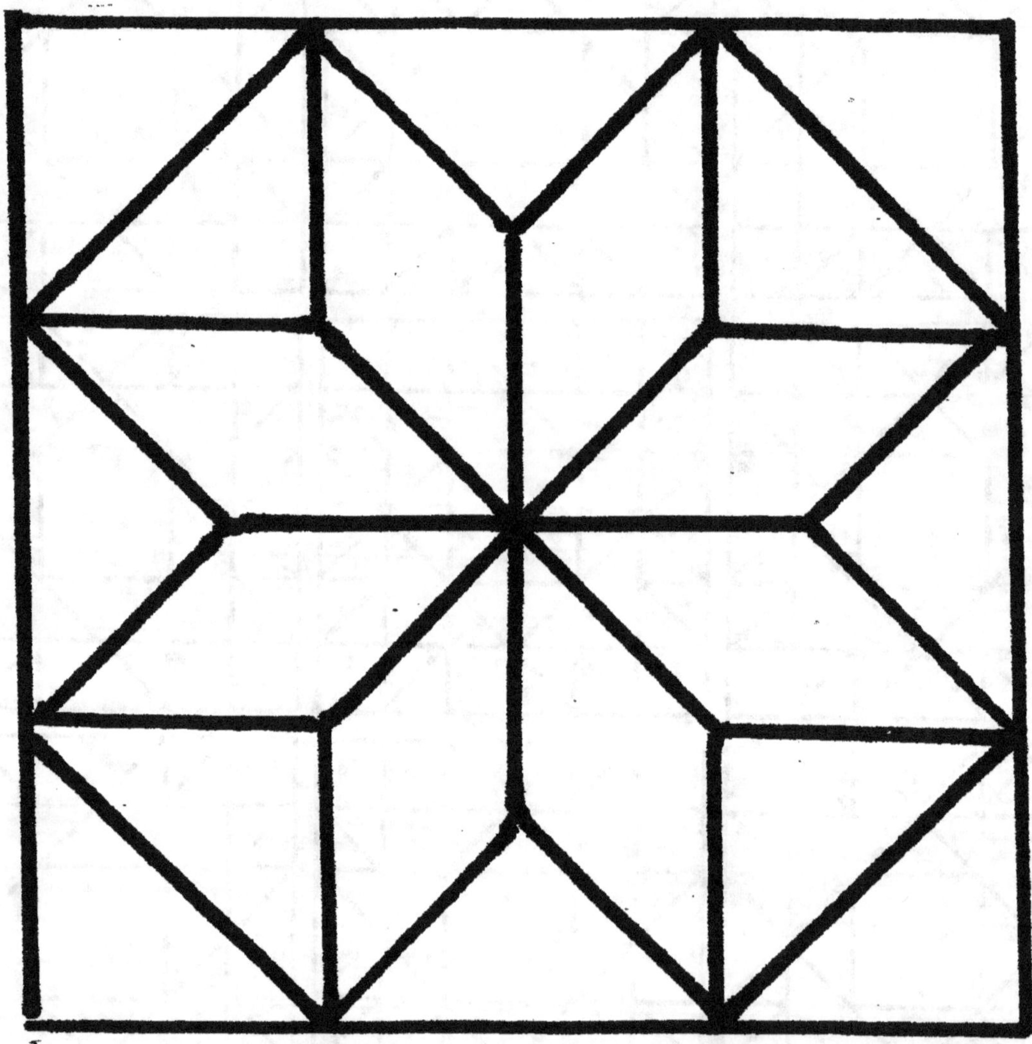

Gibson County Barn Quilt Eight Point Star

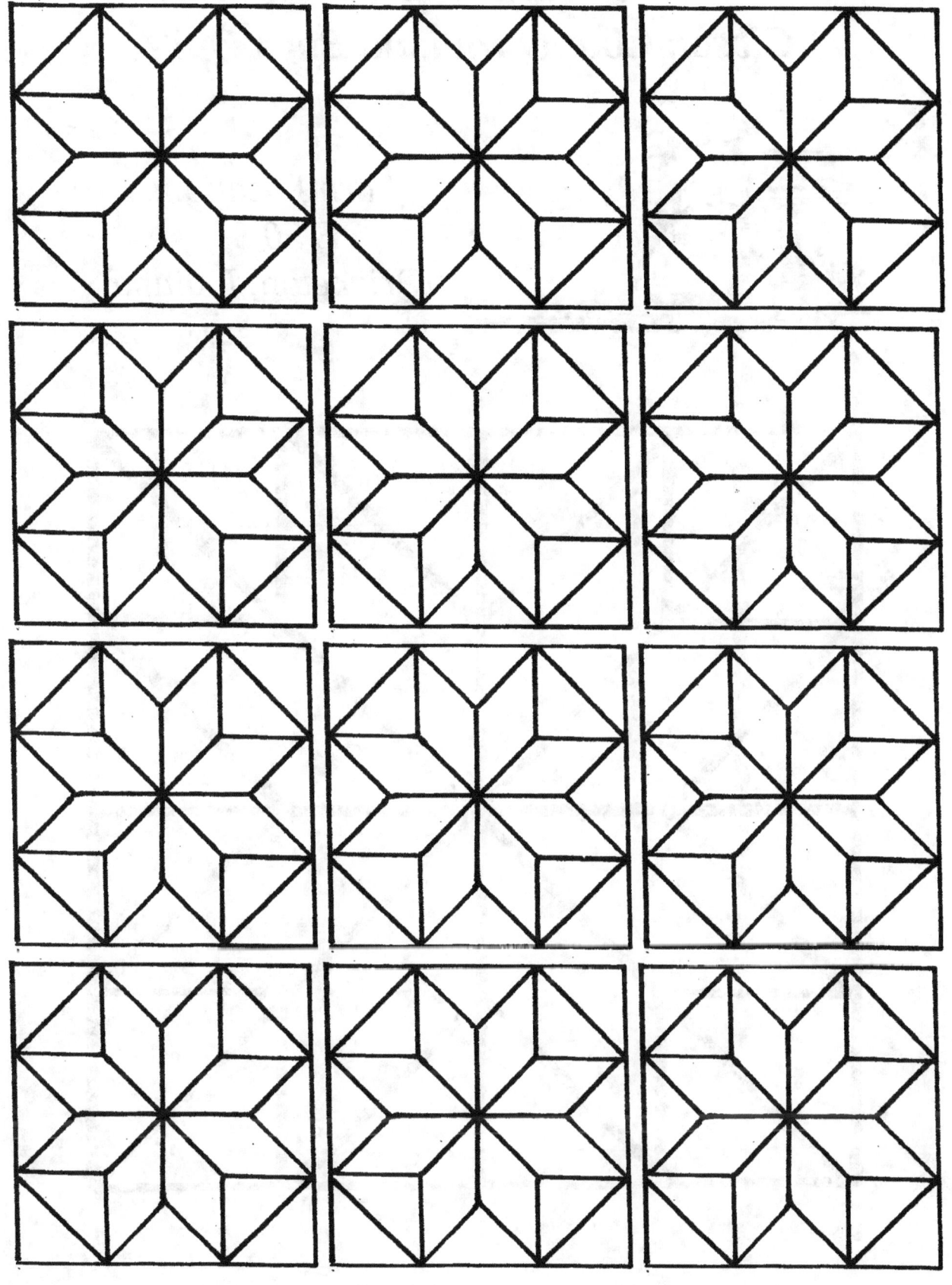

Barn Quilt Spring Star
Gibson County Indiana Barn Quilt

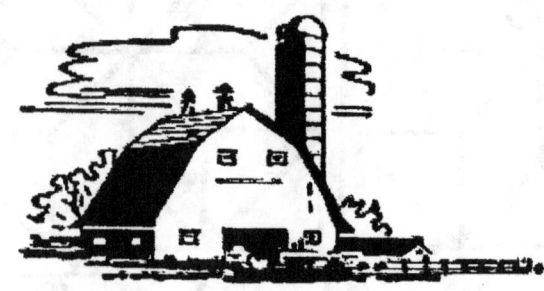

Barn Location
E 50 S
Princeton, Indiana

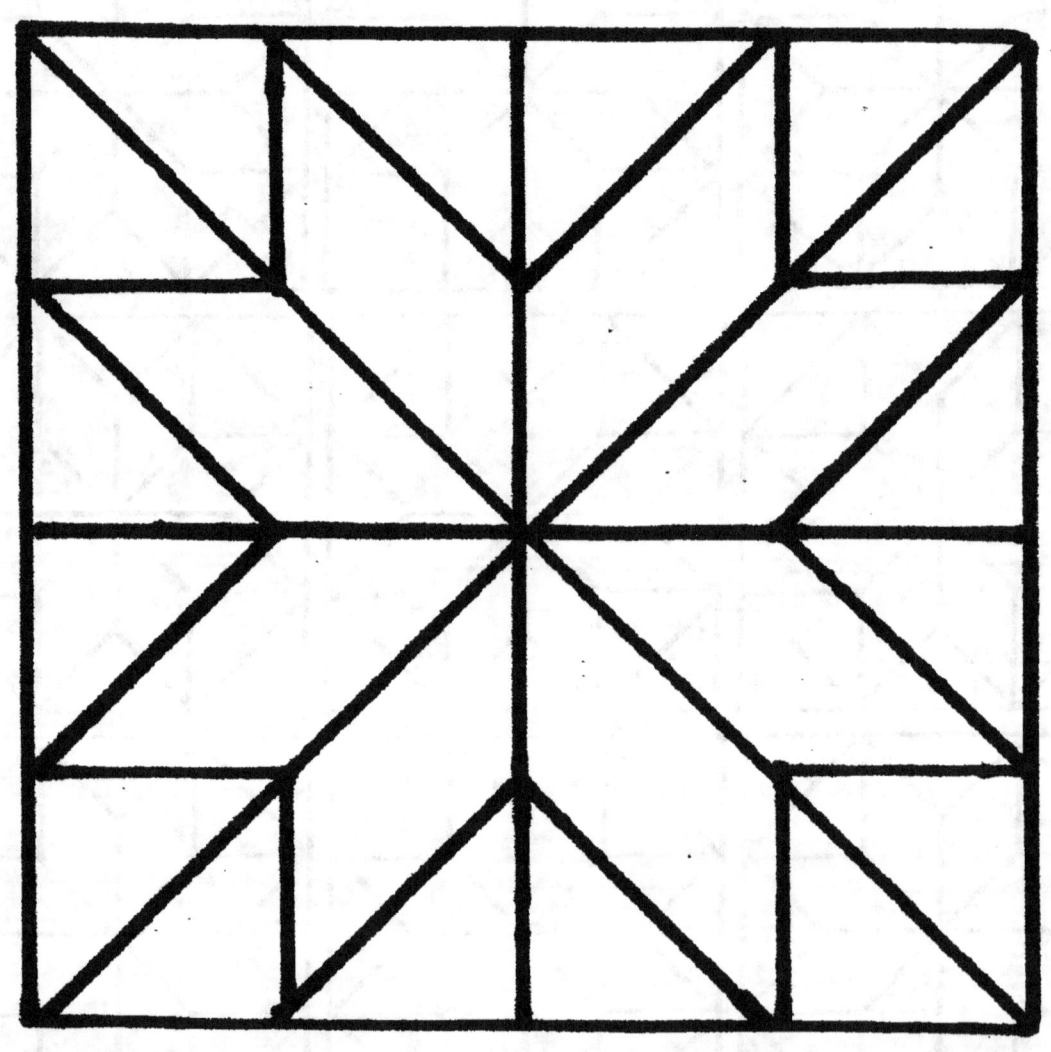

Gibson County Barn Quilt Spring Star

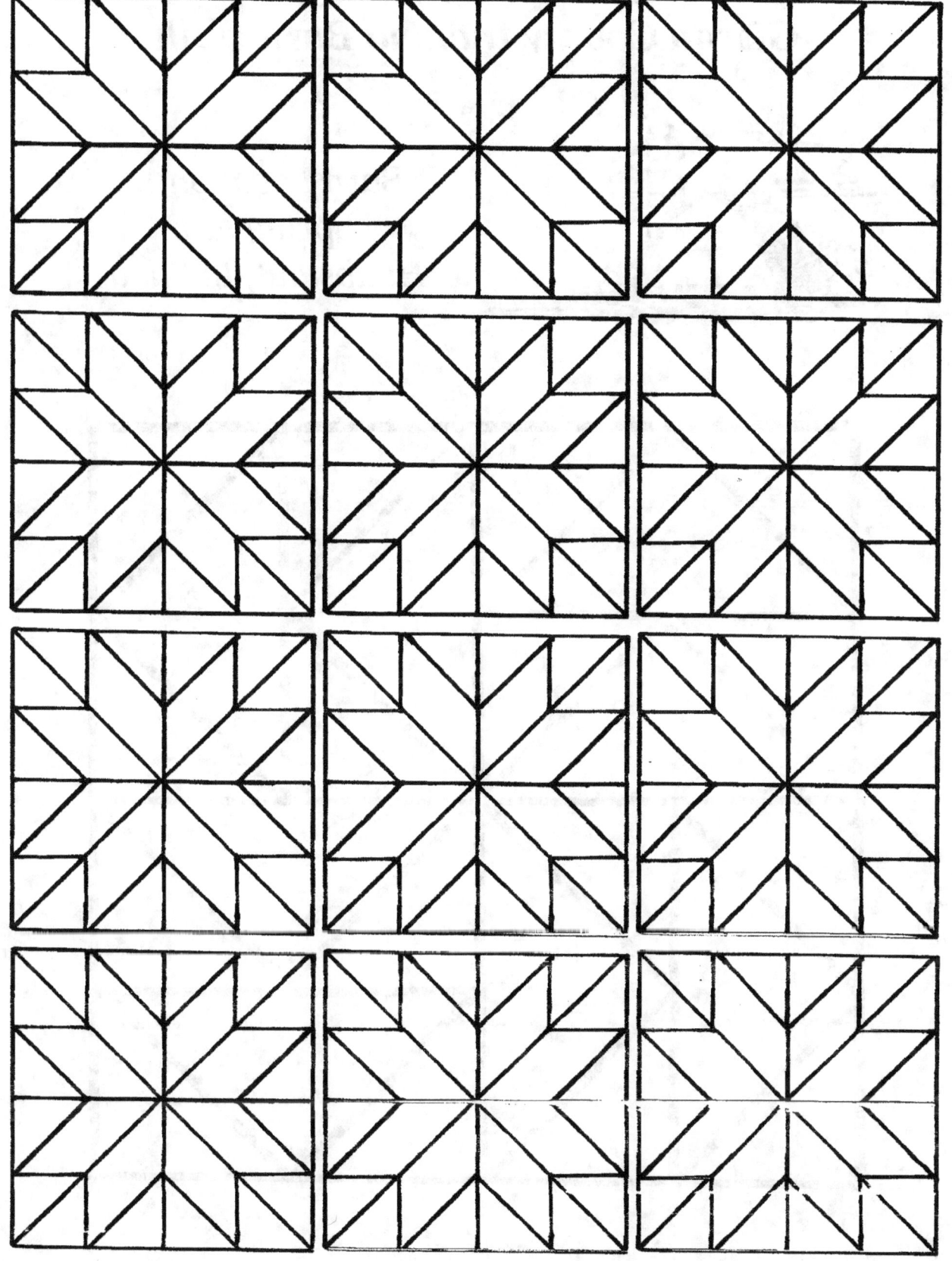

Barn Quilt Flying Geese
Gibson County Indiana Barn Quilt

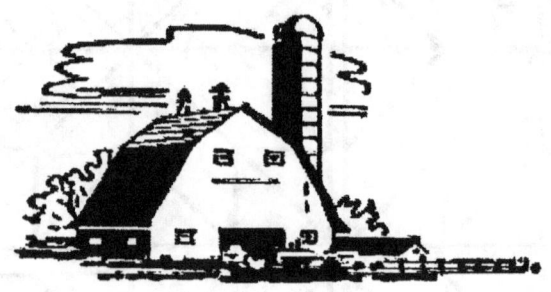

Barn Location
Spring St
Haubstadt, Indiana

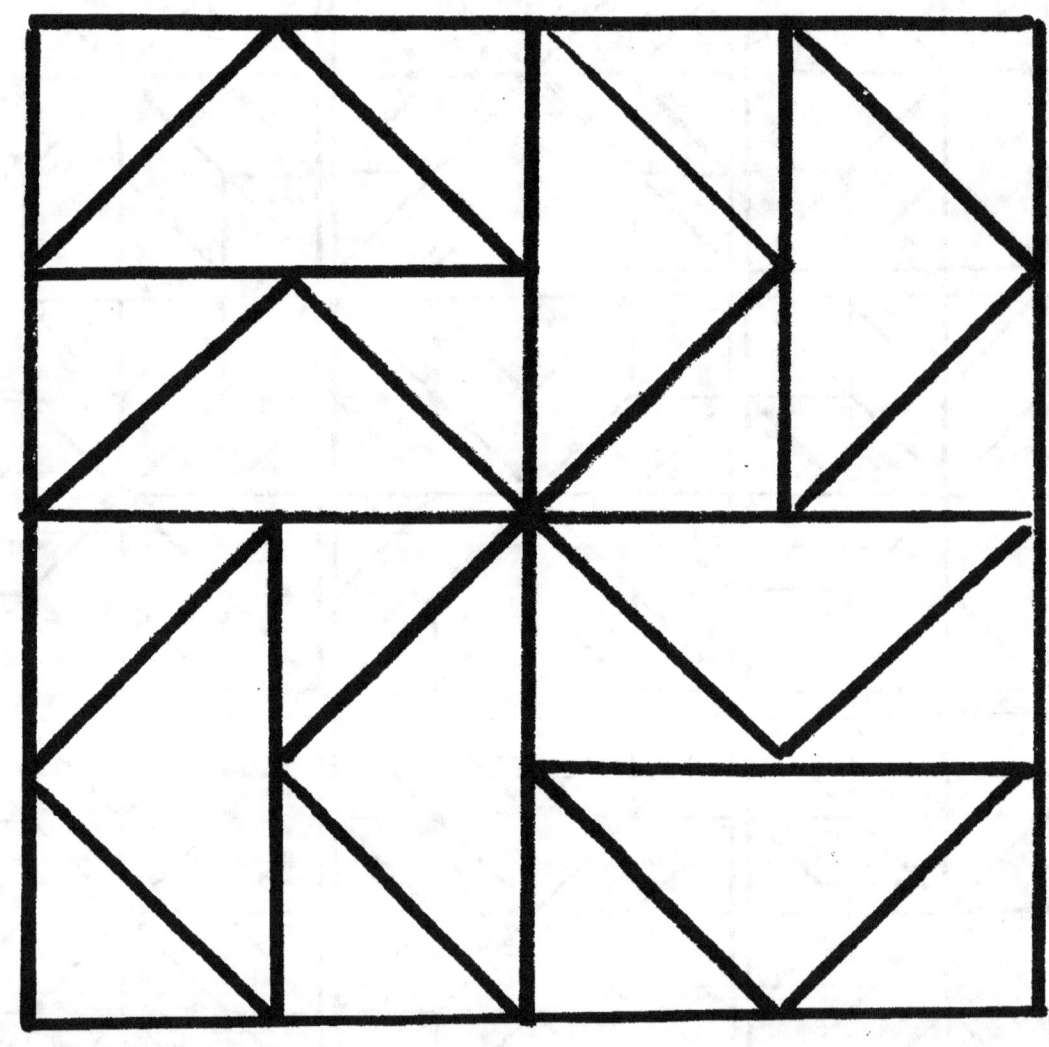

Gibson County Barn Quilt Flying Geese

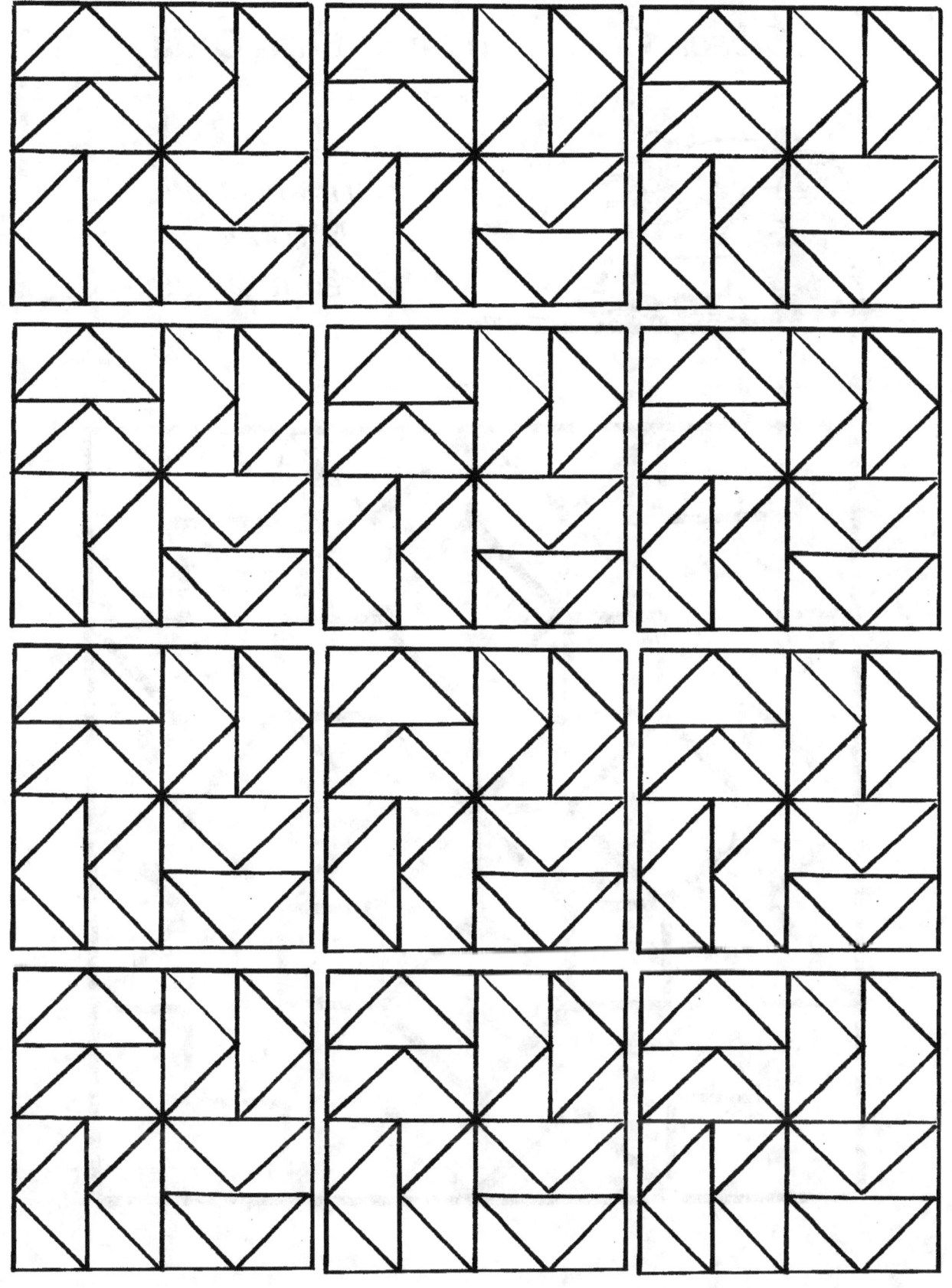

Barn Quilt Carpenter's Wheel
Gibson County Indiana Barn Quilt

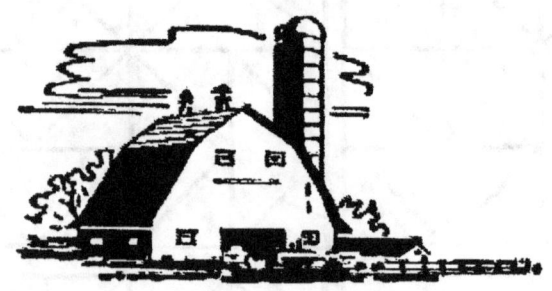

Barn Location
N 100 W
Princeton, Indiana

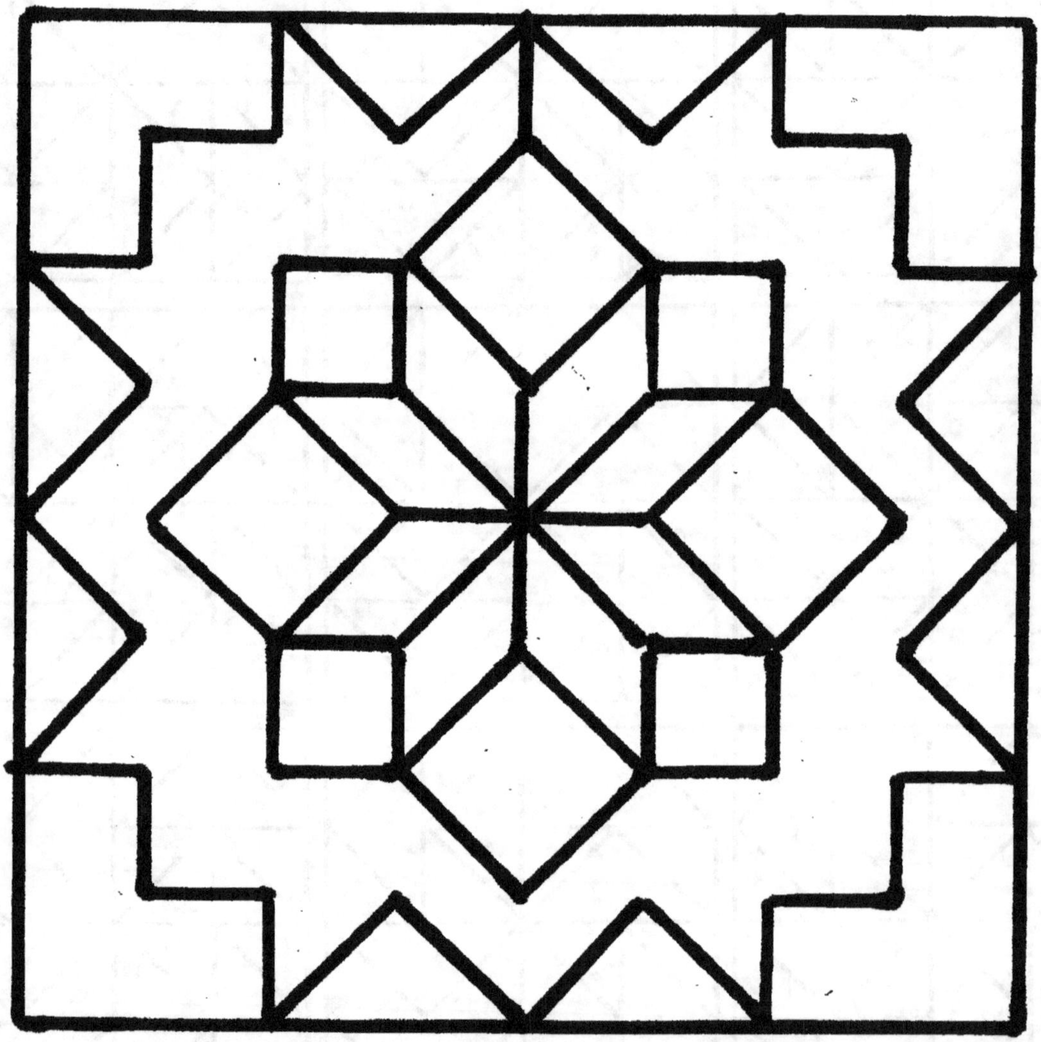

Gibson County Barn Quilt Carpenter's Wheel

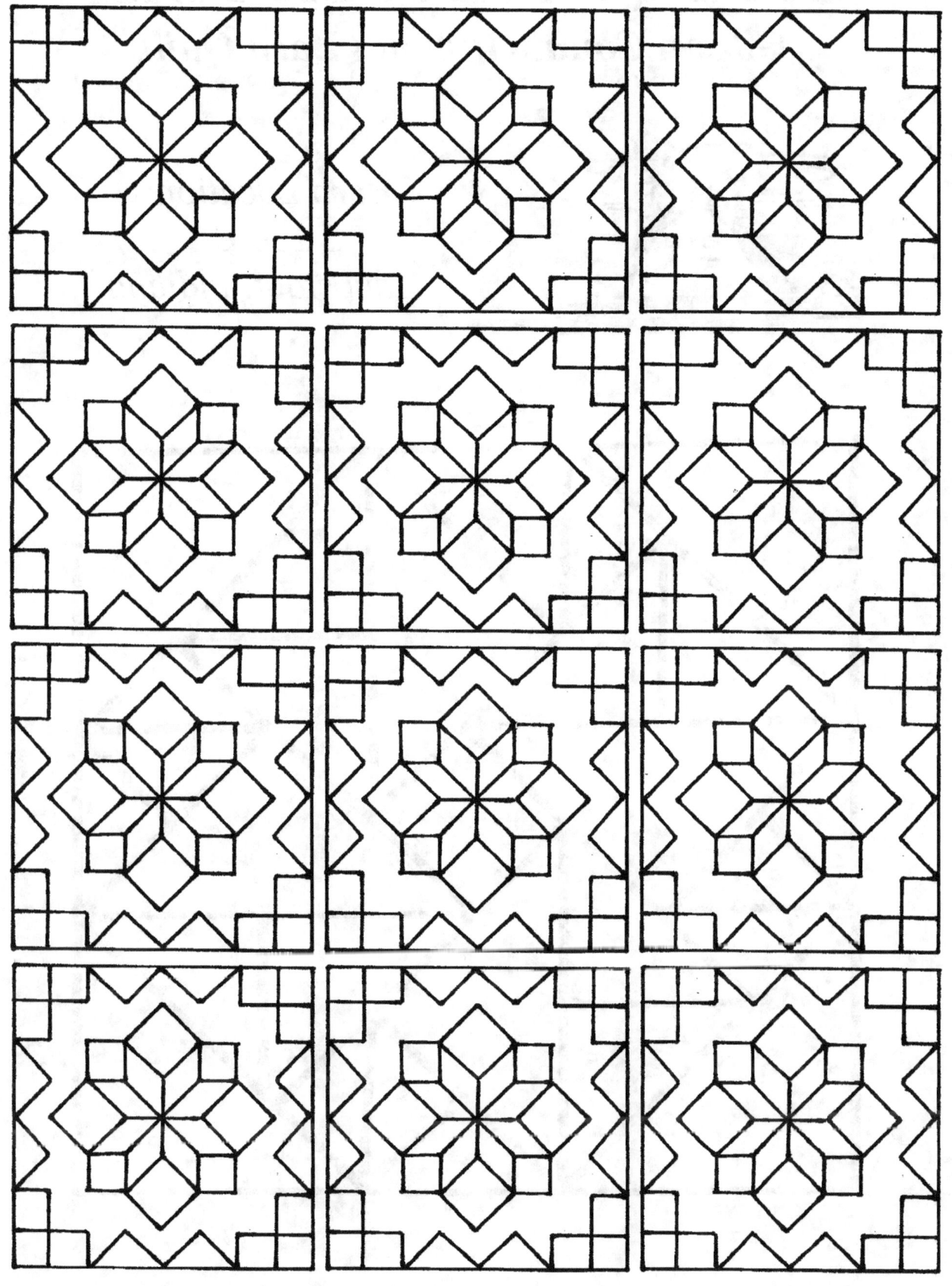

Barn Quilt Double Aster
Gibson County Indiana Barn Quilt

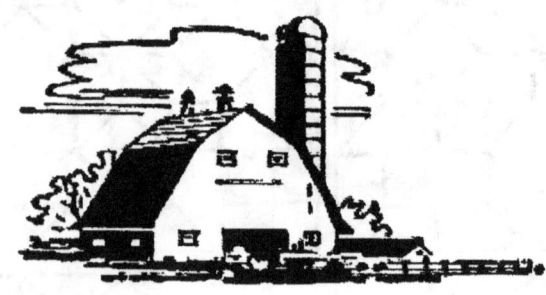

Barn Location
S 150 E
Haubstadt, Indiana

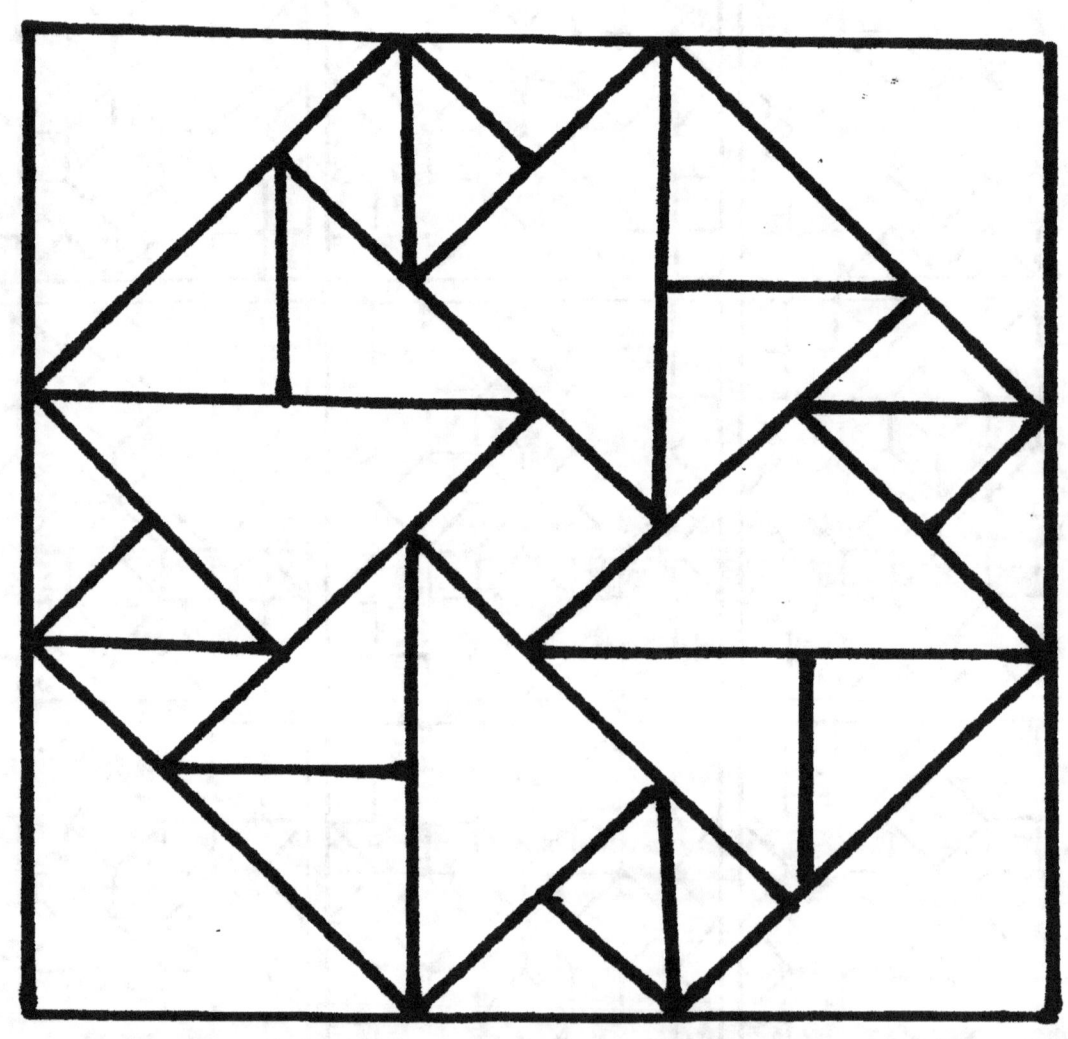

Gibson County Barn Quilt Double Aster

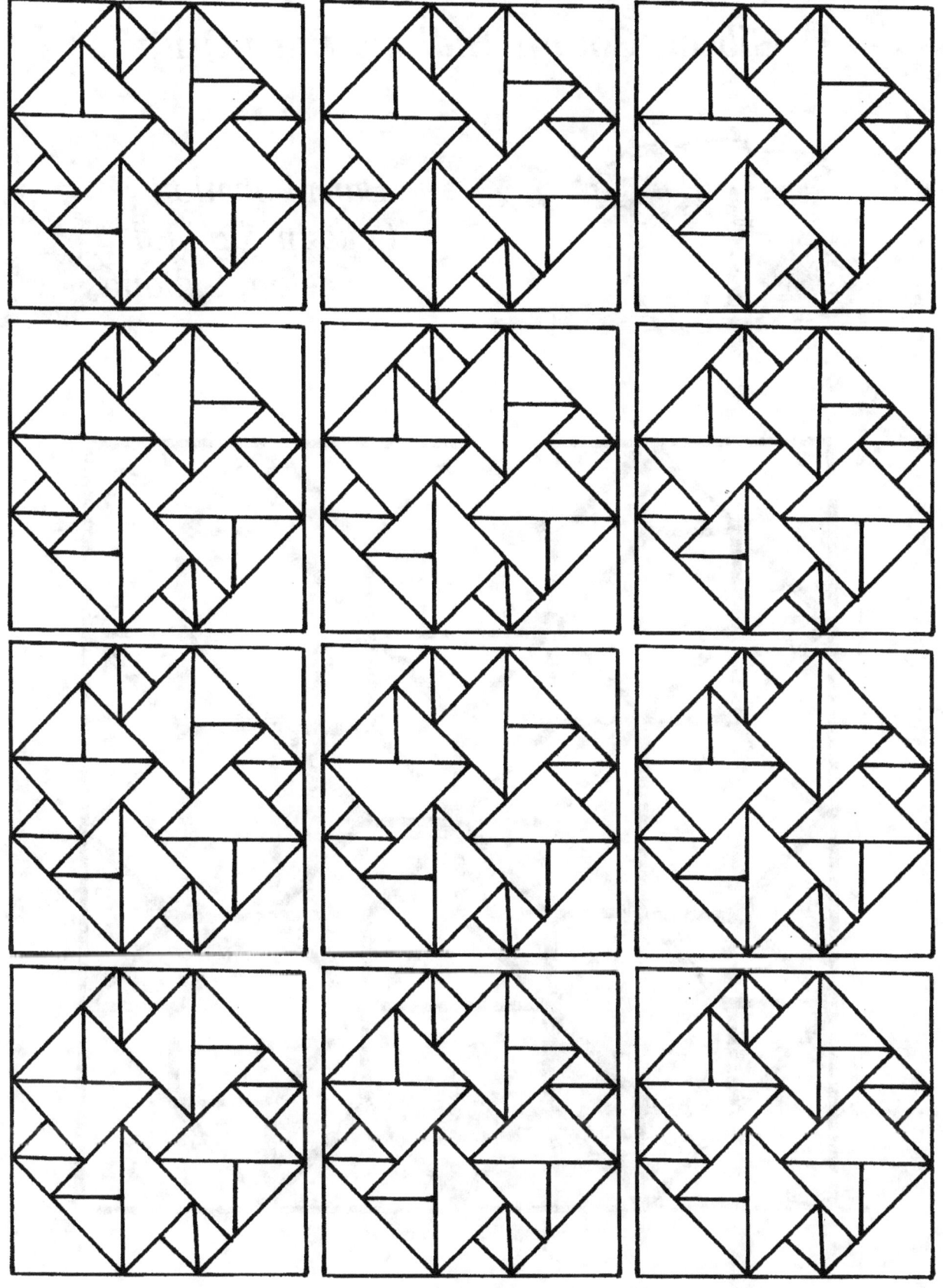

Barn Quilt Star of Bethlehem
Gibson County Indiana Barn Quilt

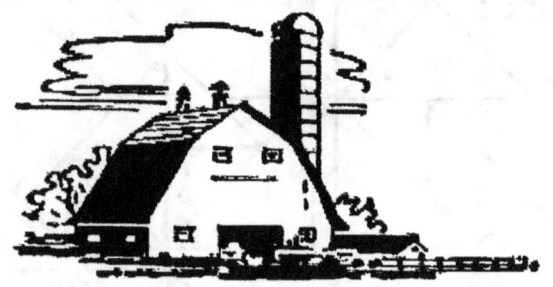

Barn Location
Lake Inwood Rd
Princeton, Indiana

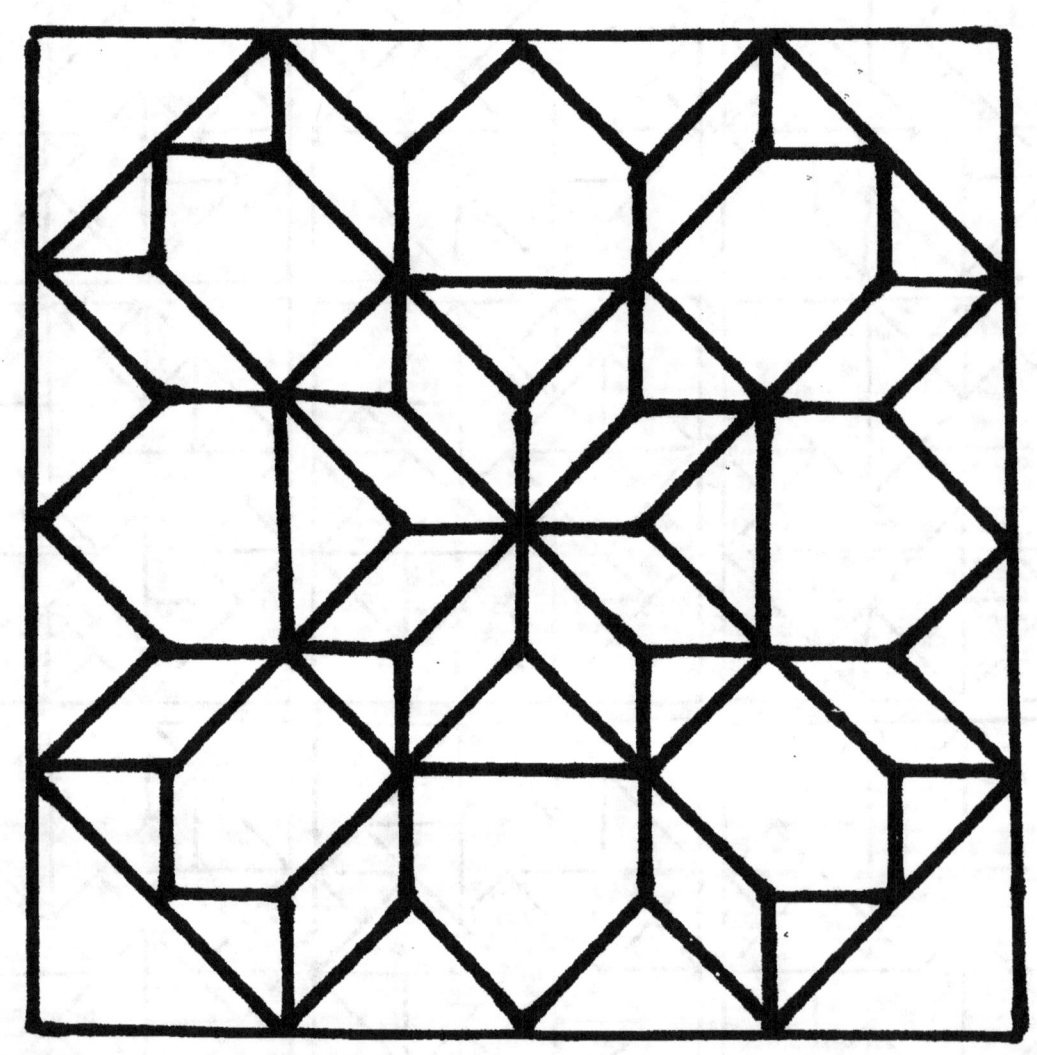

Gibson County Barn Quilt Star of Bethlehem

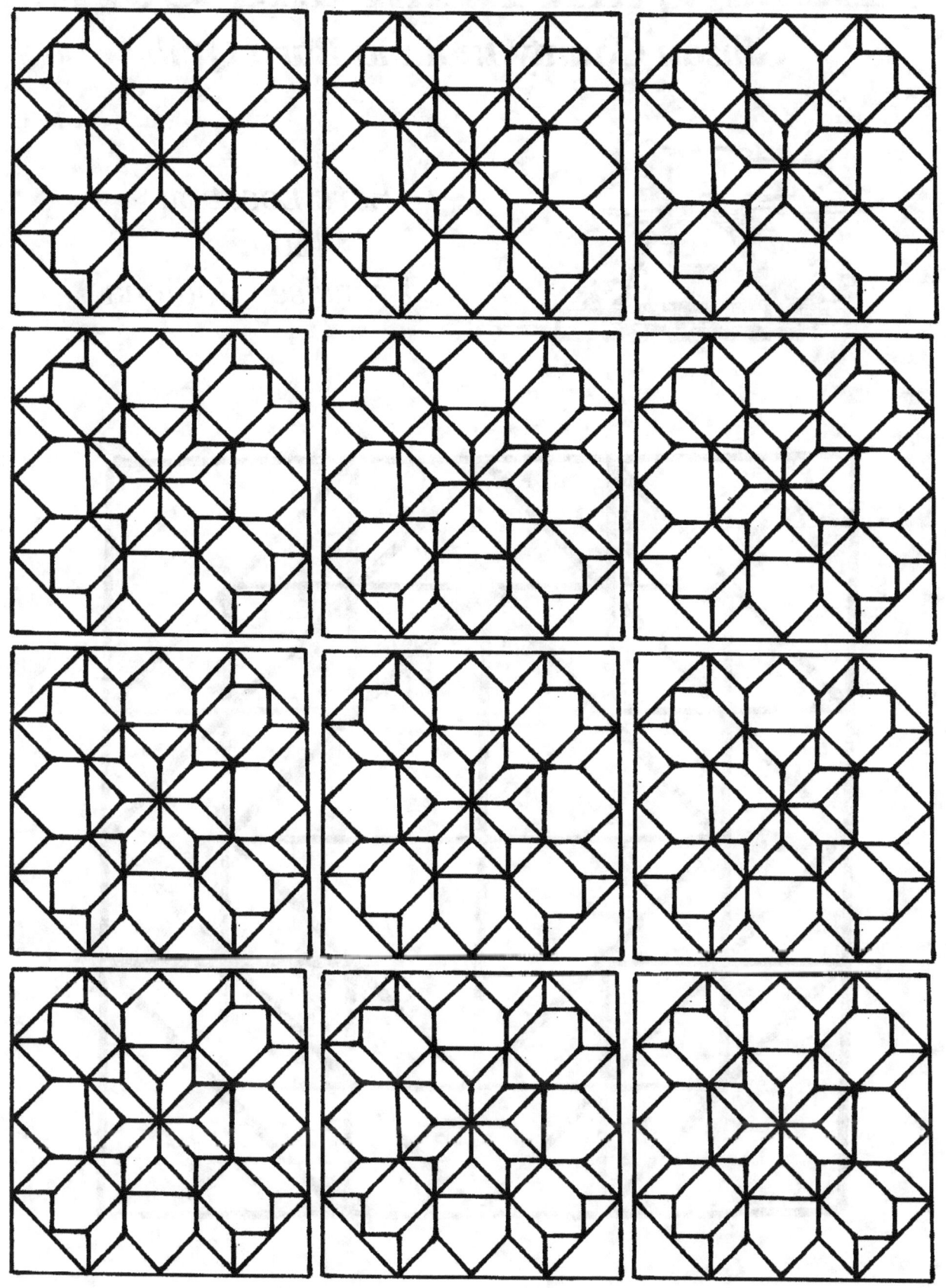

Barn Quilt Bean and Corn
Gibson County Indiana Barn Quilt

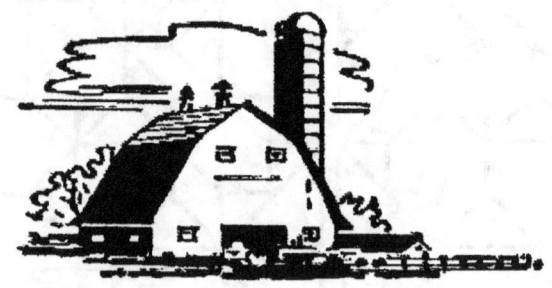

*Barn Location
450 E
Francisco, Indiana*

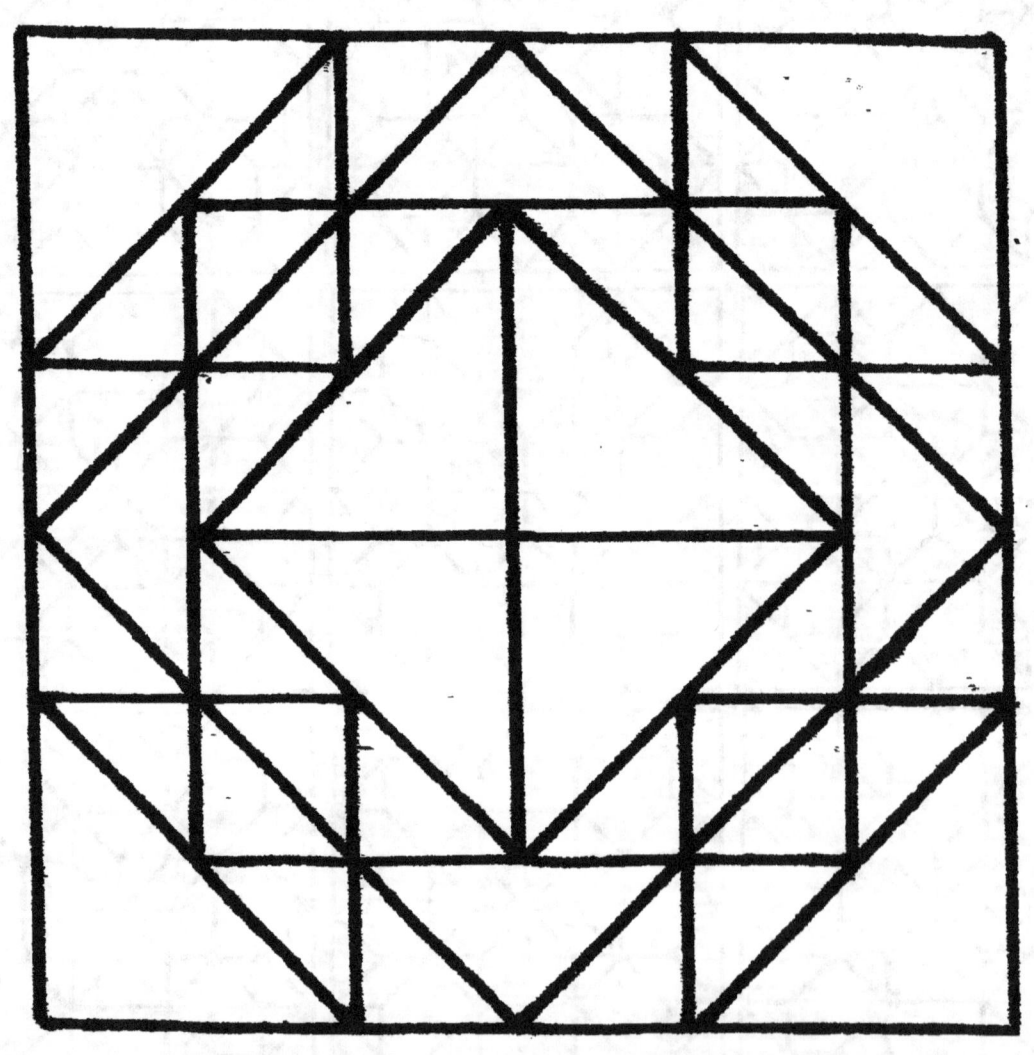

Gibson County Barn Quilt Bean & Corn

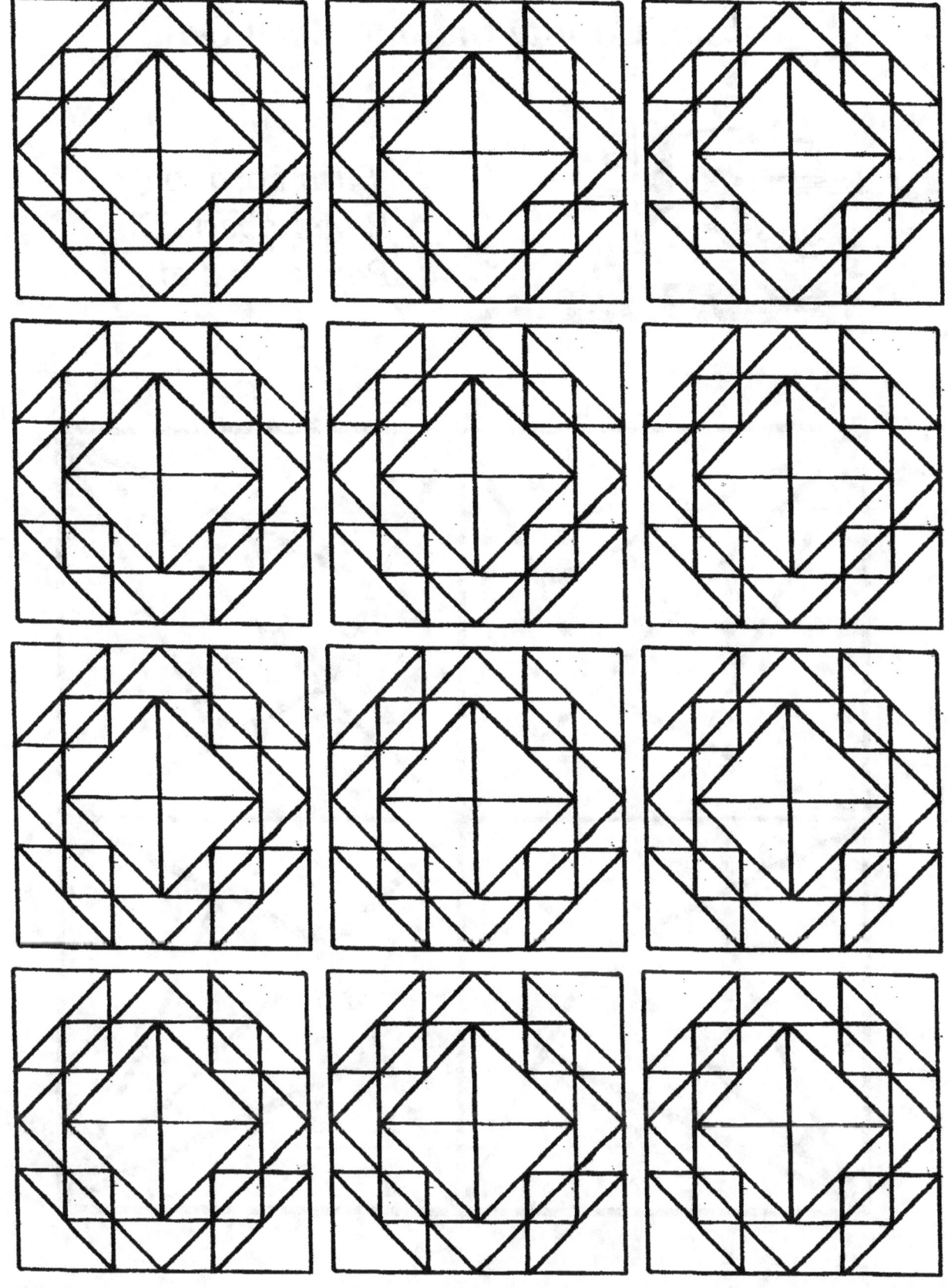

Barn Quilt Excited Star
Gibson County Indiana Barn Quilt

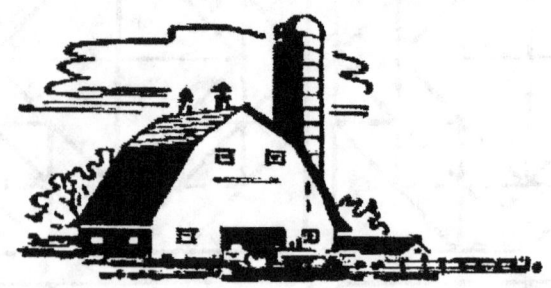

Barn Location
E McRoberts Dr
Patoka, Indiana

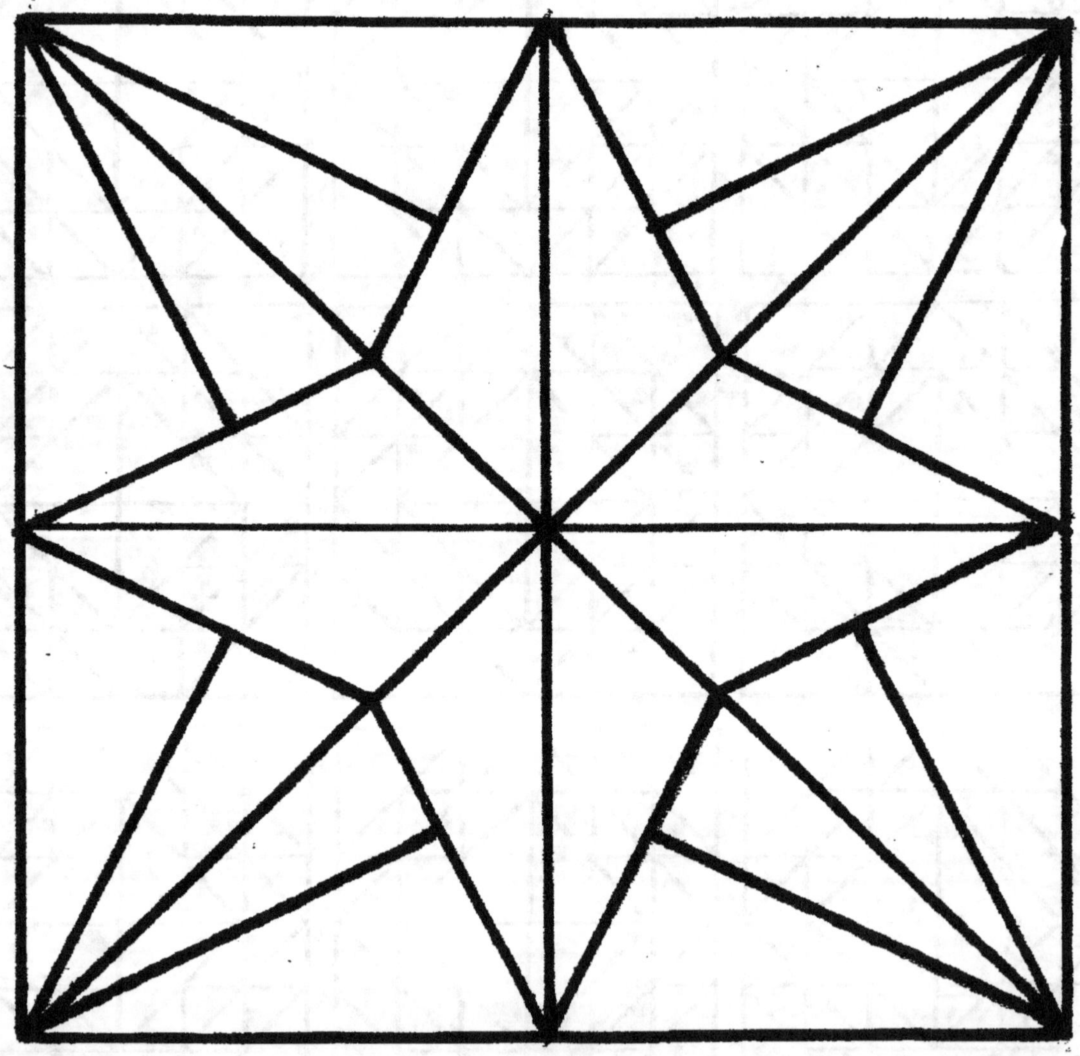

Gibson County Barn Quilt Excited Star

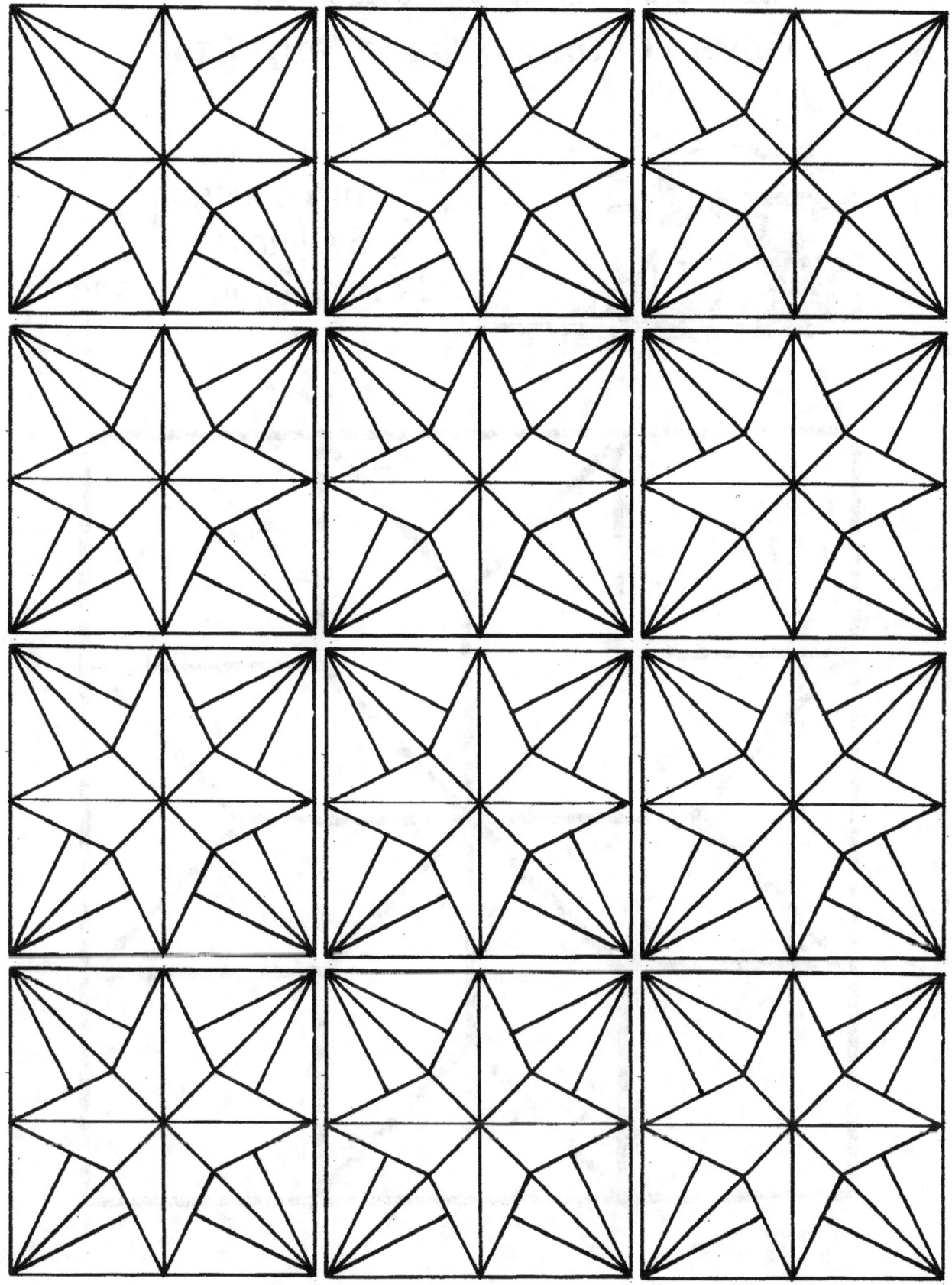

Barn Quilt X-Block
Gibson County Indiana Barn Quilt

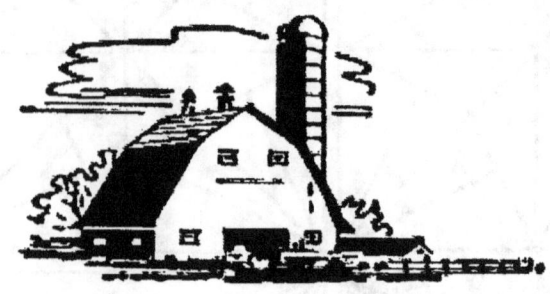

Barn Location
S Church St
Ft Branch St, Indiana

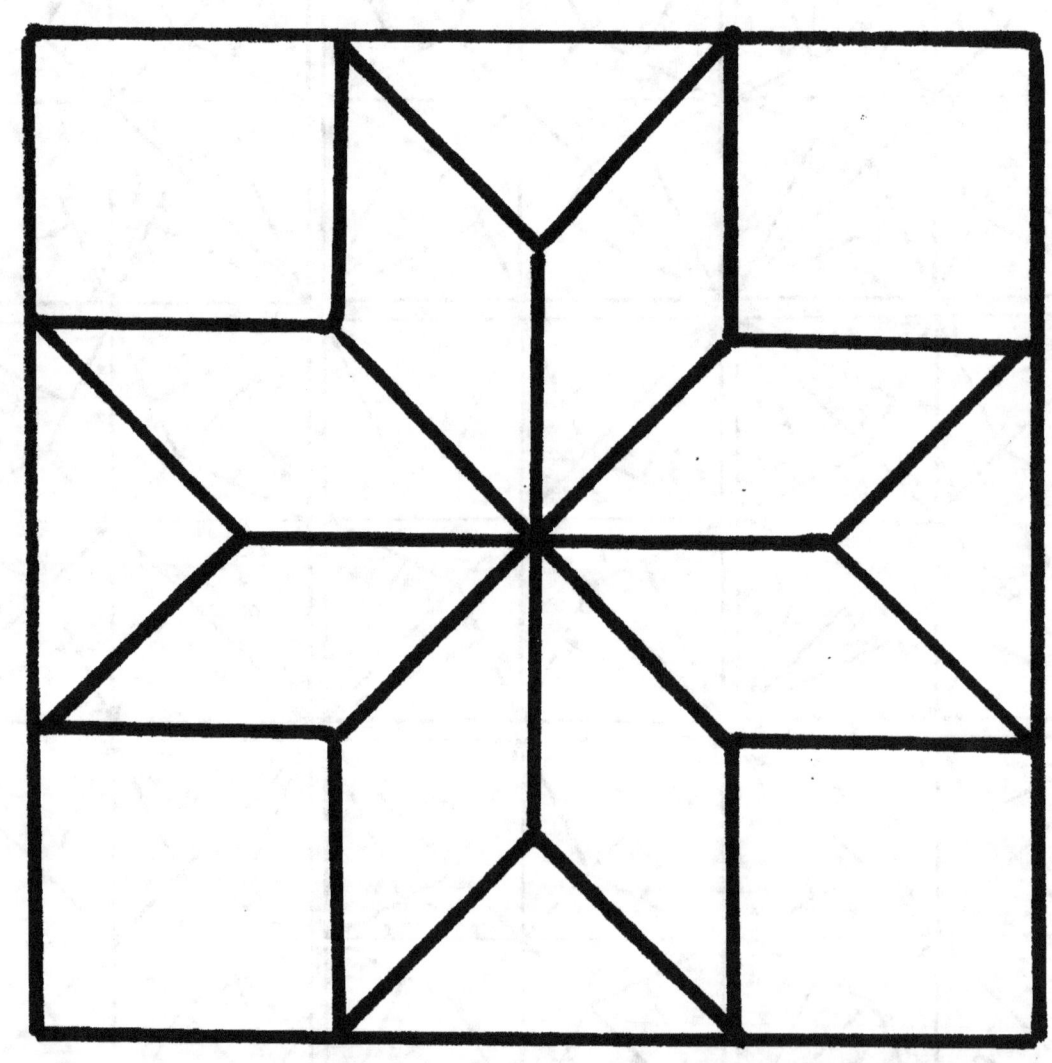

Gibson County Barn Quilt X-Block

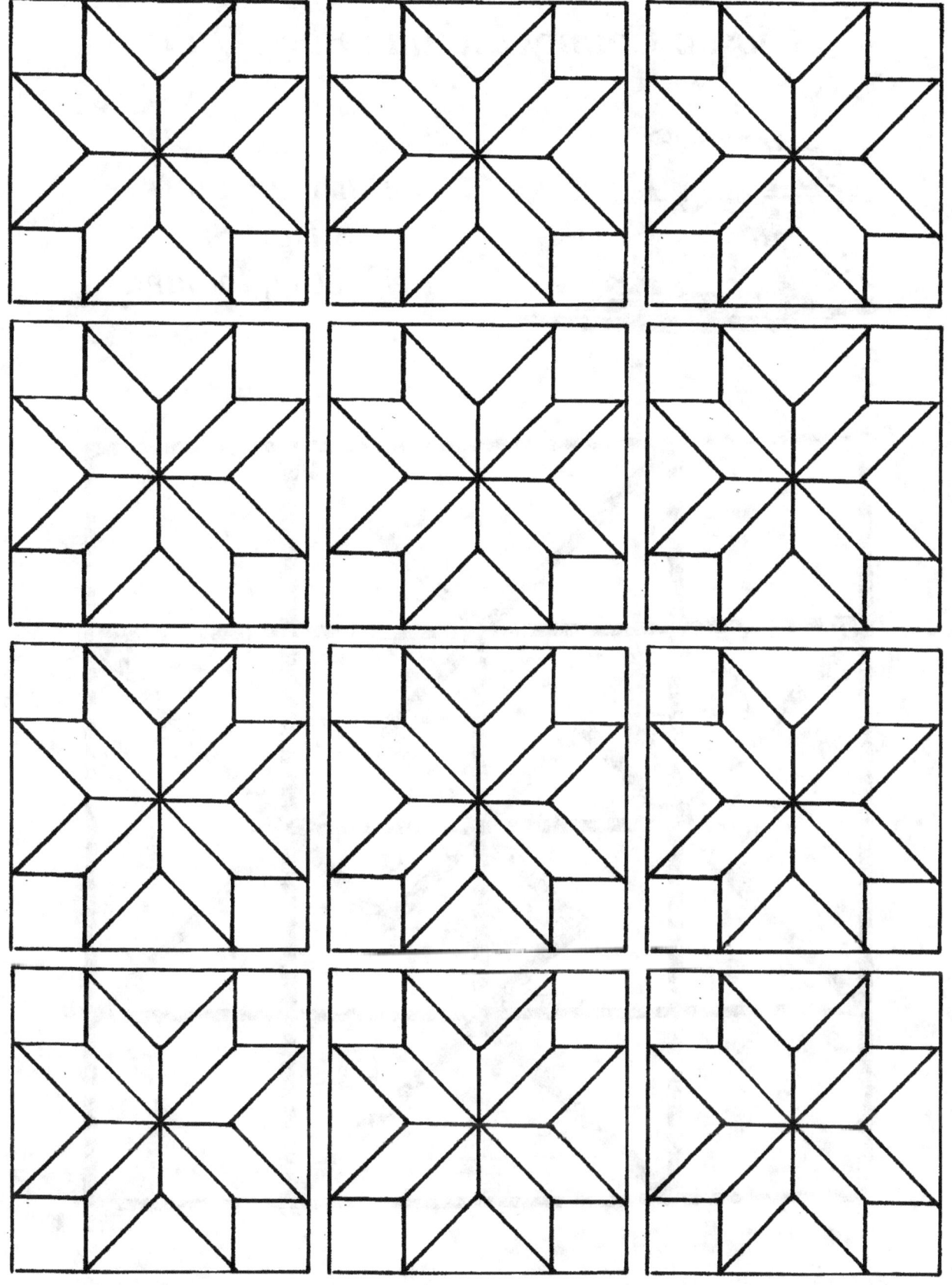

Barn Quilt Dewey's Victory
Gibson County Indiana Barn Quilt

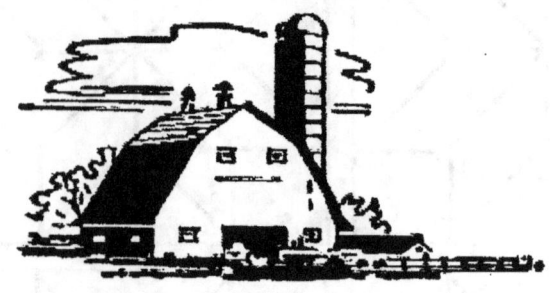

Barn Location
S Hart St
Princeton, Indiana

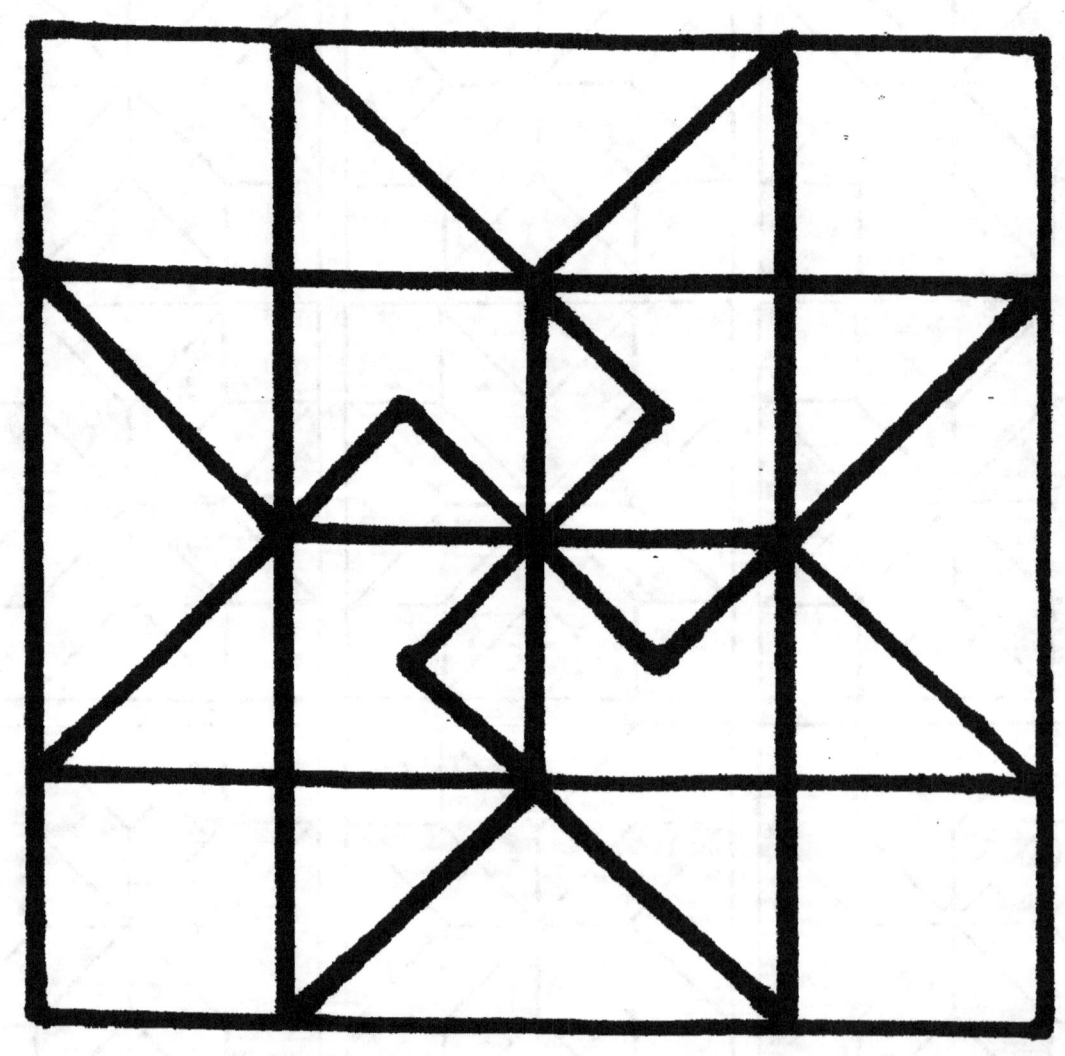

Gibson County Barn Quilt Dewey's Victory

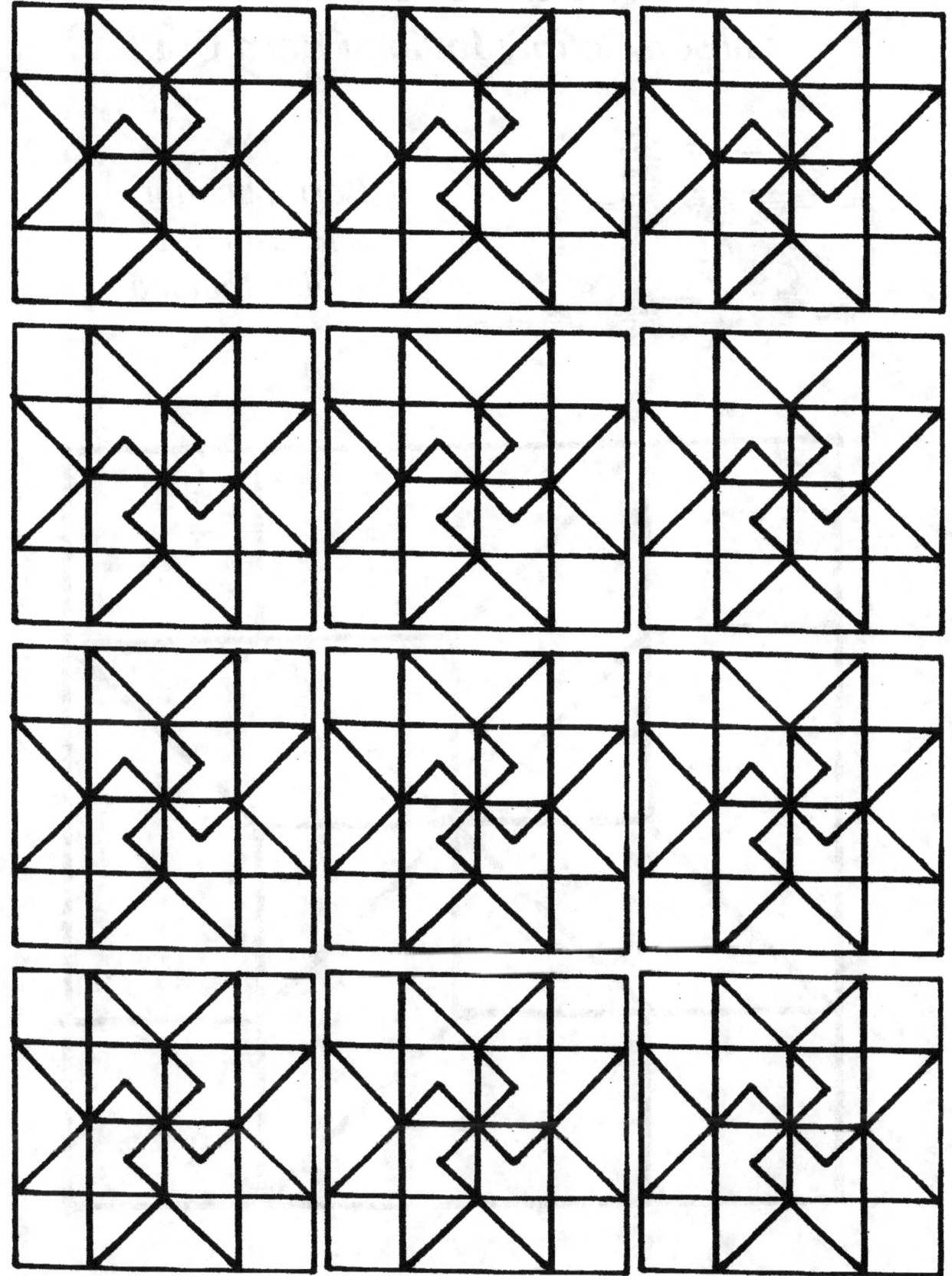

Barn Quilt Clay's Choice
Gibson County Indiana Barn Quilt

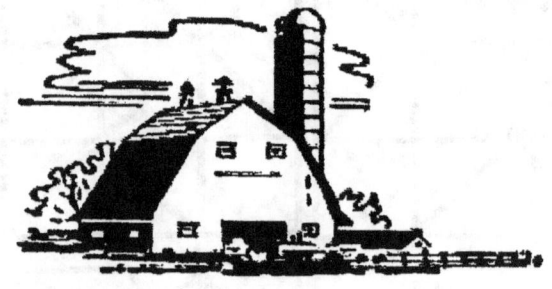

Barn Location
S Hudson Rd
Patoka, Indiana

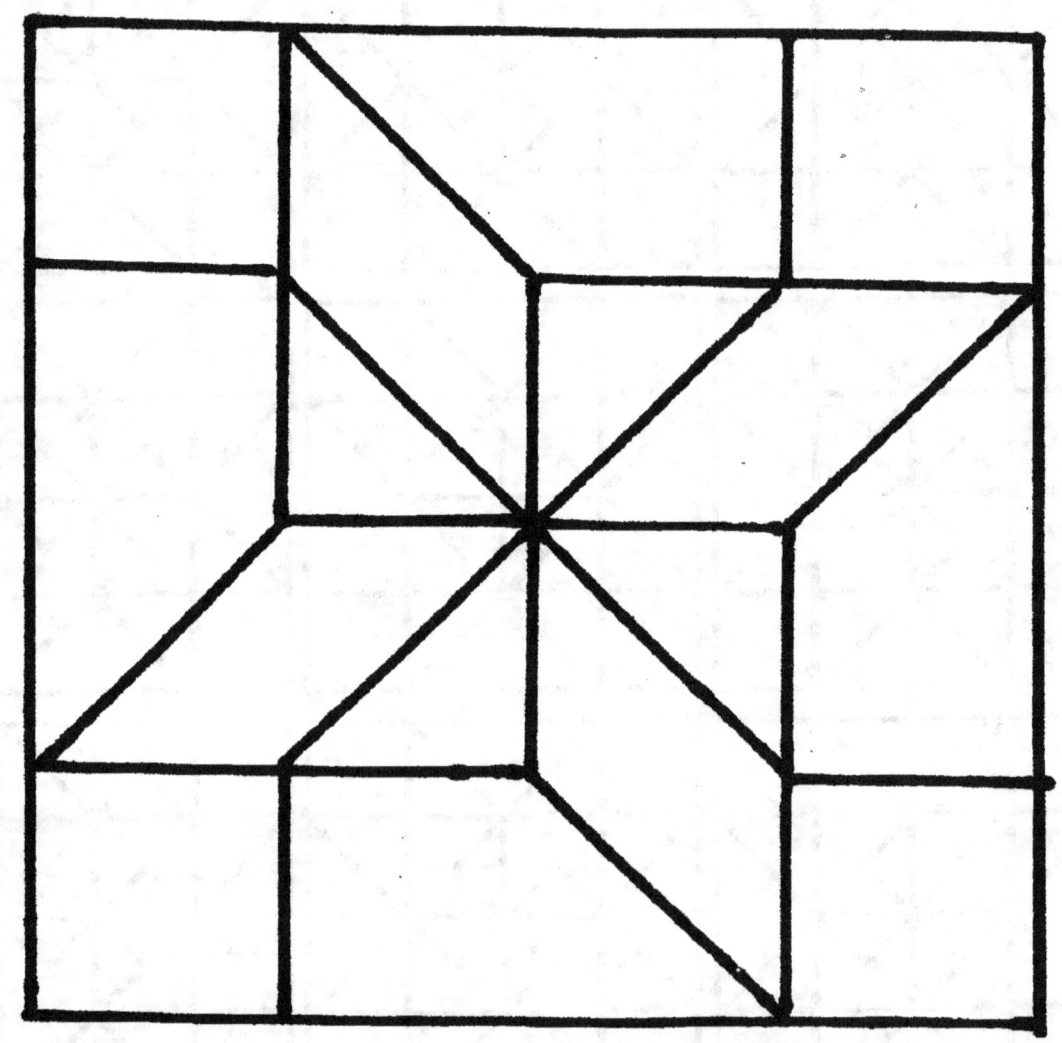

Gibson County Barn Quilt Clay's Choice

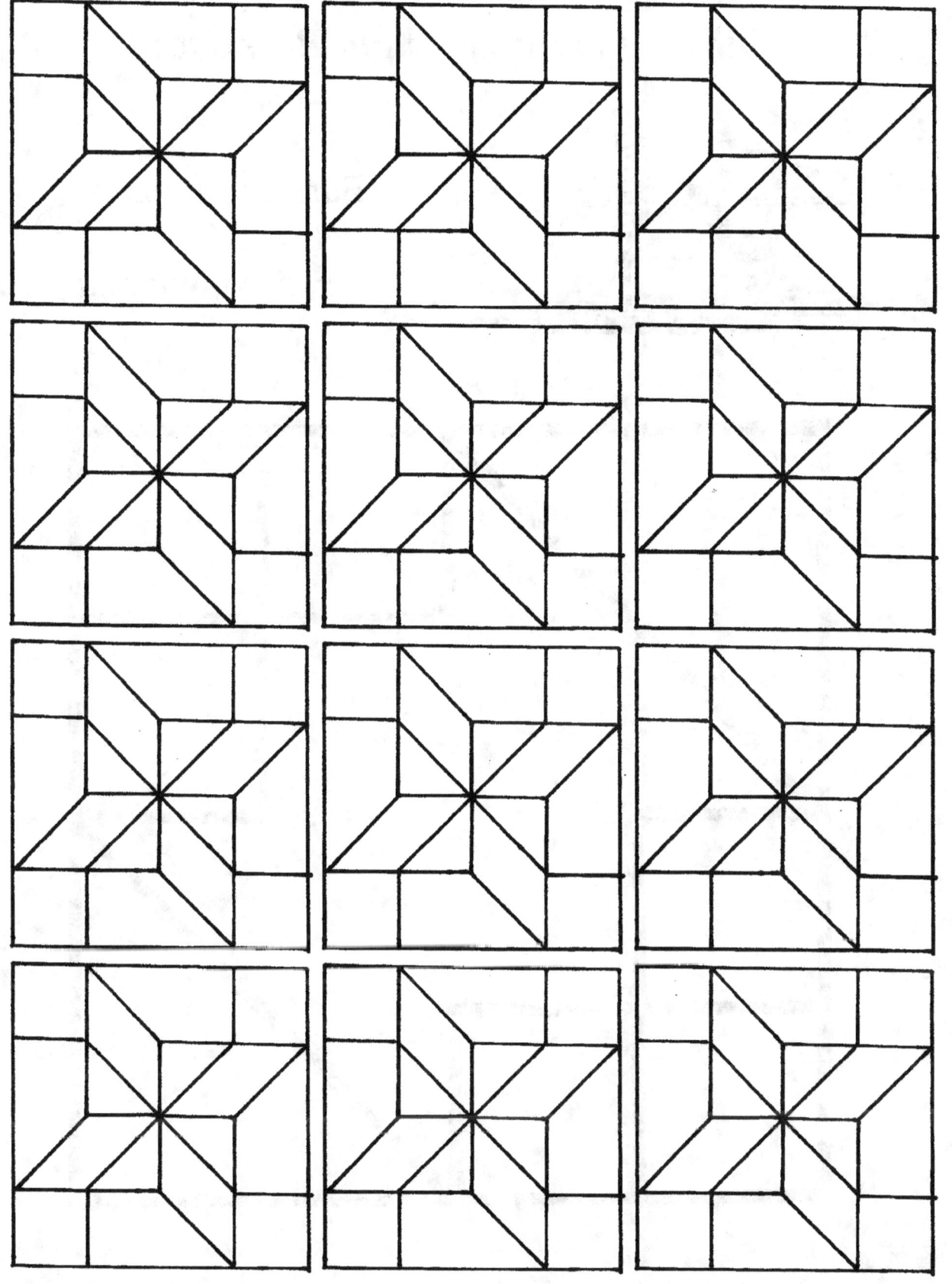

Barn Quilt Jacob's Ladder
Gibson County Indiana Barn Quilt

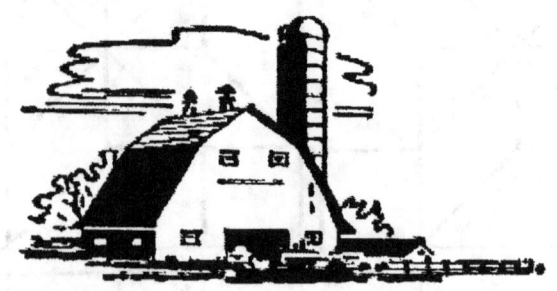

Barn Location
E 175 S
Francisco, Indiana

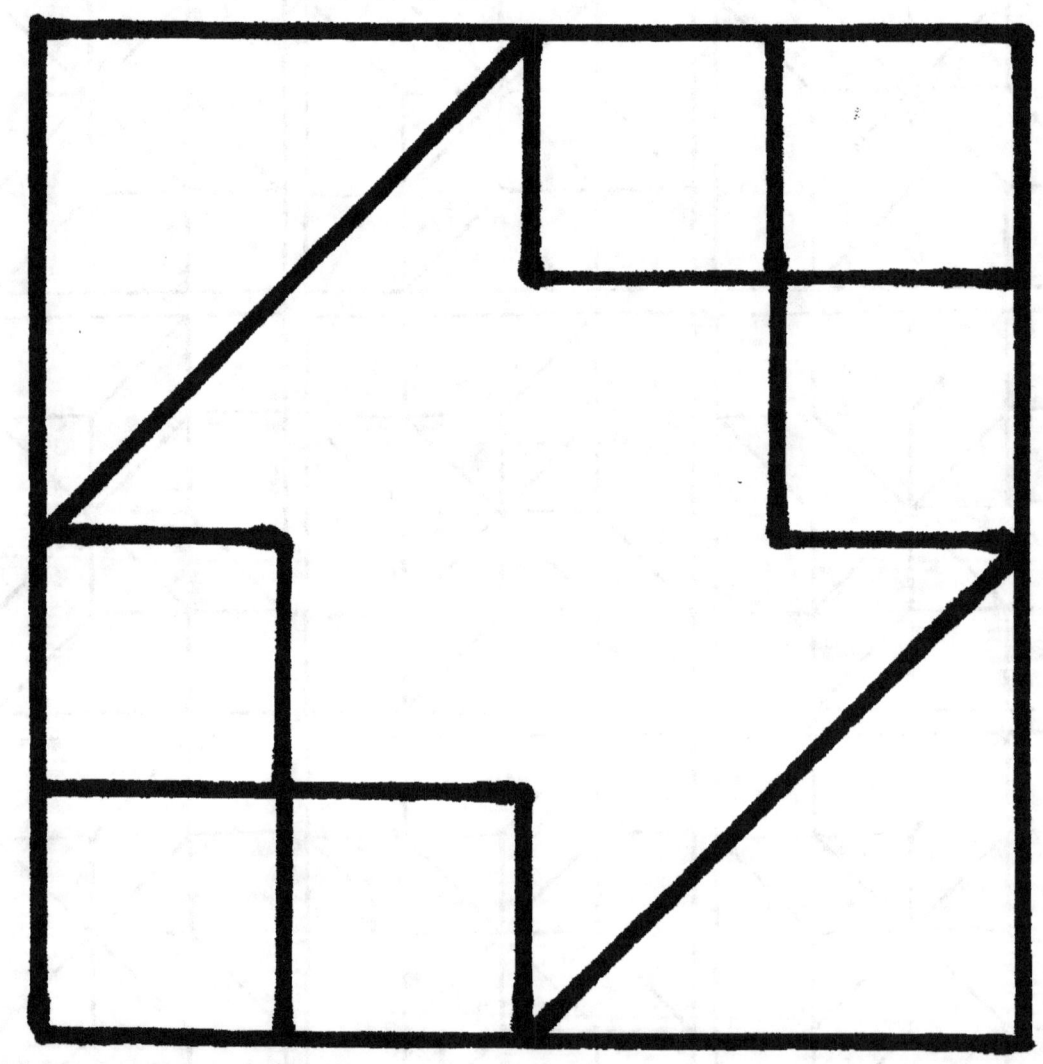

Gibson County Barn Quilt Jacob's Ladder

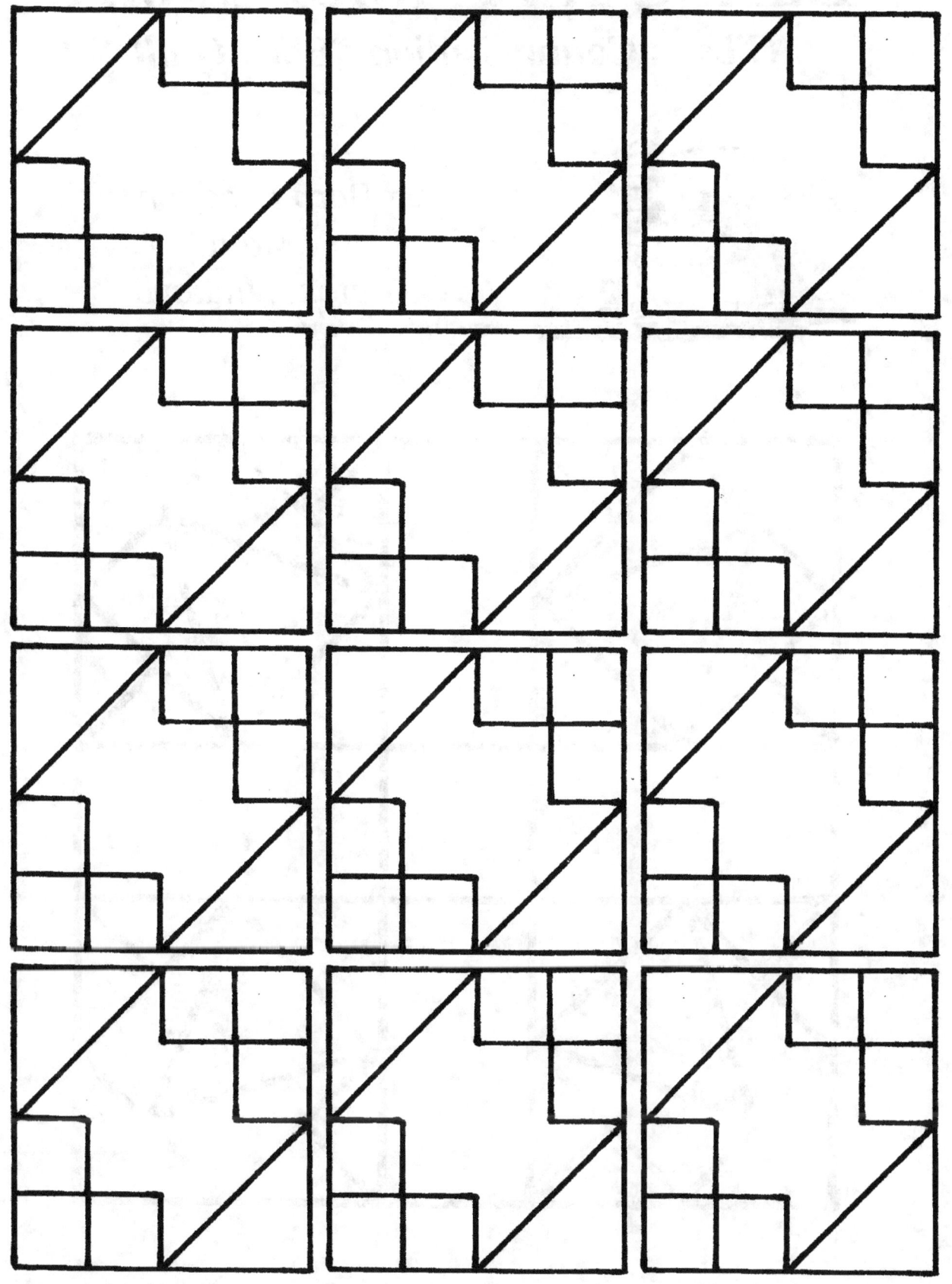

Barn Quilt Ladies Choice

Gibson County Indiana Barn Quilt

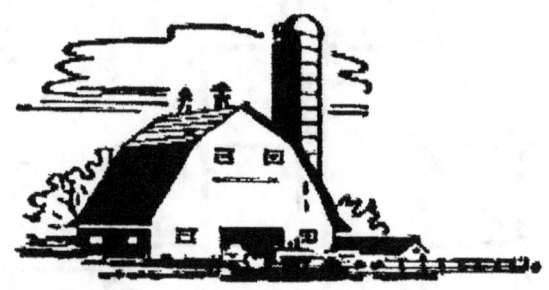

Barn Location
N Main
Patoka, Indiana

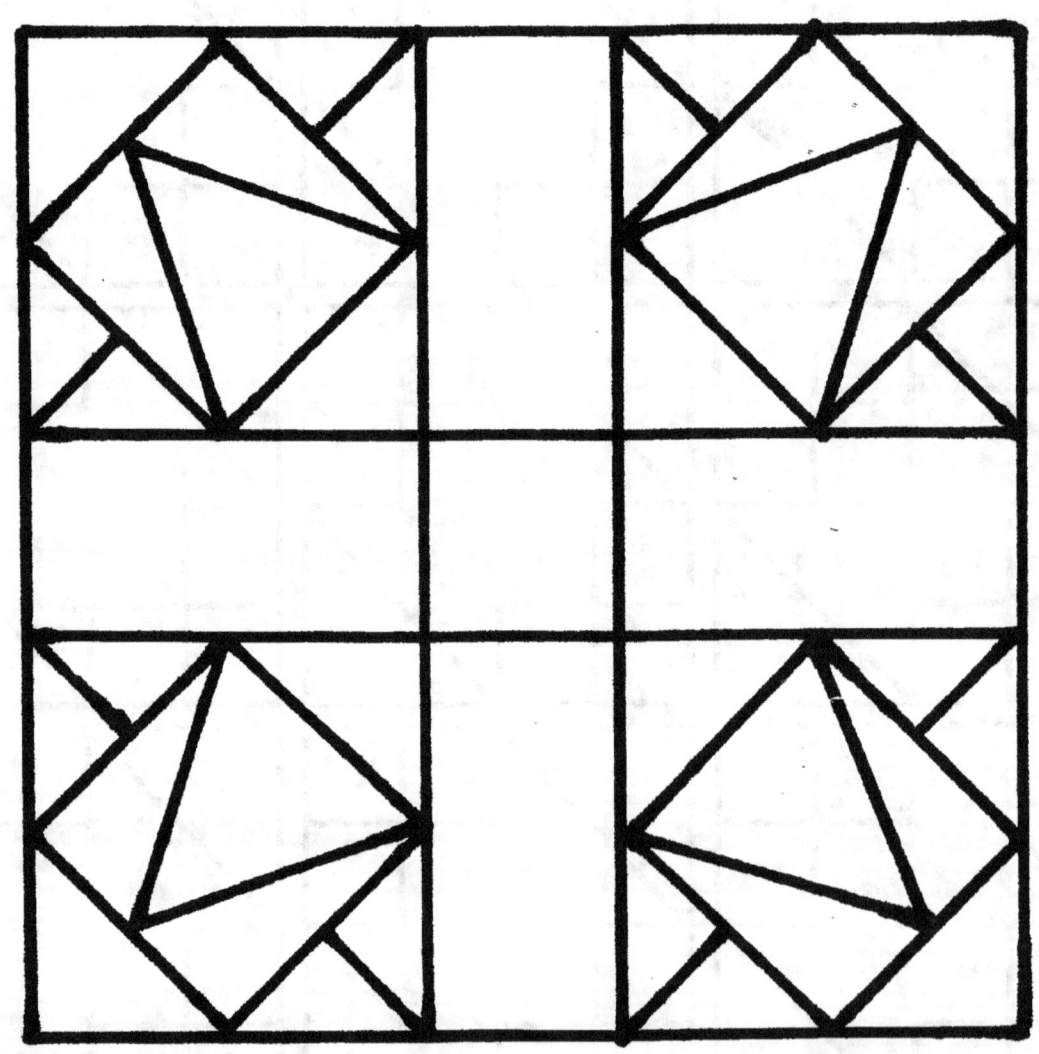

Gibson County Barn Quilt Ladies Choice

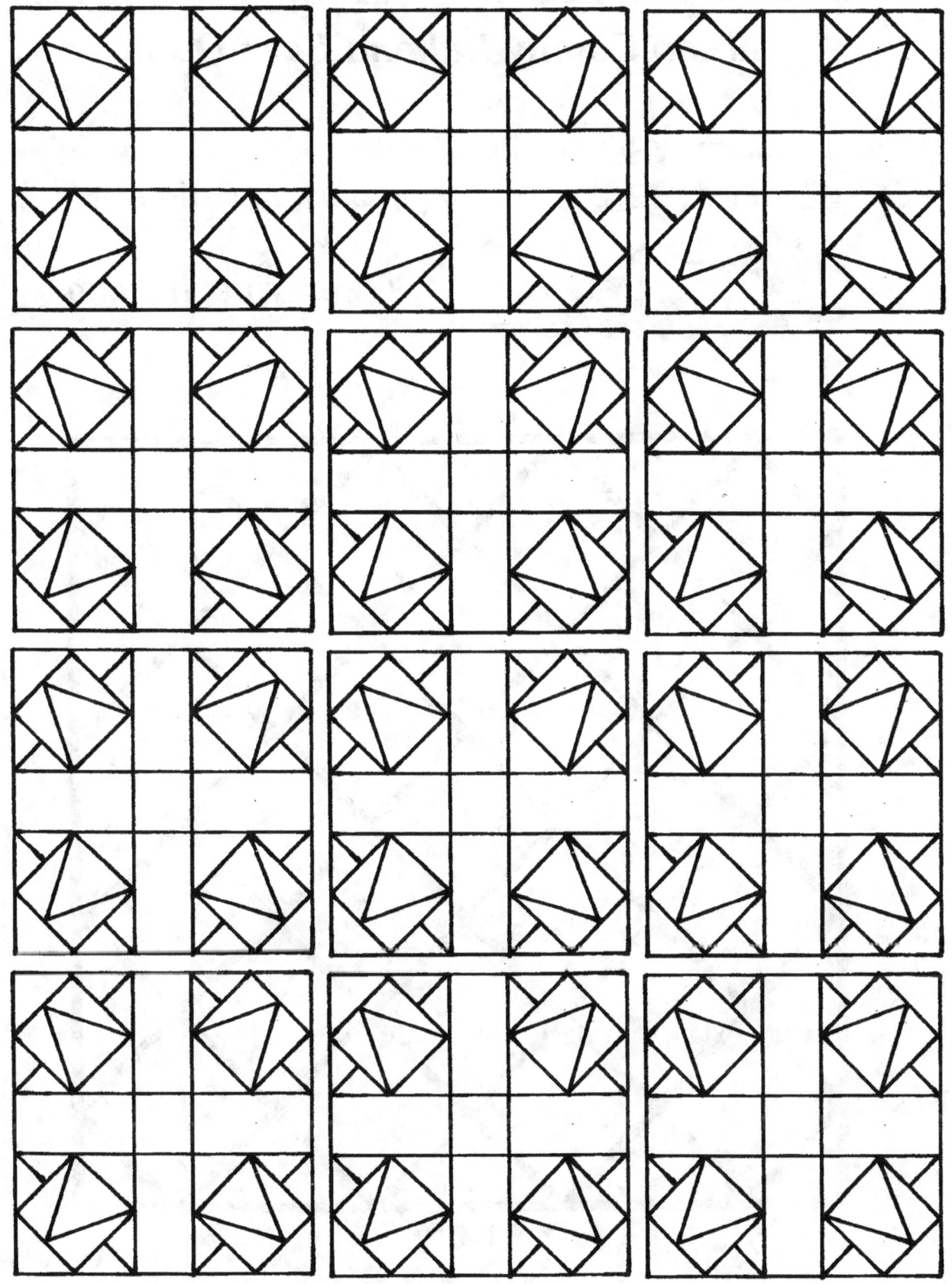

Barn Quilt Granny Square
Gibson County Indiana Barn Quilt

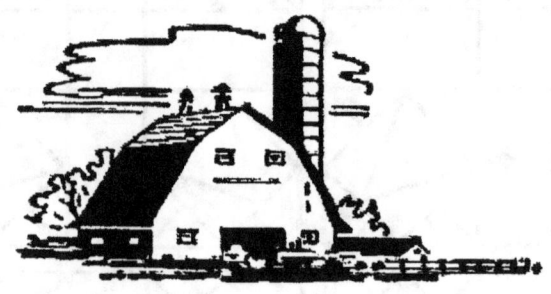

Barn Location
W 1000 S
Owensville, Indiana

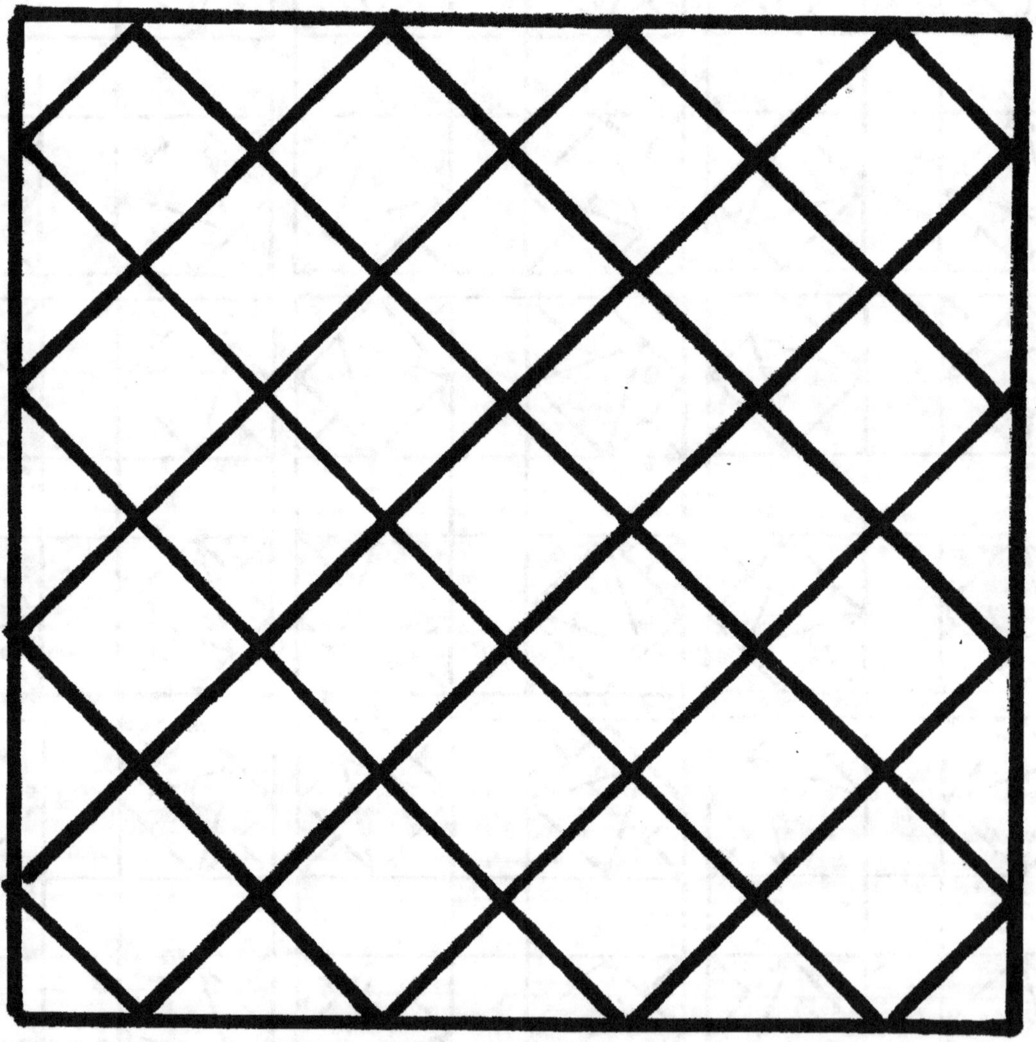

Gibson County Barn Quilt Granny Square

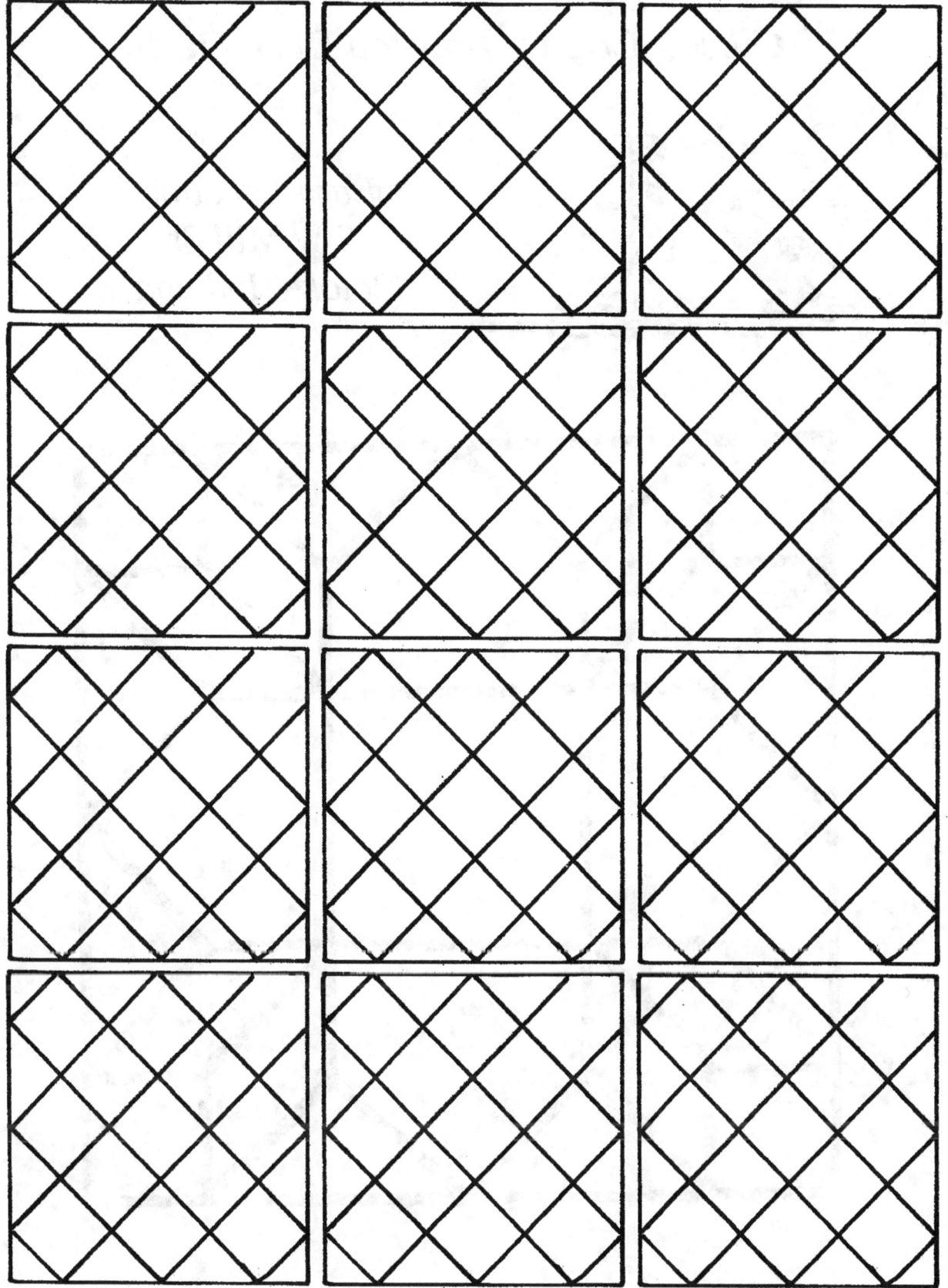

Barn Quilt Weather Vane
Gibson County Indiana Barn Quilt

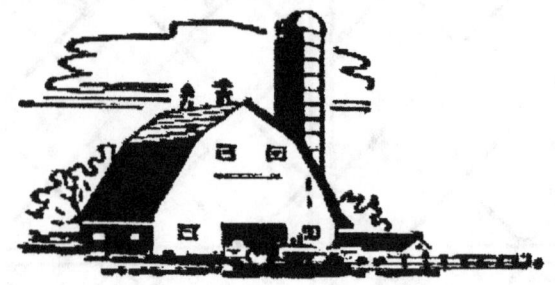

Barn Location
S W Mill St
Patoka, Indiana

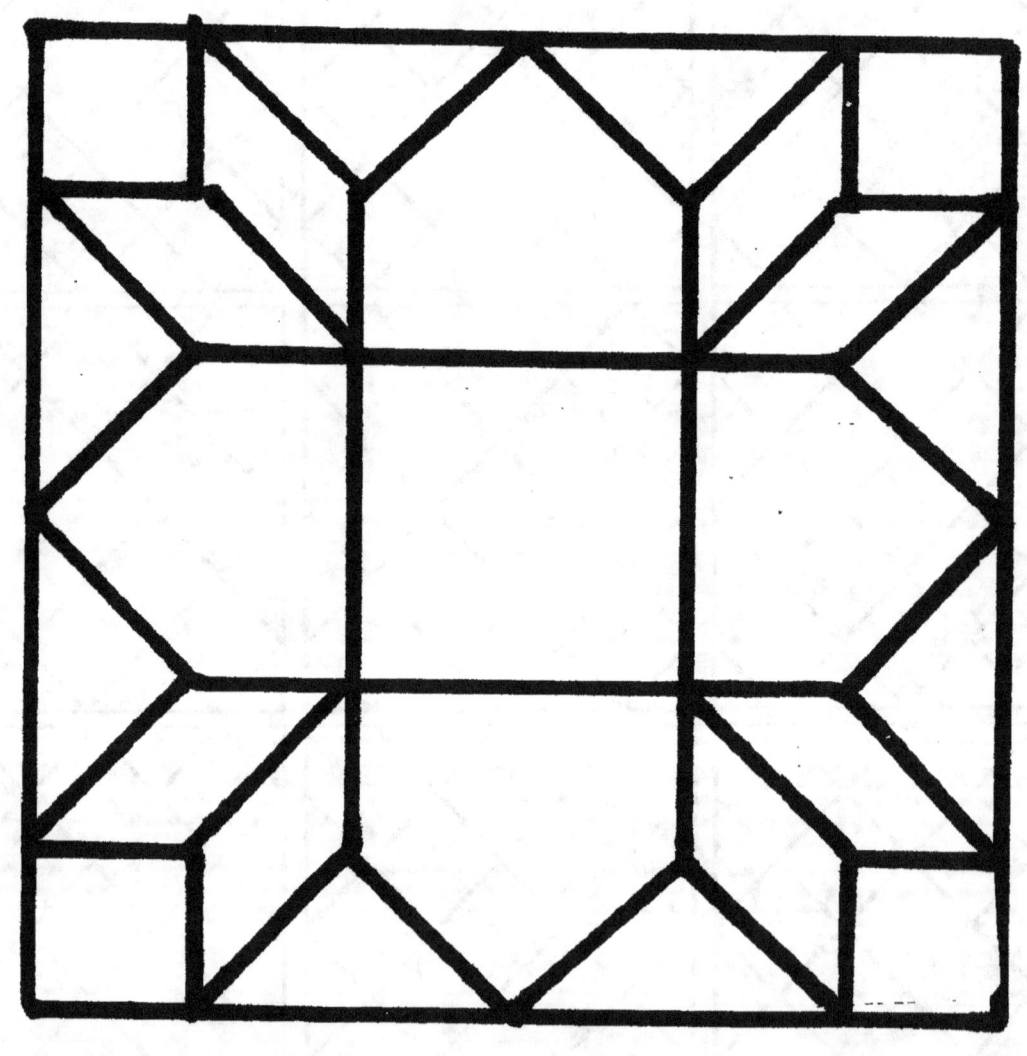

Gibson County Barn Quilt Weather Vane

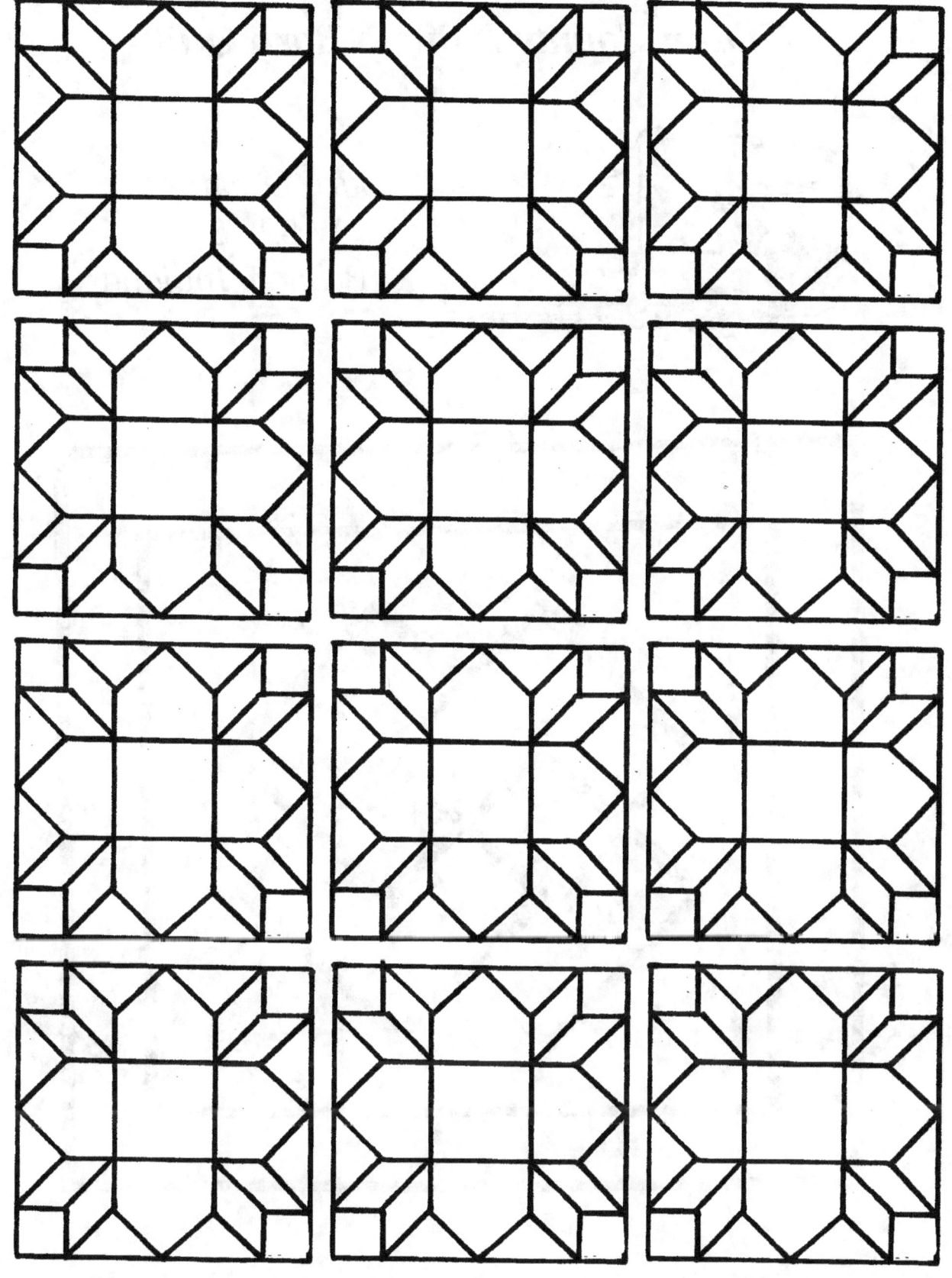

Barn Quilt Card Trick
Gibson County Indiana Barn Quilt

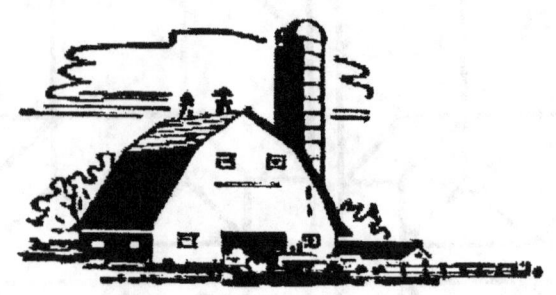

Barn Location
W 525 S
Ft Branch, Indiana

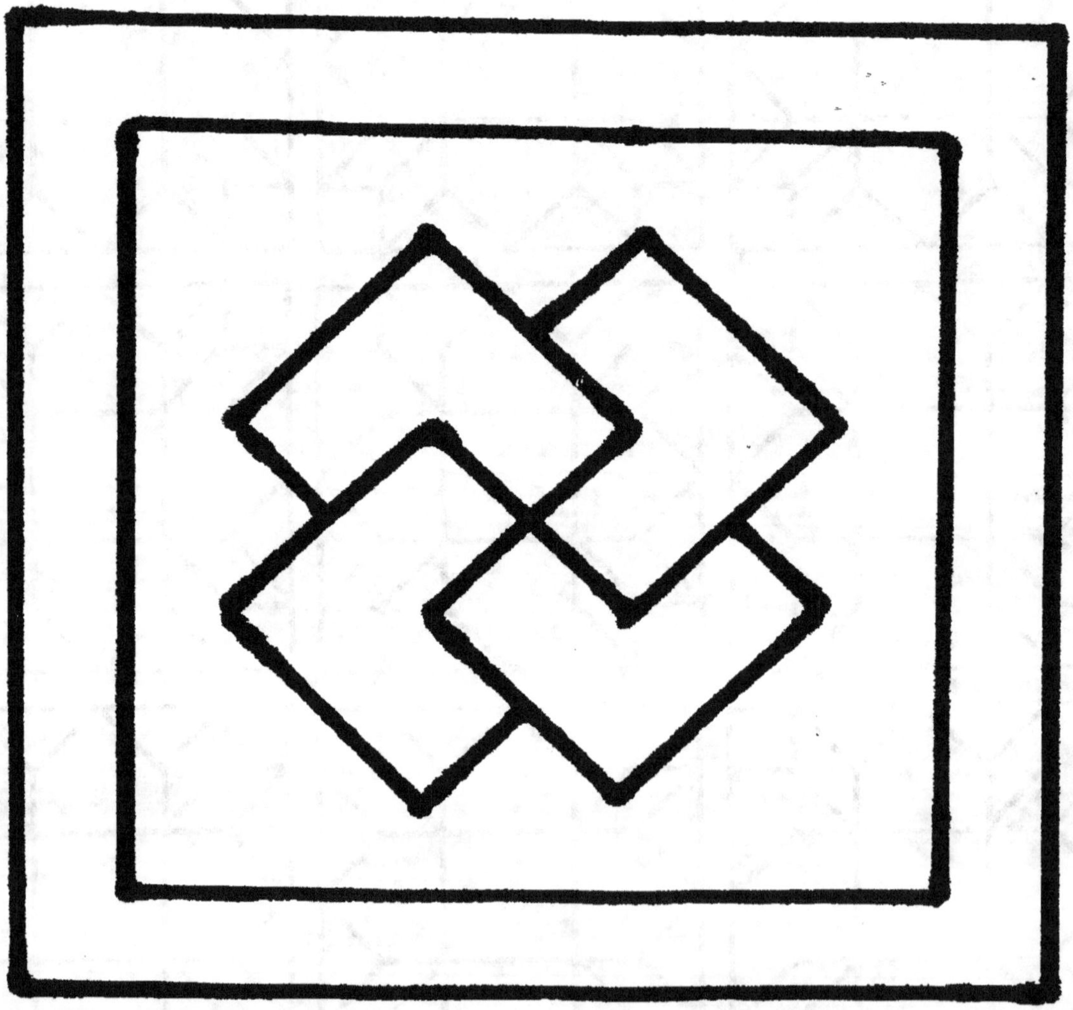

Gibson County Barn Quilt Card Trick

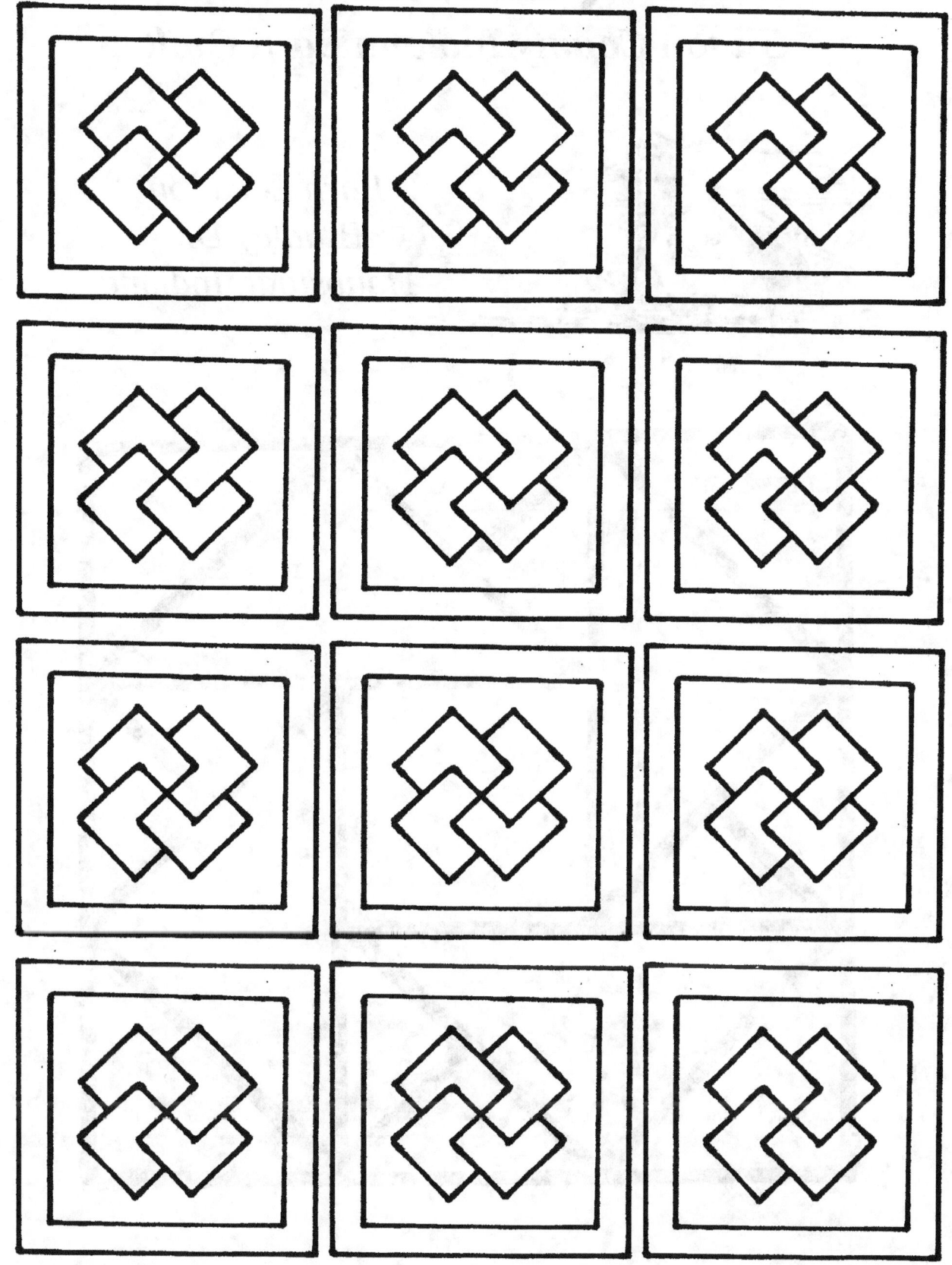

Barn Quilt Air Castle
Gibson County Indiana Barn Quilt

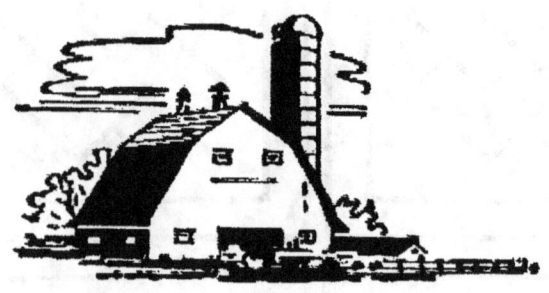

Barn Location
Bradley Dr
Haubstadt, Indiana

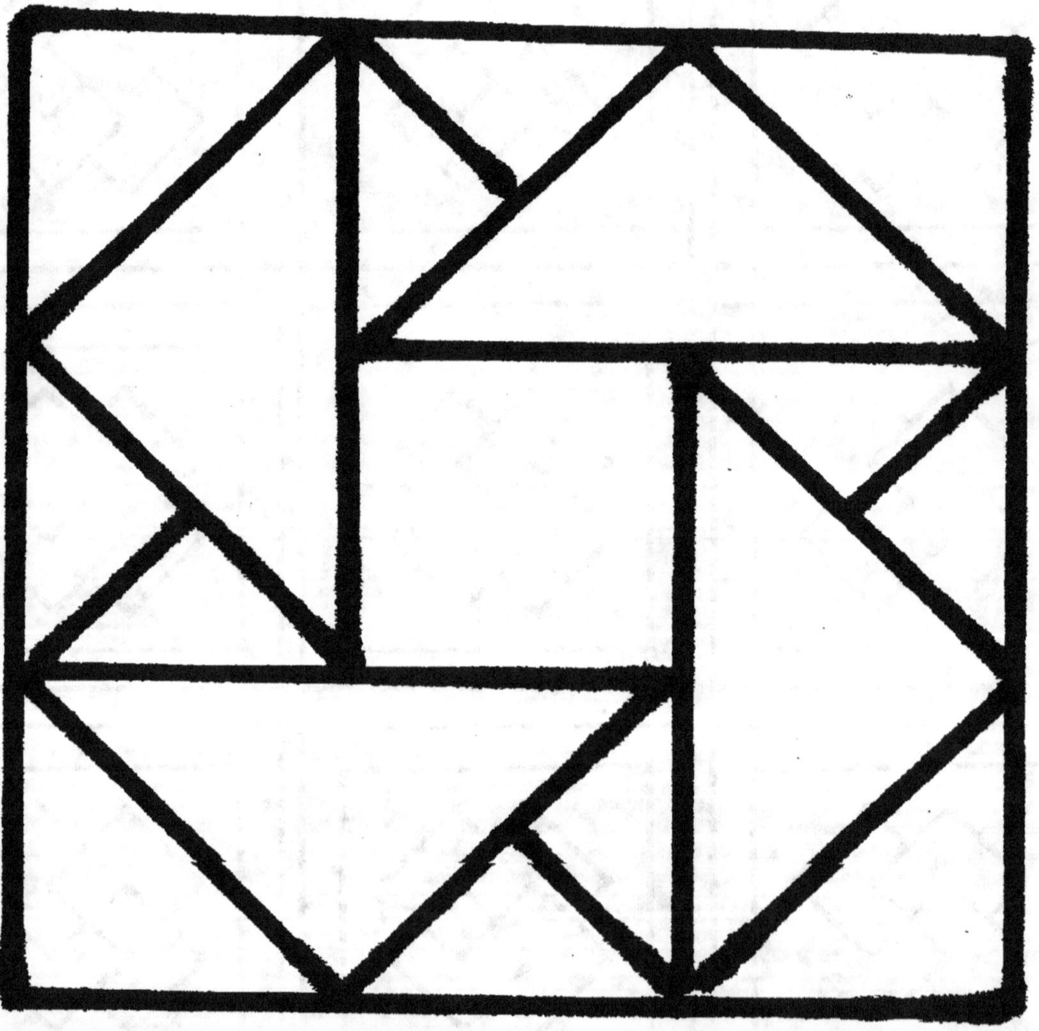

Gibson County Barn Quilt Air Castle

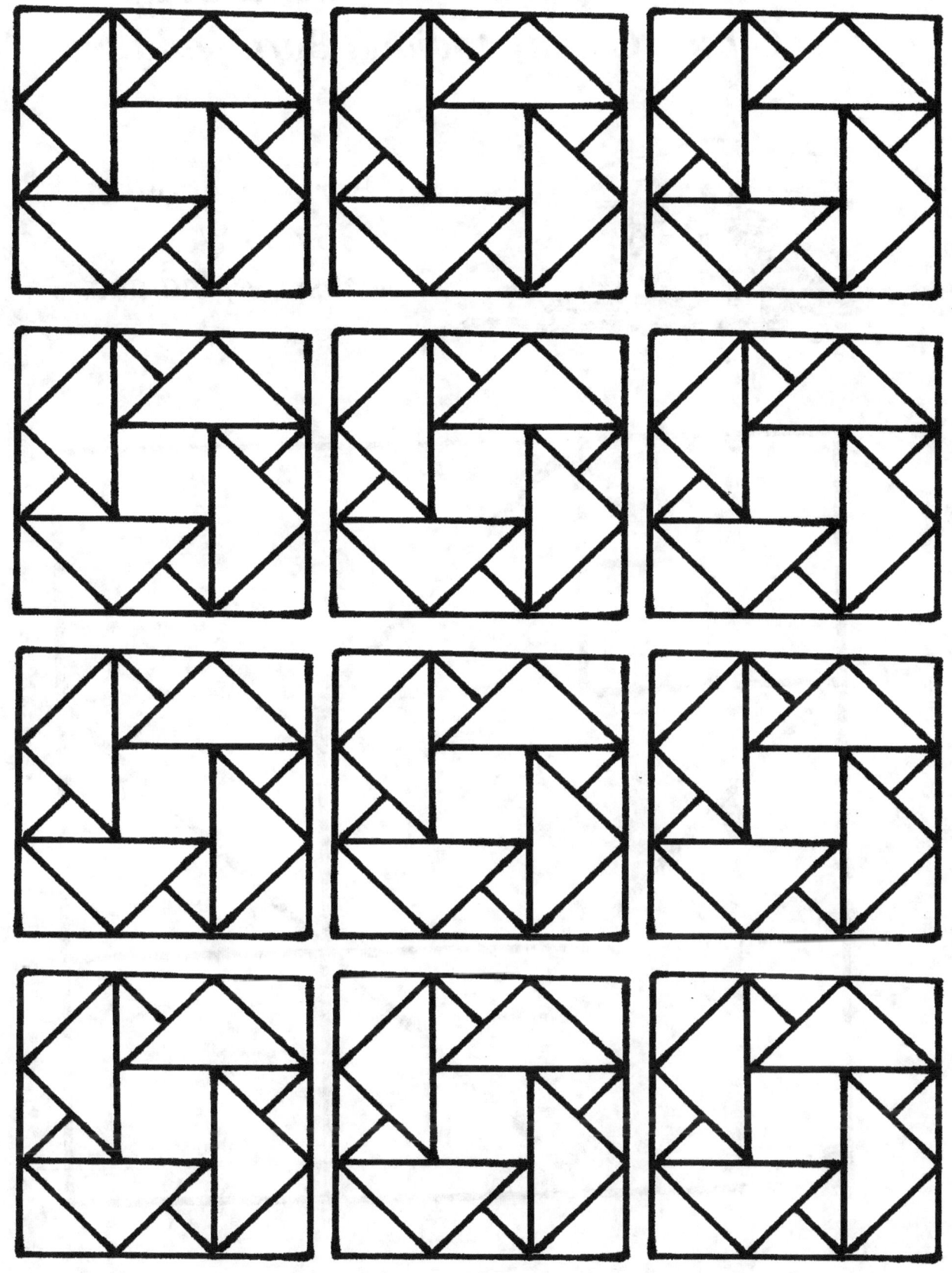

Barn Quilt Buttercup
Gibson County Indiana Barn Quilt

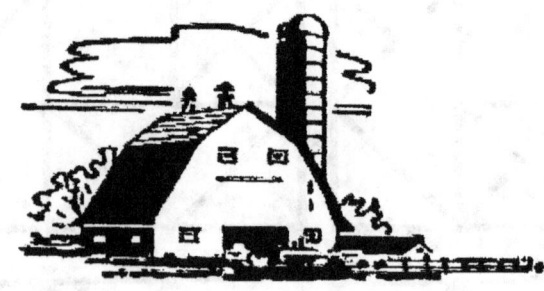

Barn Location
S 450 W
Owensville, Indiana

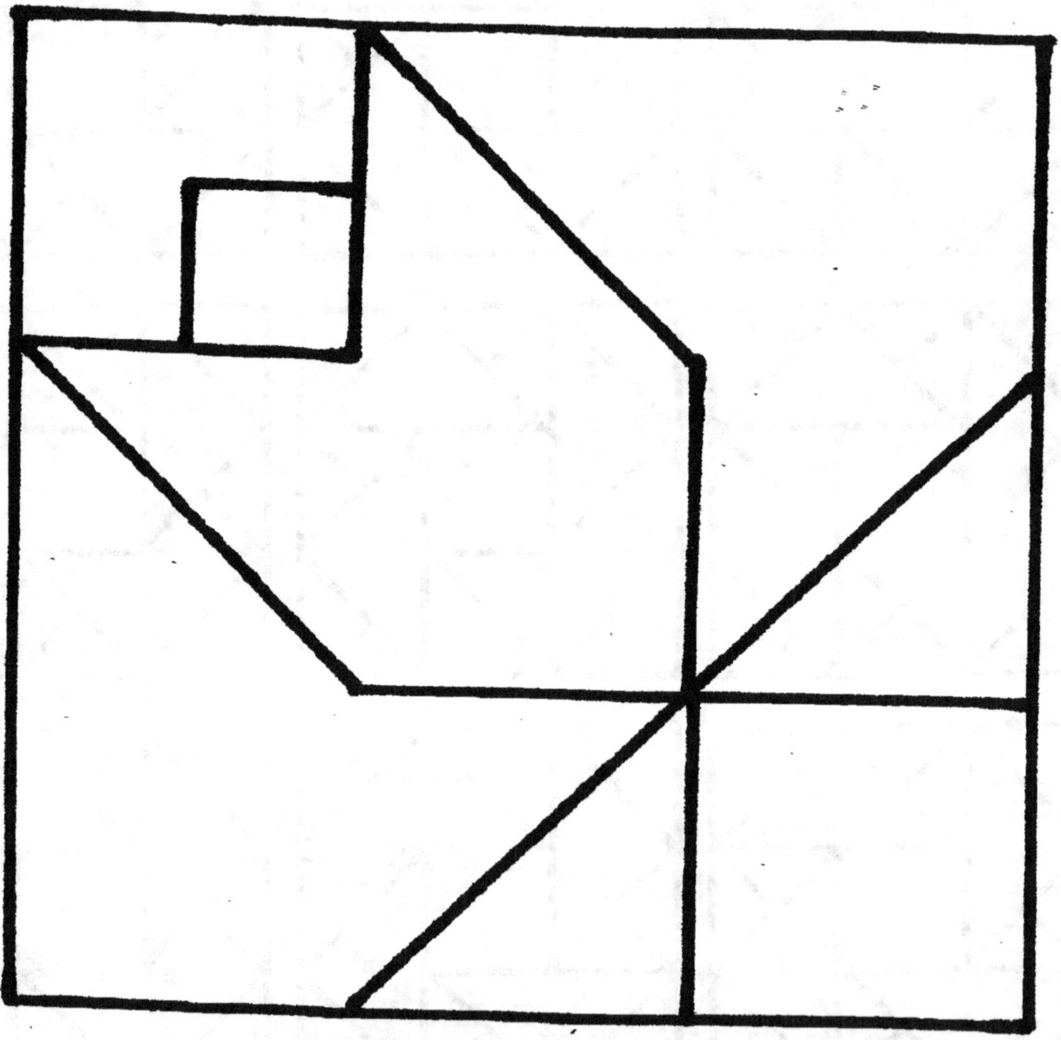

Gibson County Barn Quilt Buttercup

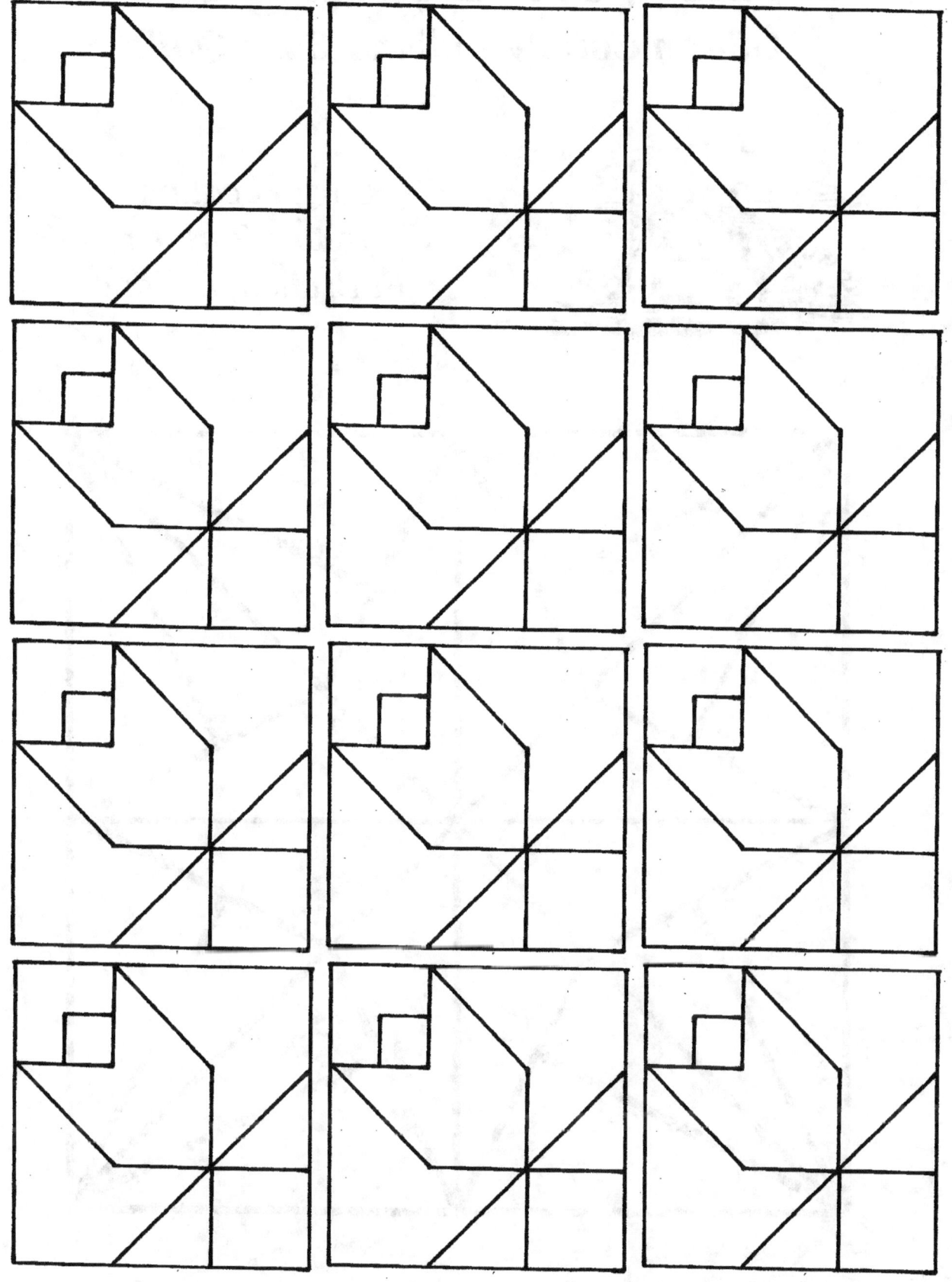

Barn Quilt Blazing Star
Gibson County Indiana Barn Quilt

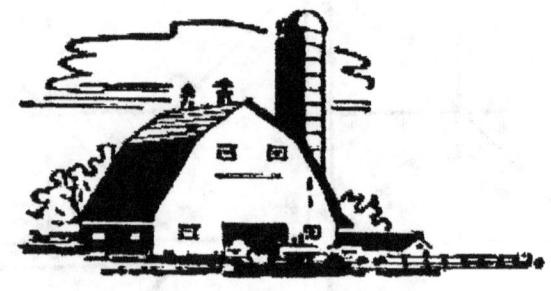

Barn Location
Tretter Park Dr
Ft Branch, Indiana

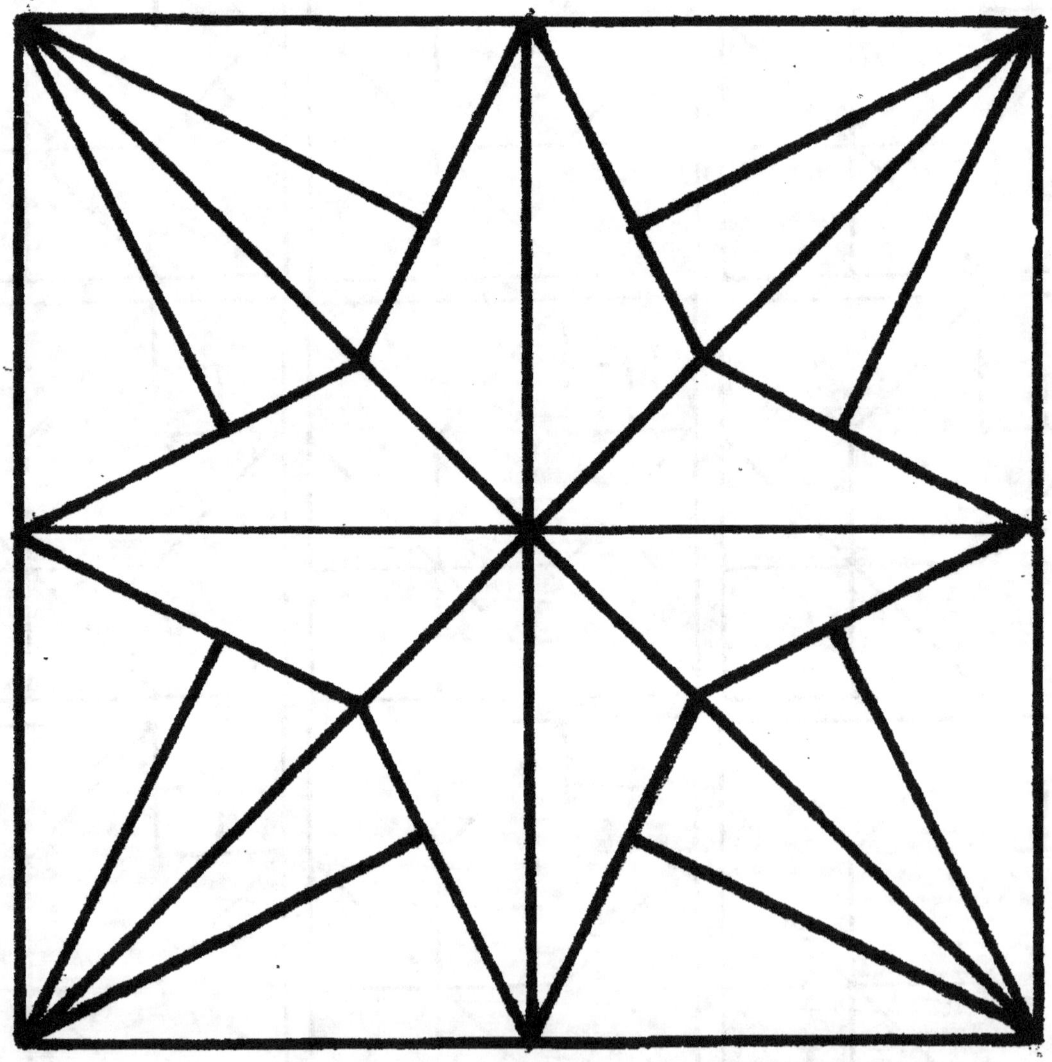

Gibson County Barn Quilt Blazing Star

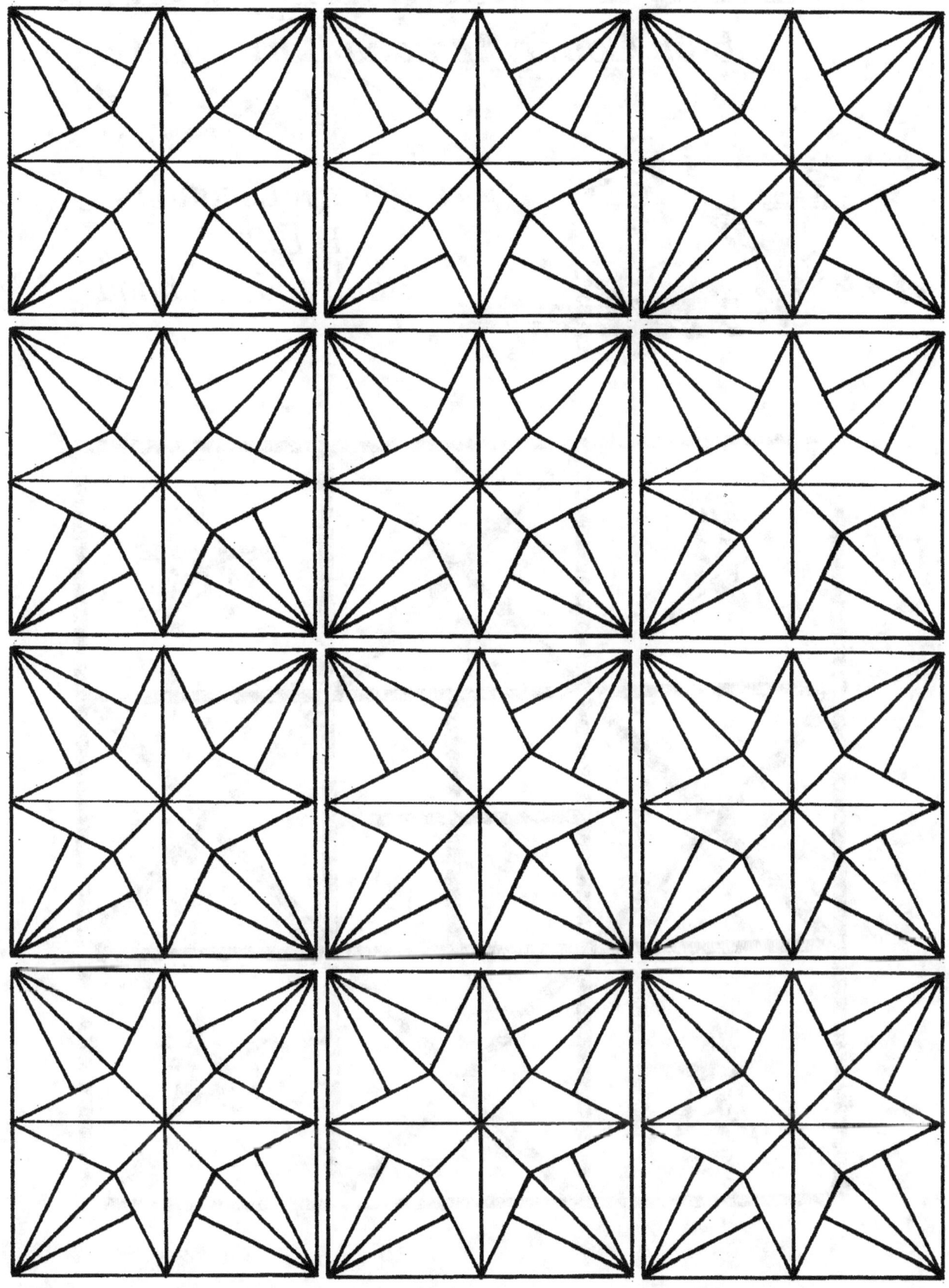

Barn Quilt Country Farm
Gibson County Indiana Barn Quilt

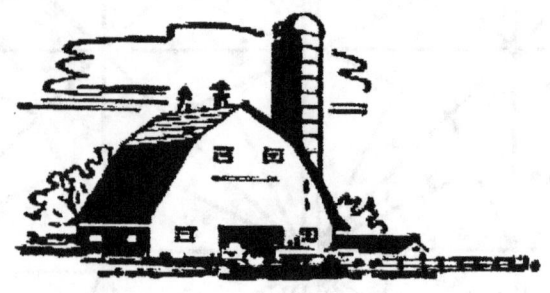

Barn Location
E 1025 S
Haubstadt, Indiana

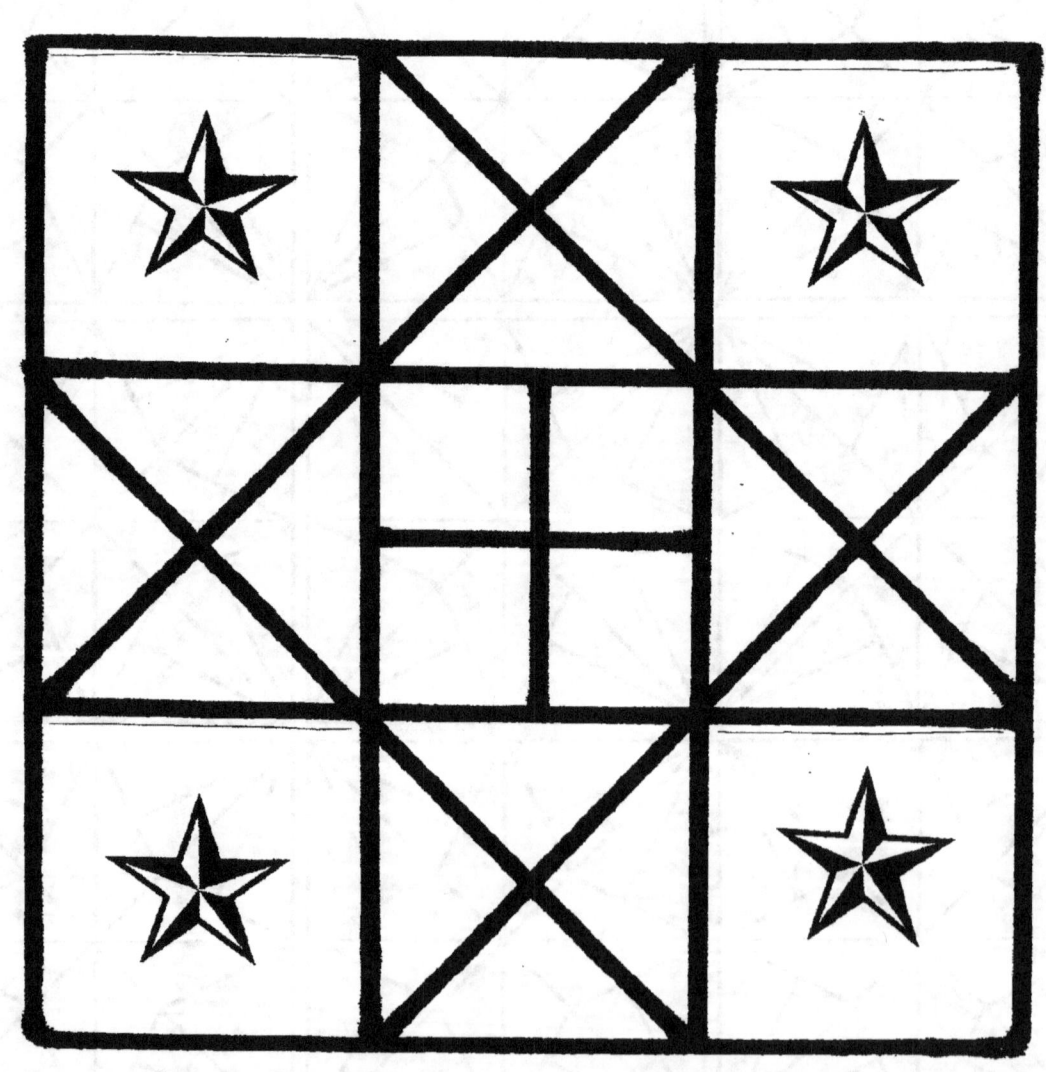

Gibson County Barn Quilt Country Farm

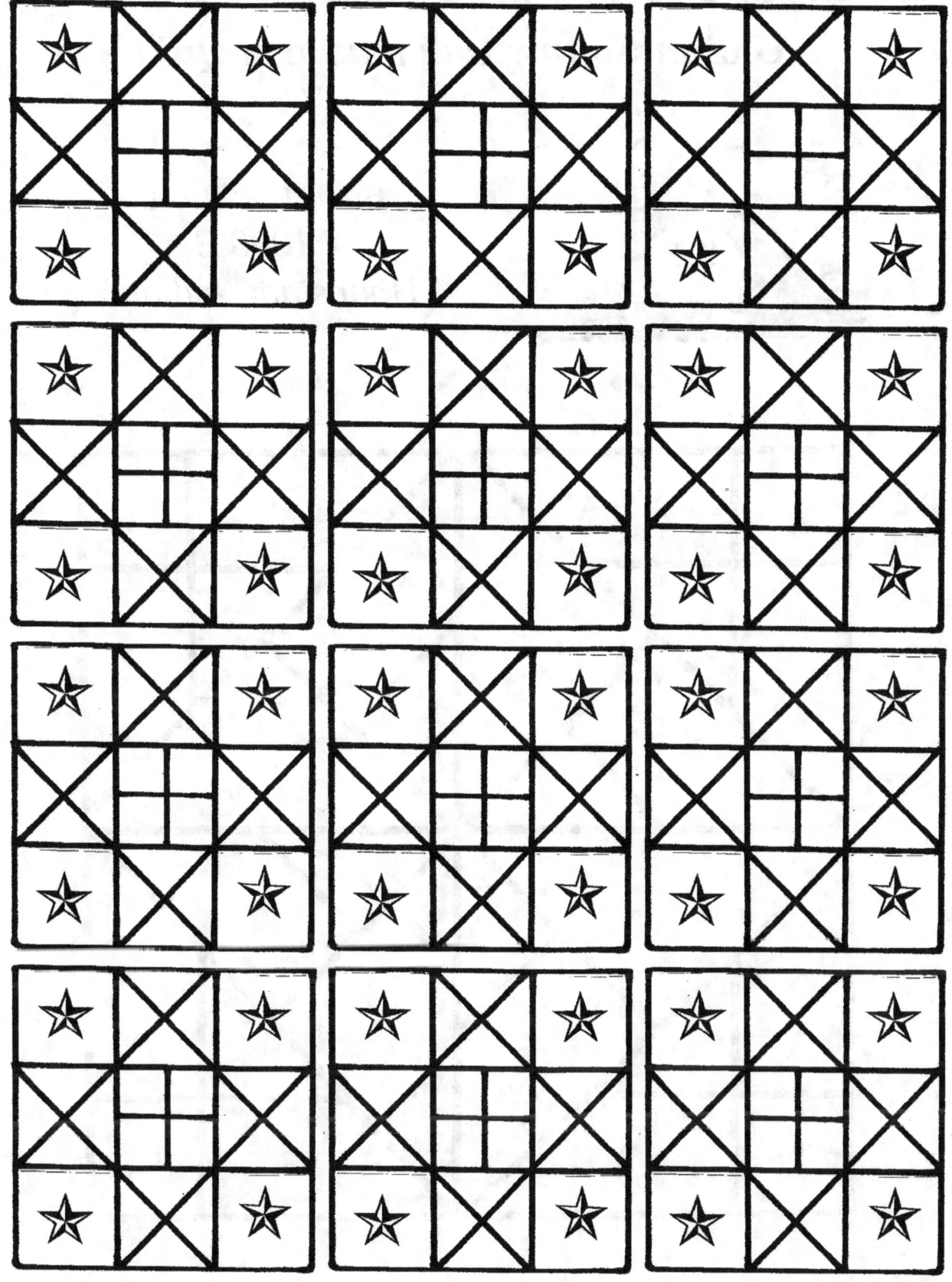

Barn Quilt December Days

Gibson County Indiana Barn Quilt

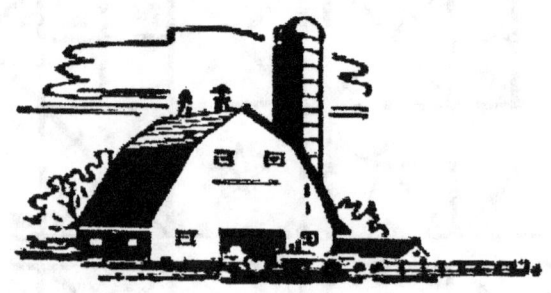

Barn Location
W 1000 E
Haubstadt, Indiana

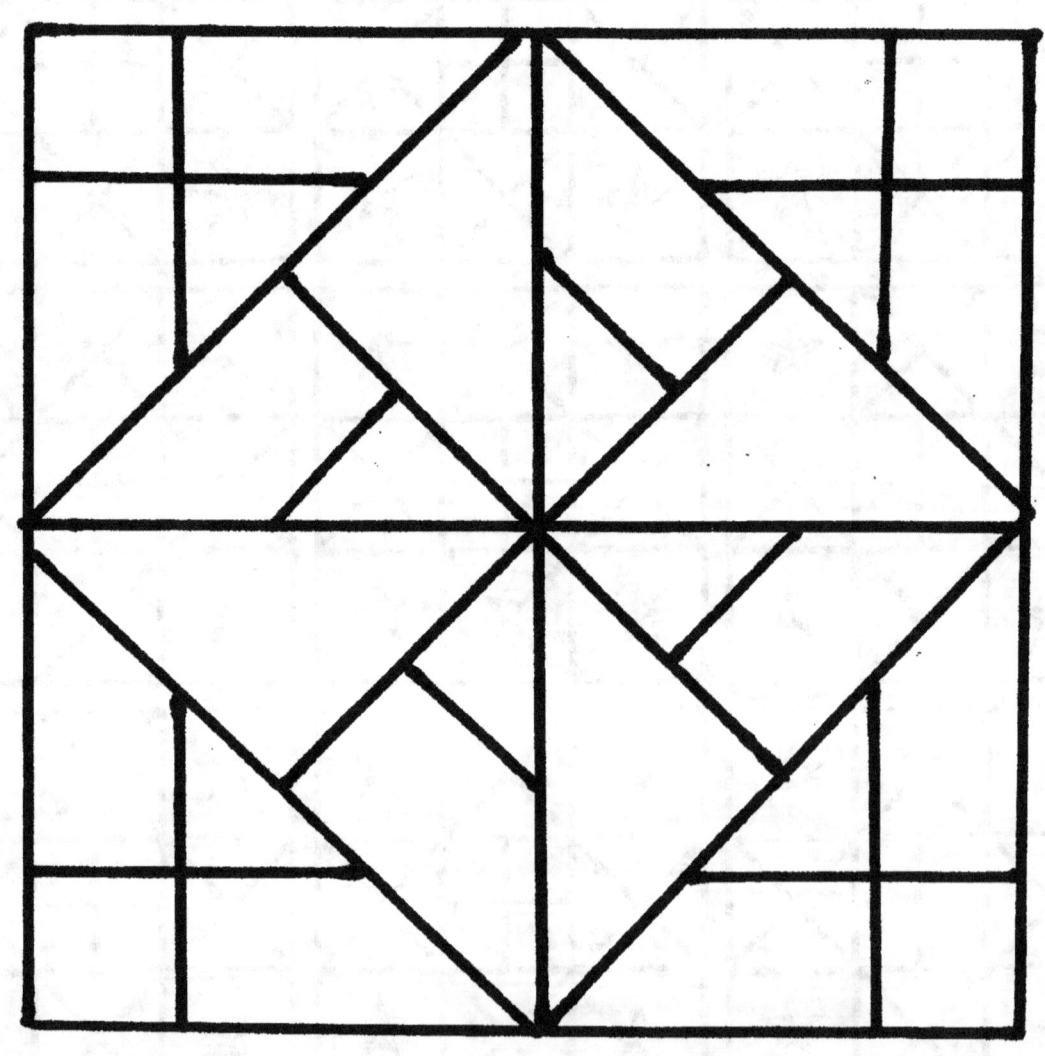

Gibson County Barn Quilt December Days

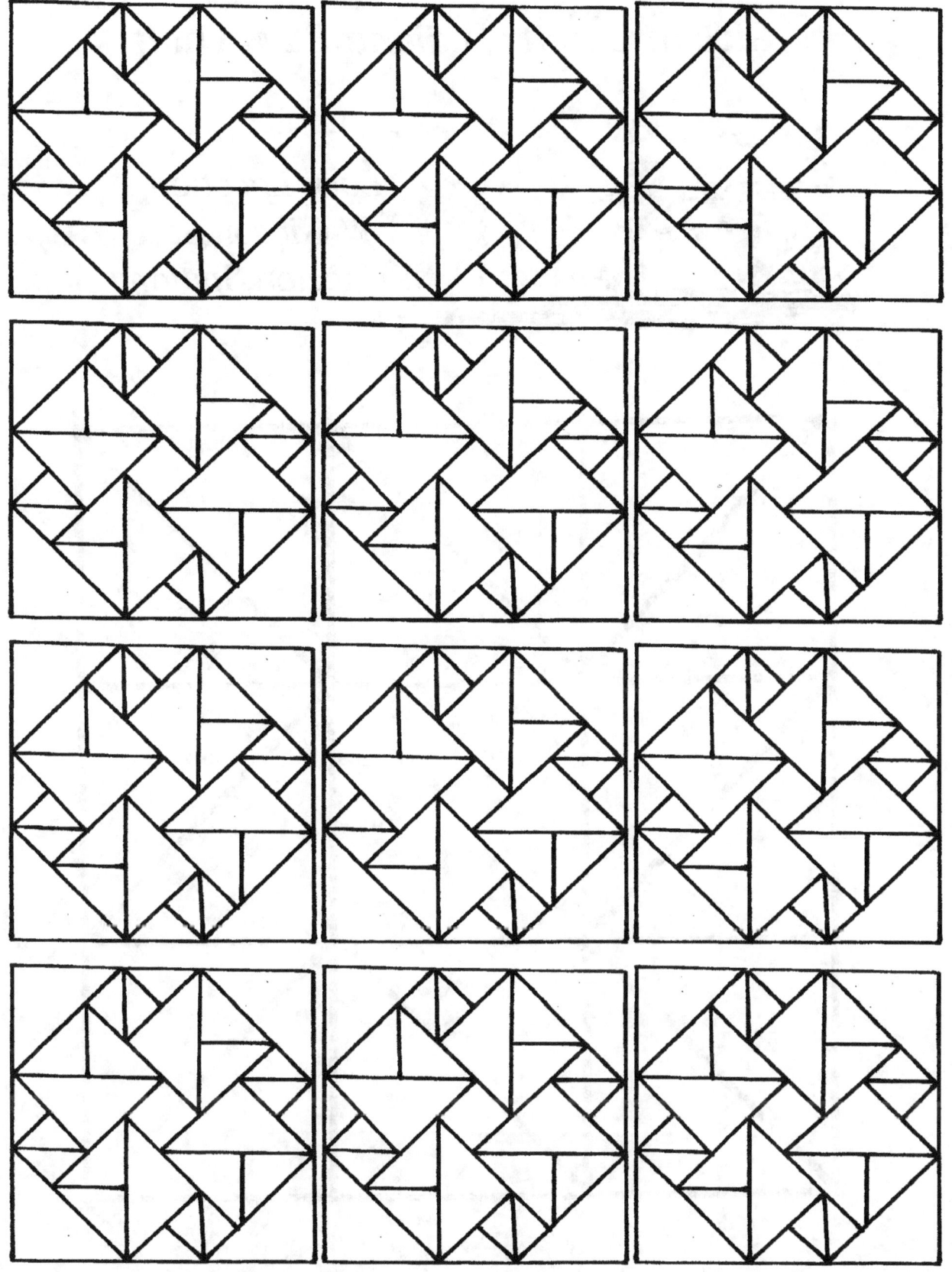

Barn Quilt Gathering Stars

Gibson County Indiana Barn Quilt

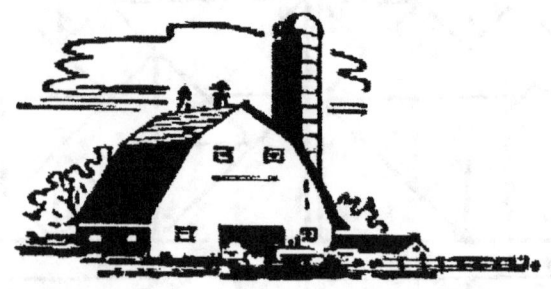

Barn Location
W Gibson St
Princeton, Indiana

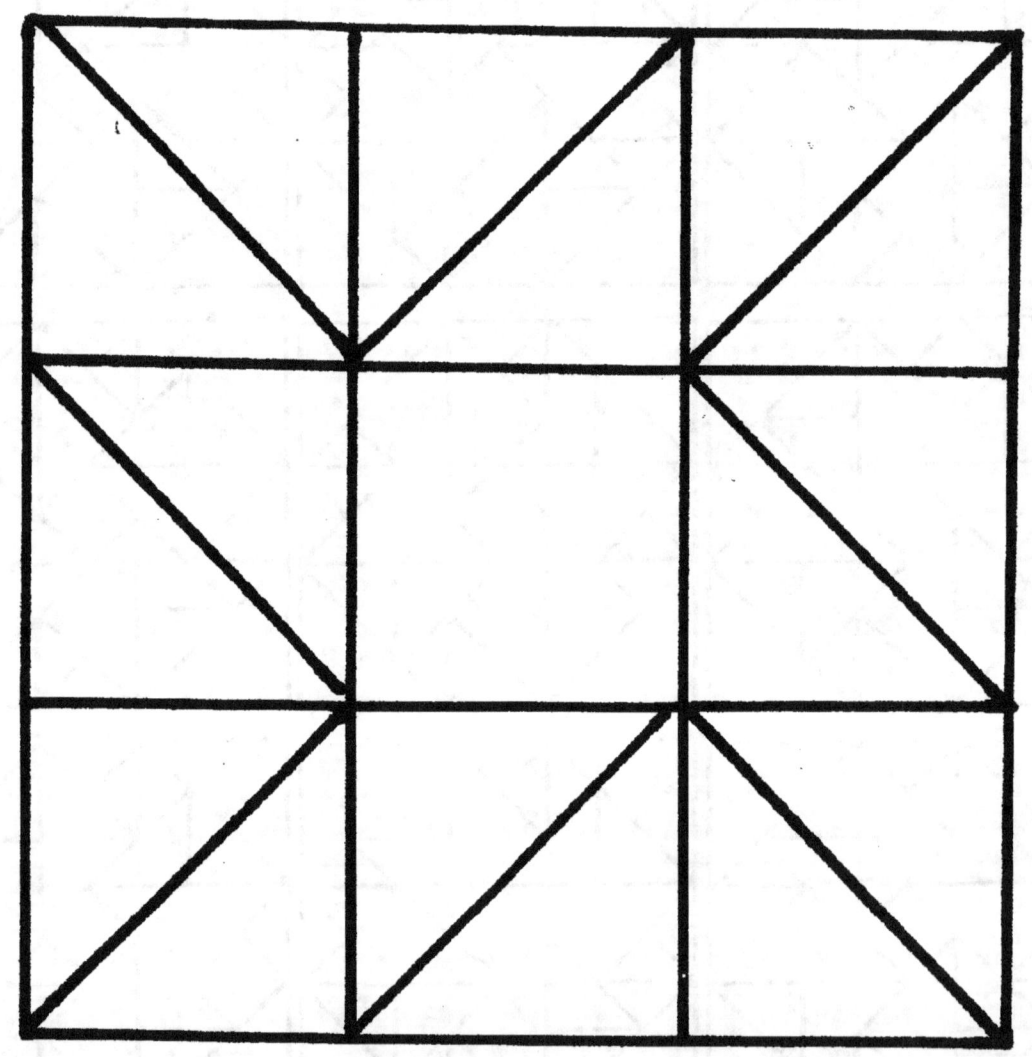

Gibson County Barn Quilt Gathering Stars

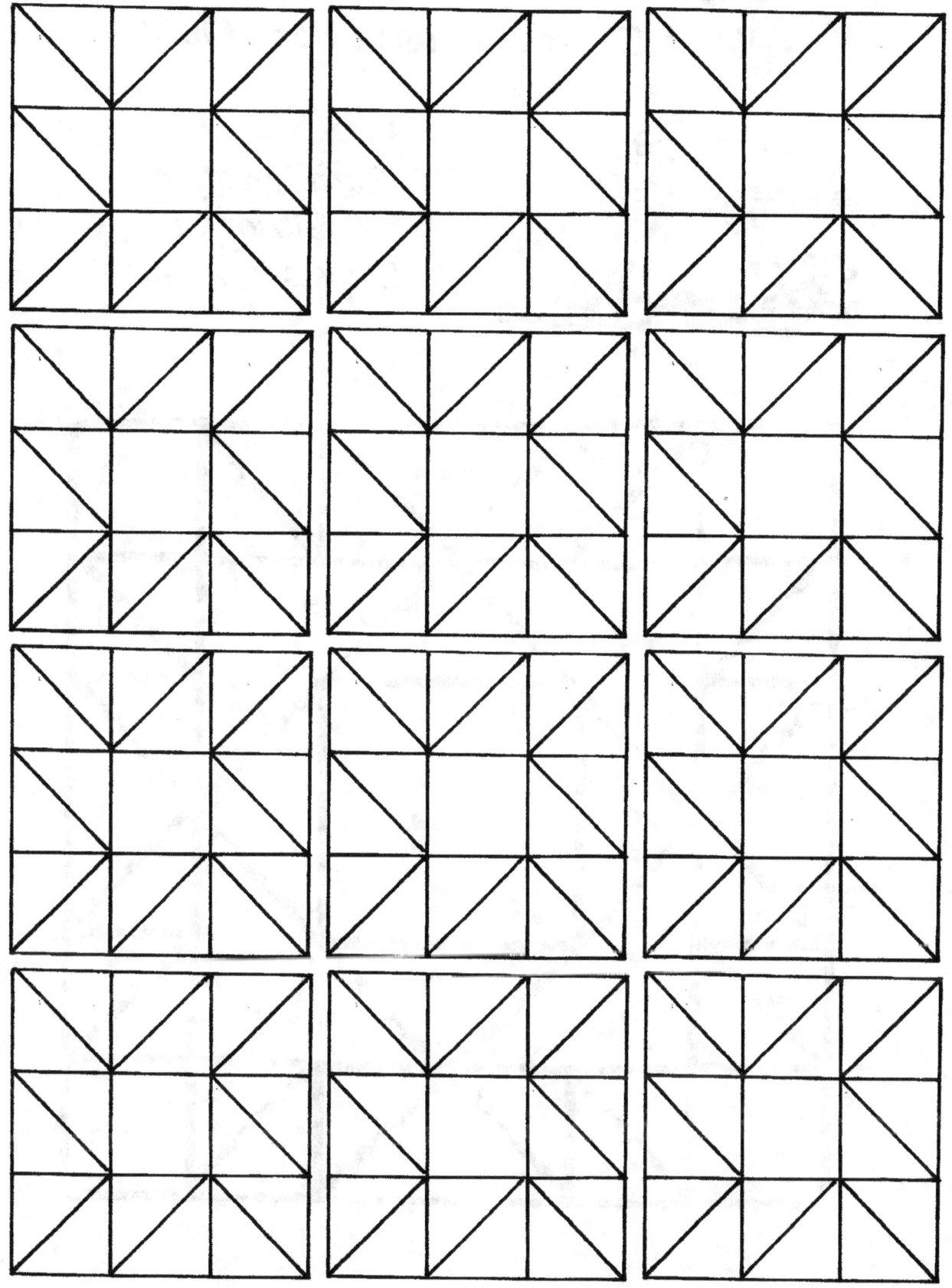

Barn Quilt Cat Paw
Gibson County Indiana Barn Quilt

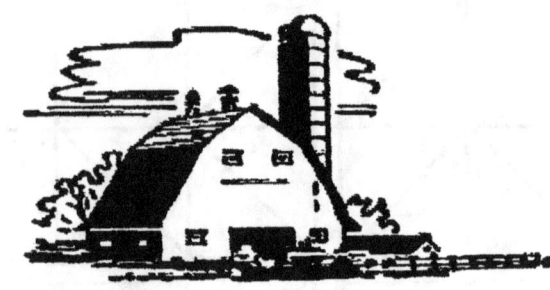

Barn Location
W Gibson St
Haubstadt, Indiana

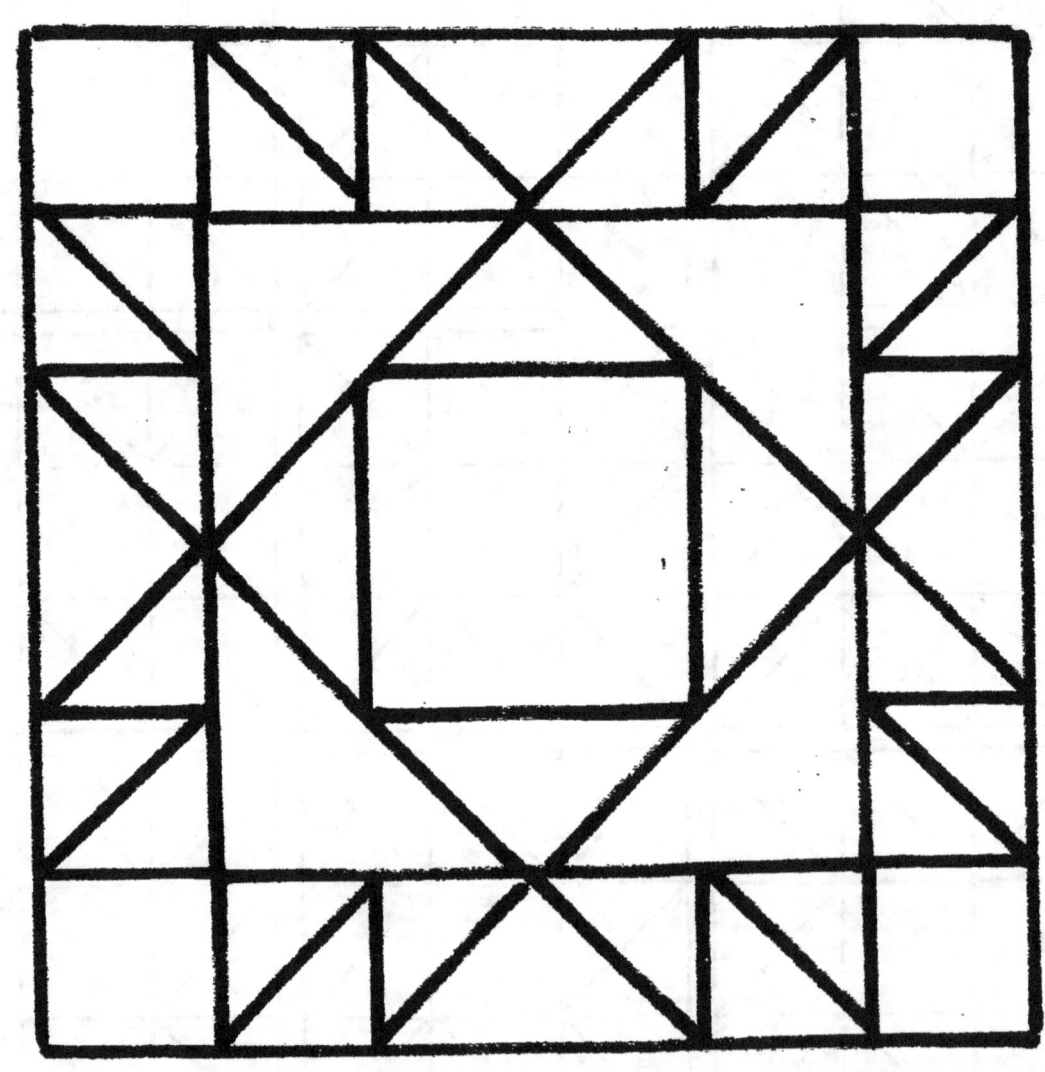

Gibson County Barn Quilt Cat Paw

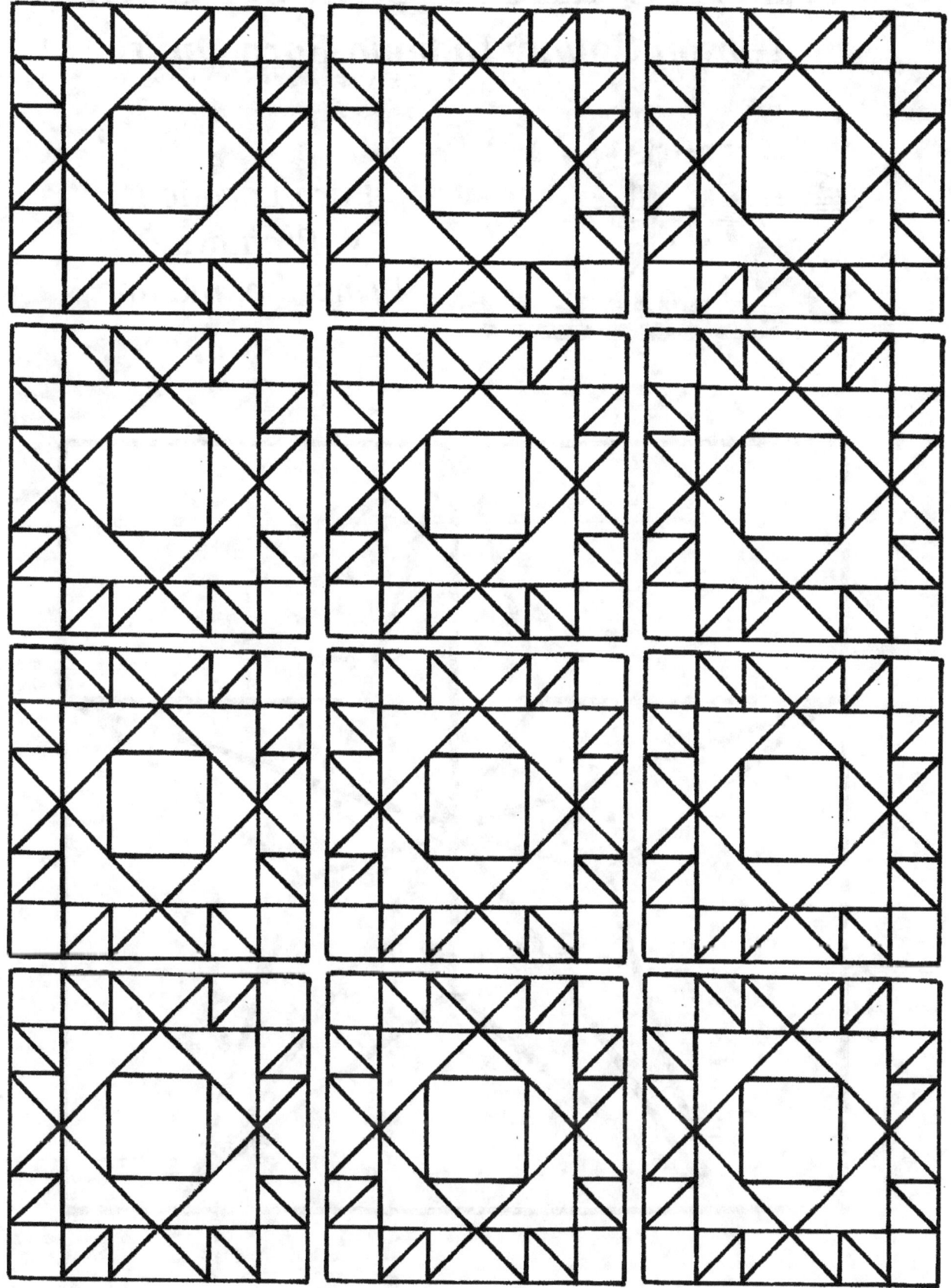

Barn Quilt Bisected Star
Gibson County Indiana Barn Quilt

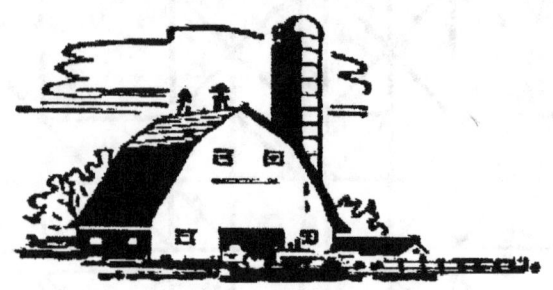

Barn Location
W Broadway
Princeton, Indiana

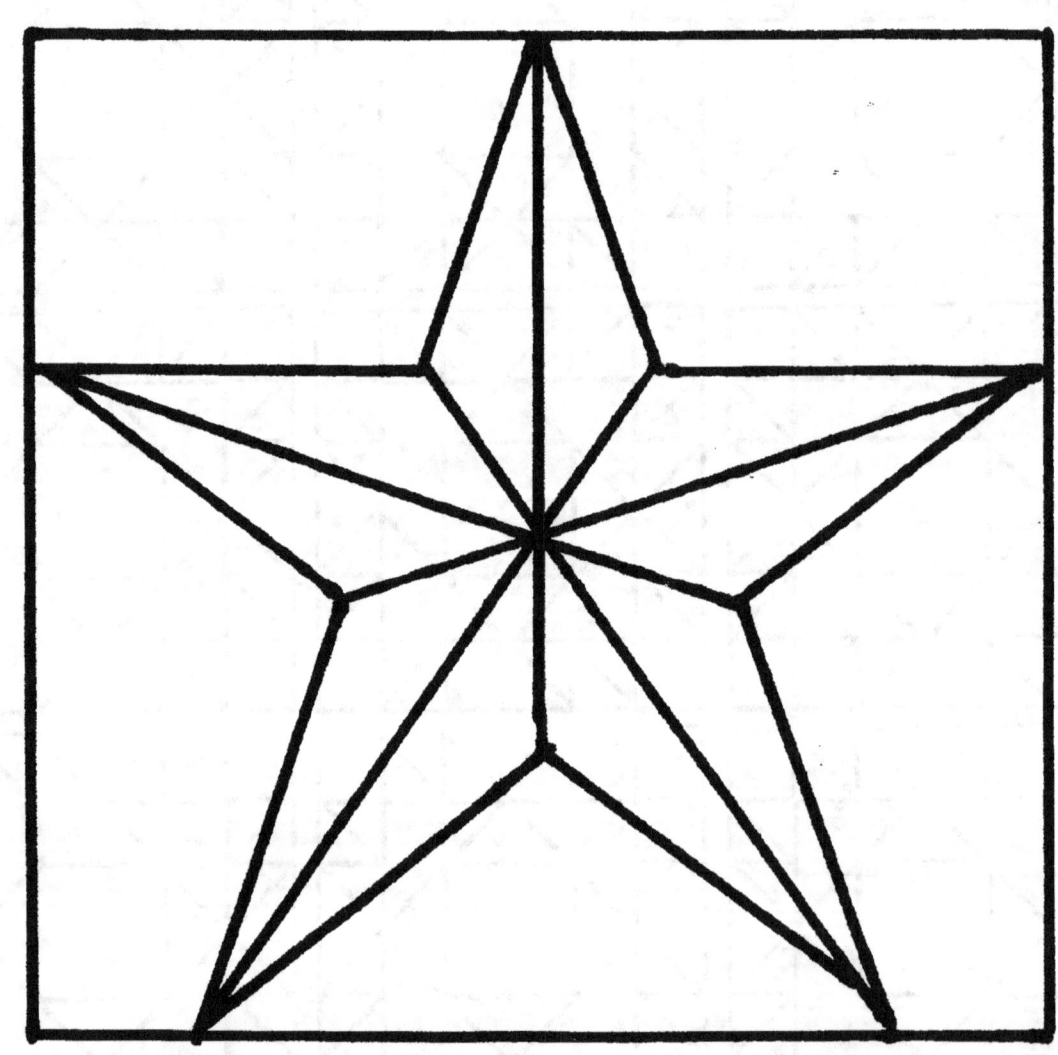

Gibson County Barn Quilt Bisected Star

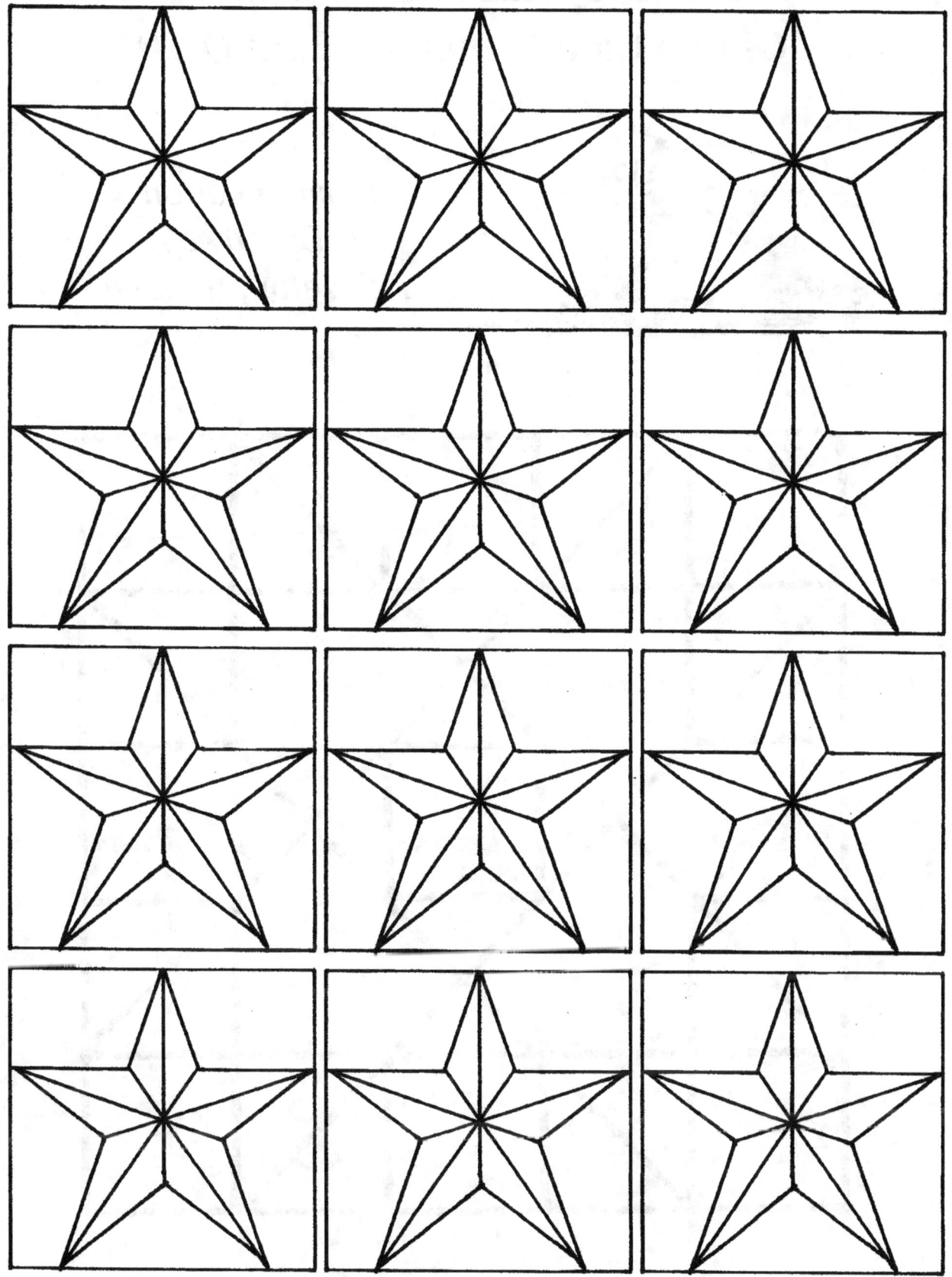

Barn Quilt Crossings
Gibson County Indiana Barn Quilt

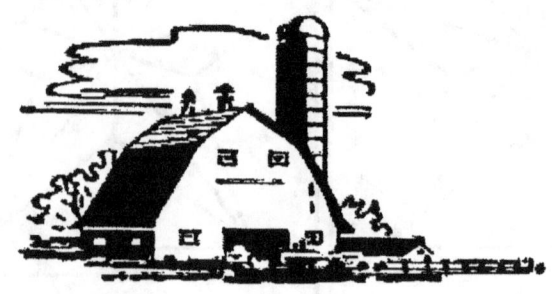

Barn Location
W Broadway
Princeton, Indiana

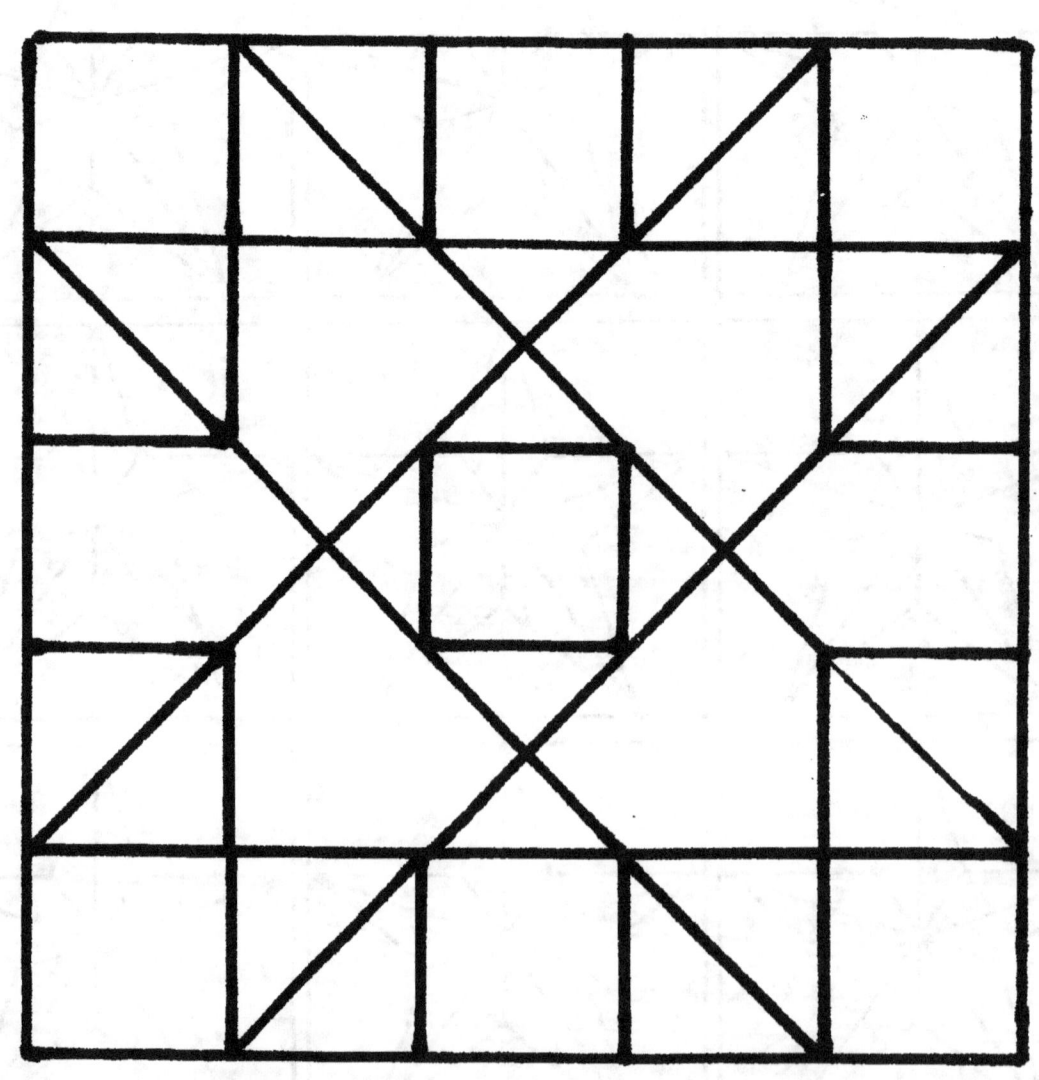

Gibson County Barn Quilt Crossings

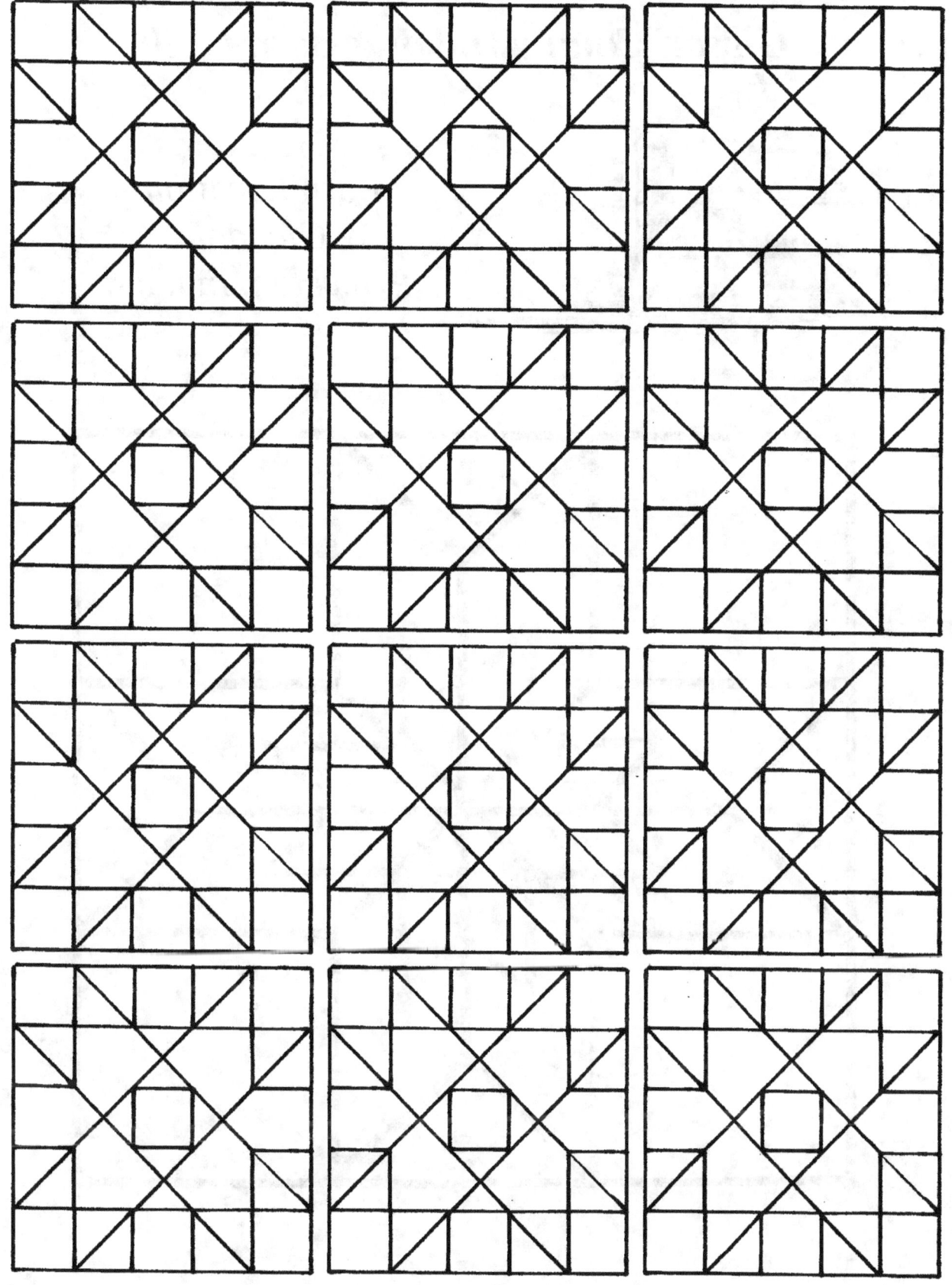

Barn Quilt Janie's Star
Gibson County Indiana Barn Quilt

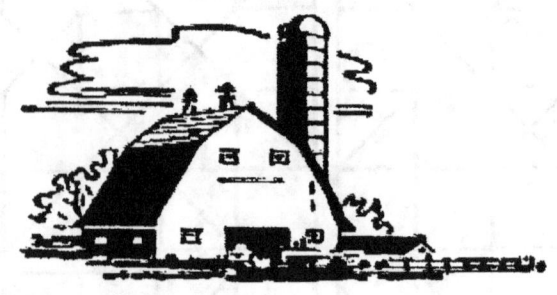

Barn Location
W Glendale
Princeton, Indiana

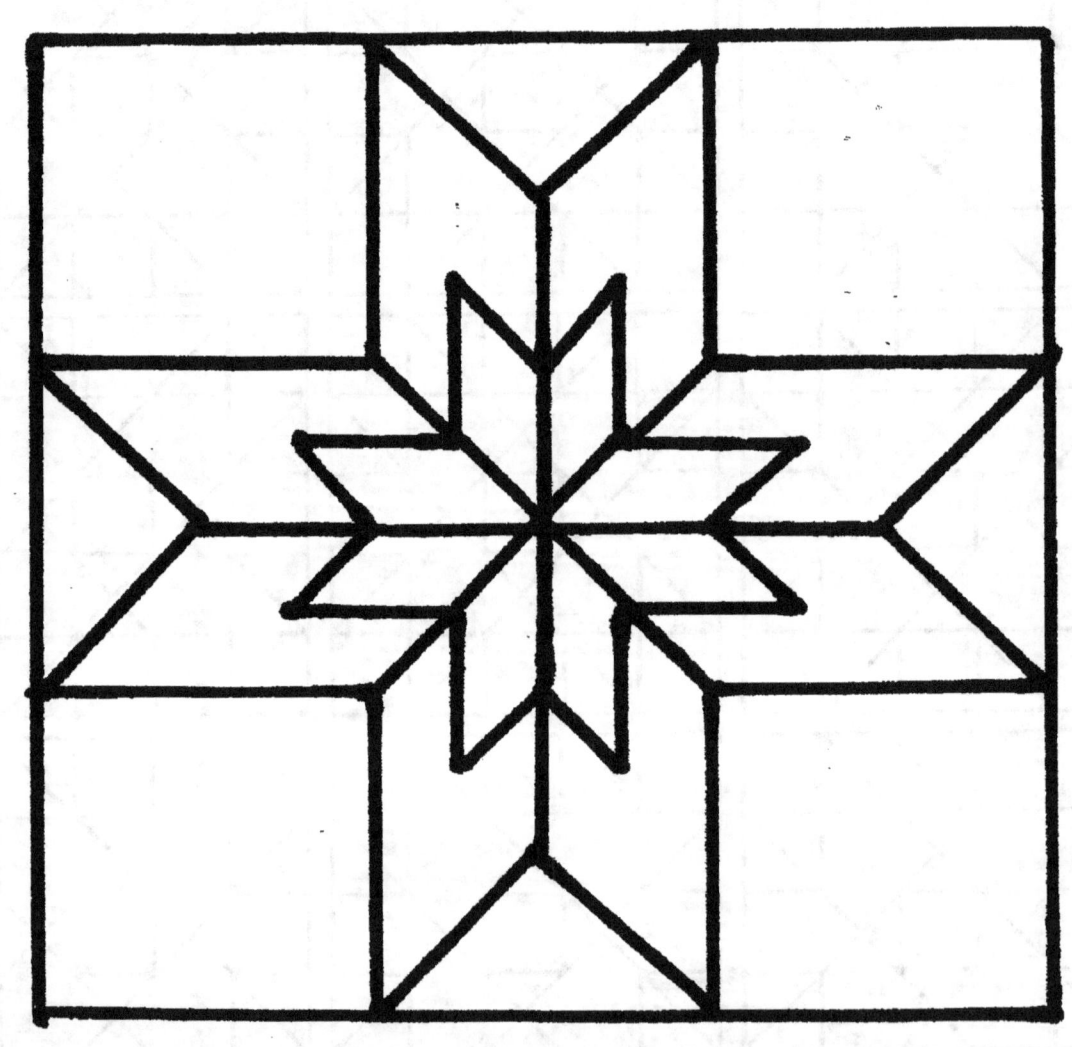

Gibson County Barn Quilt Janie's Star

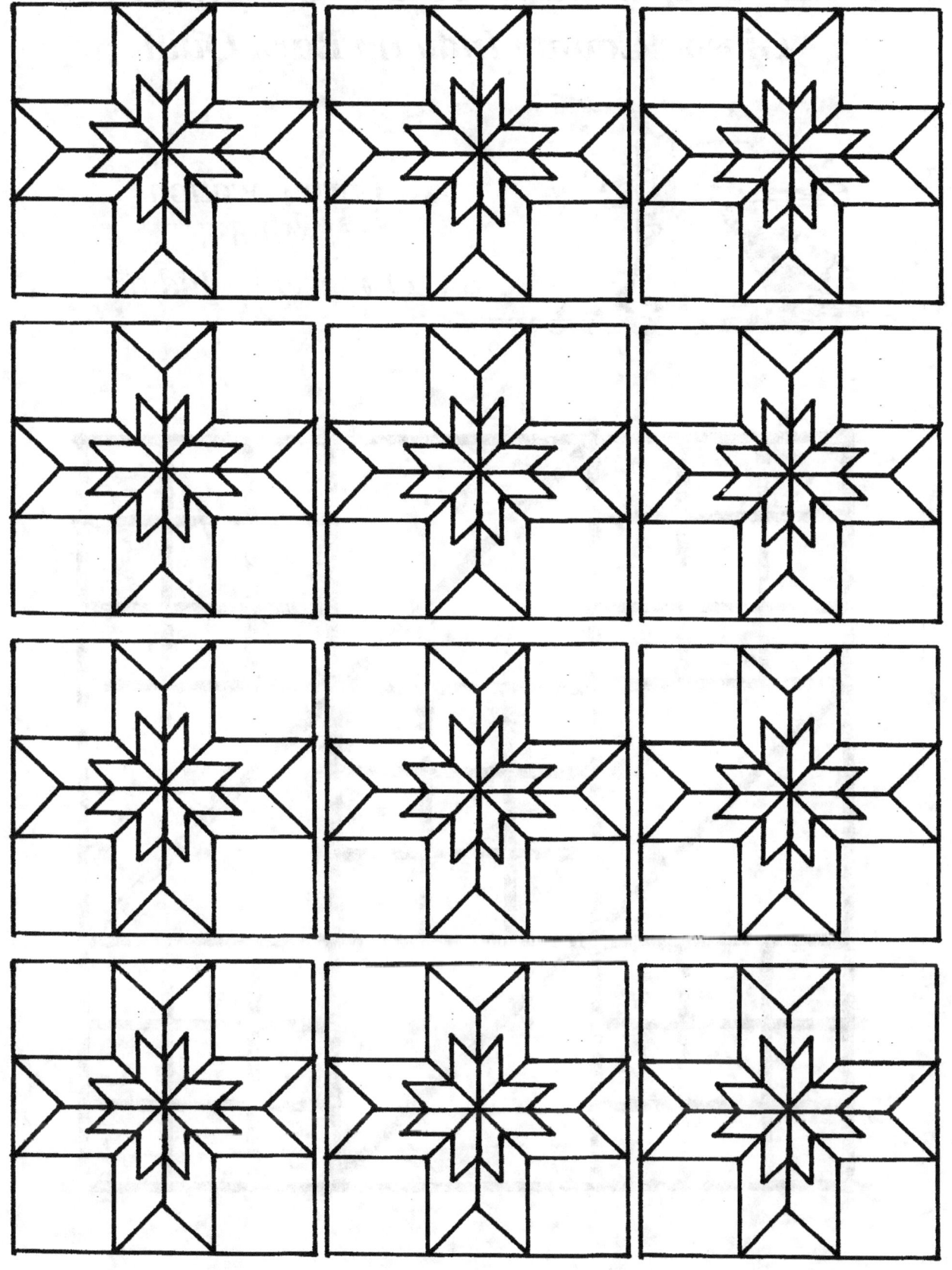

Barn Quilt Jacob's Ladder
Gibson County Indiana Barn Quilt

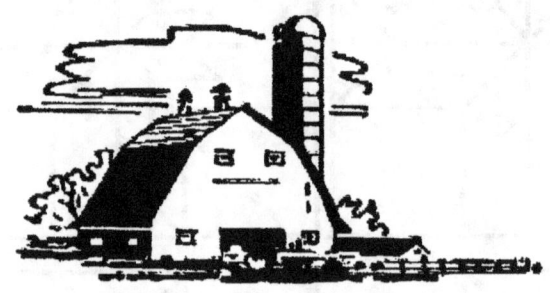

Barn Location
N Main St
Ownesville, Indiana

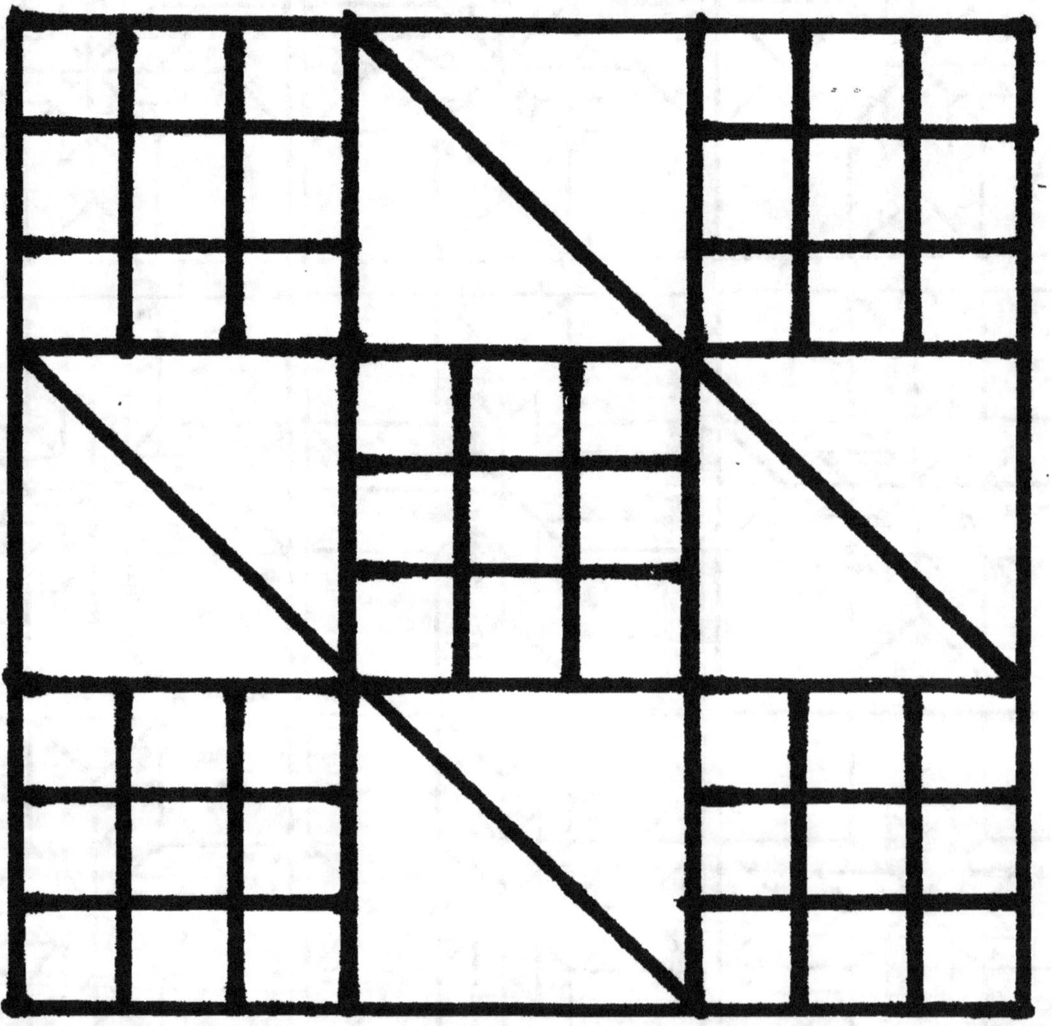

Gibson County Barn Quilt Jacob's Ladder

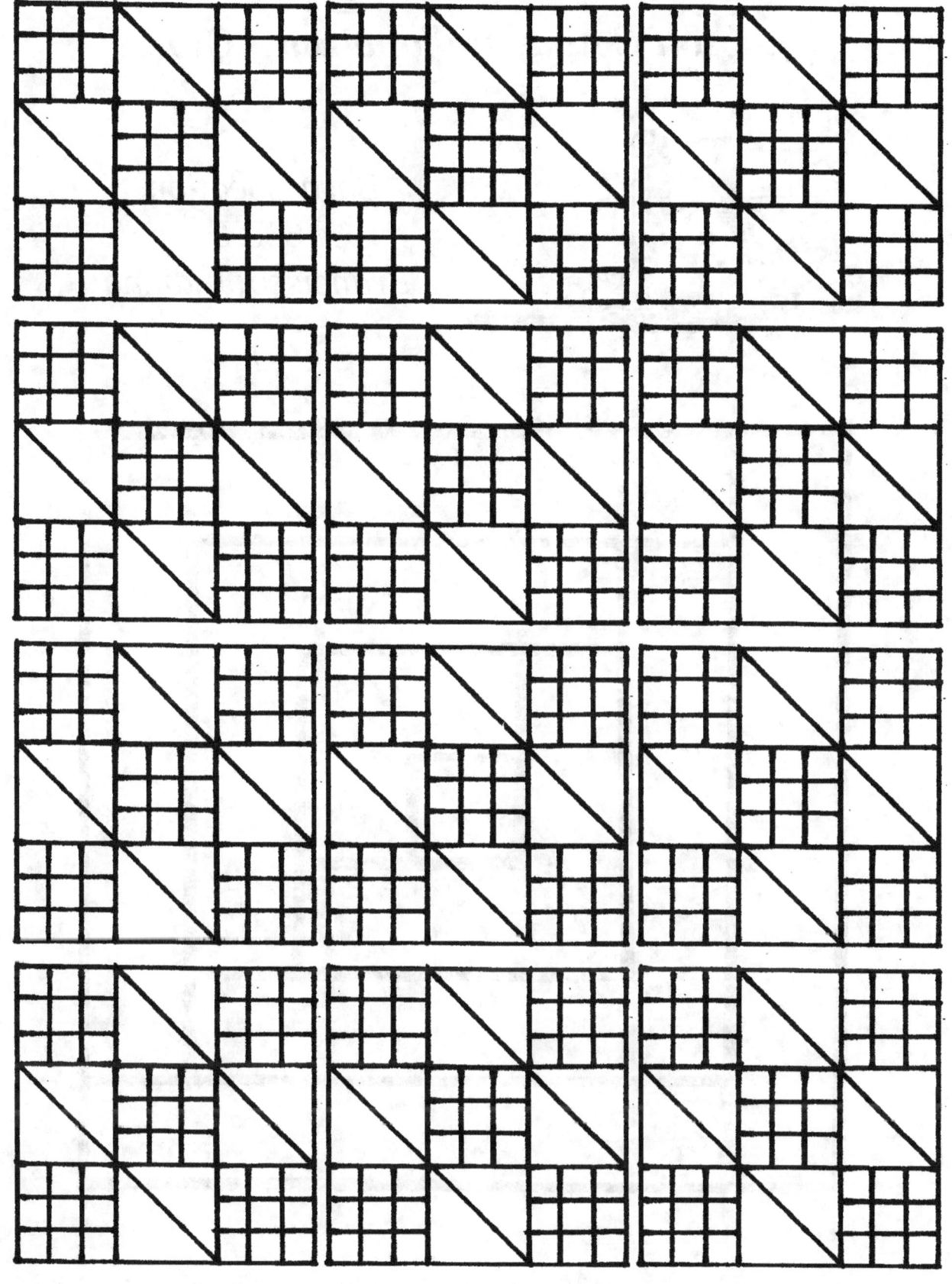

Barn Quilt Log Cabin
Gibson County Indiana Barn Quilt

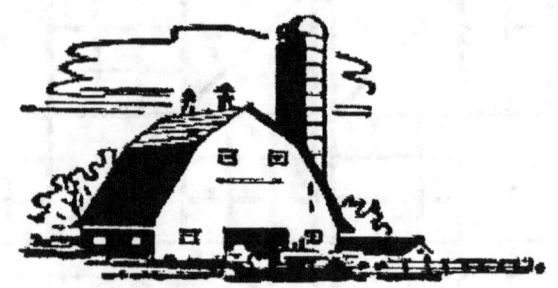

Barn Location
N 650 E
Francisco, Indiana

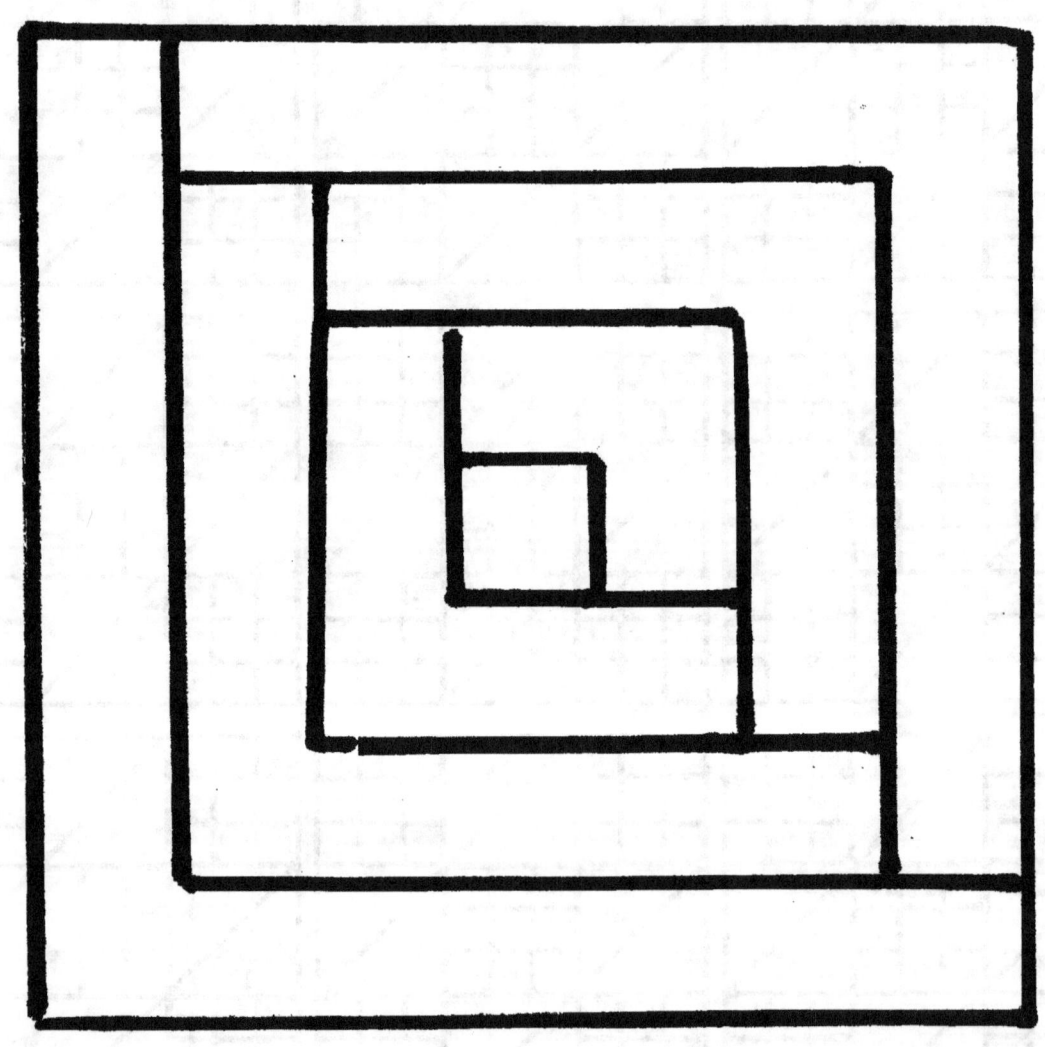

Gibson County Barn Quilt Log Cabin

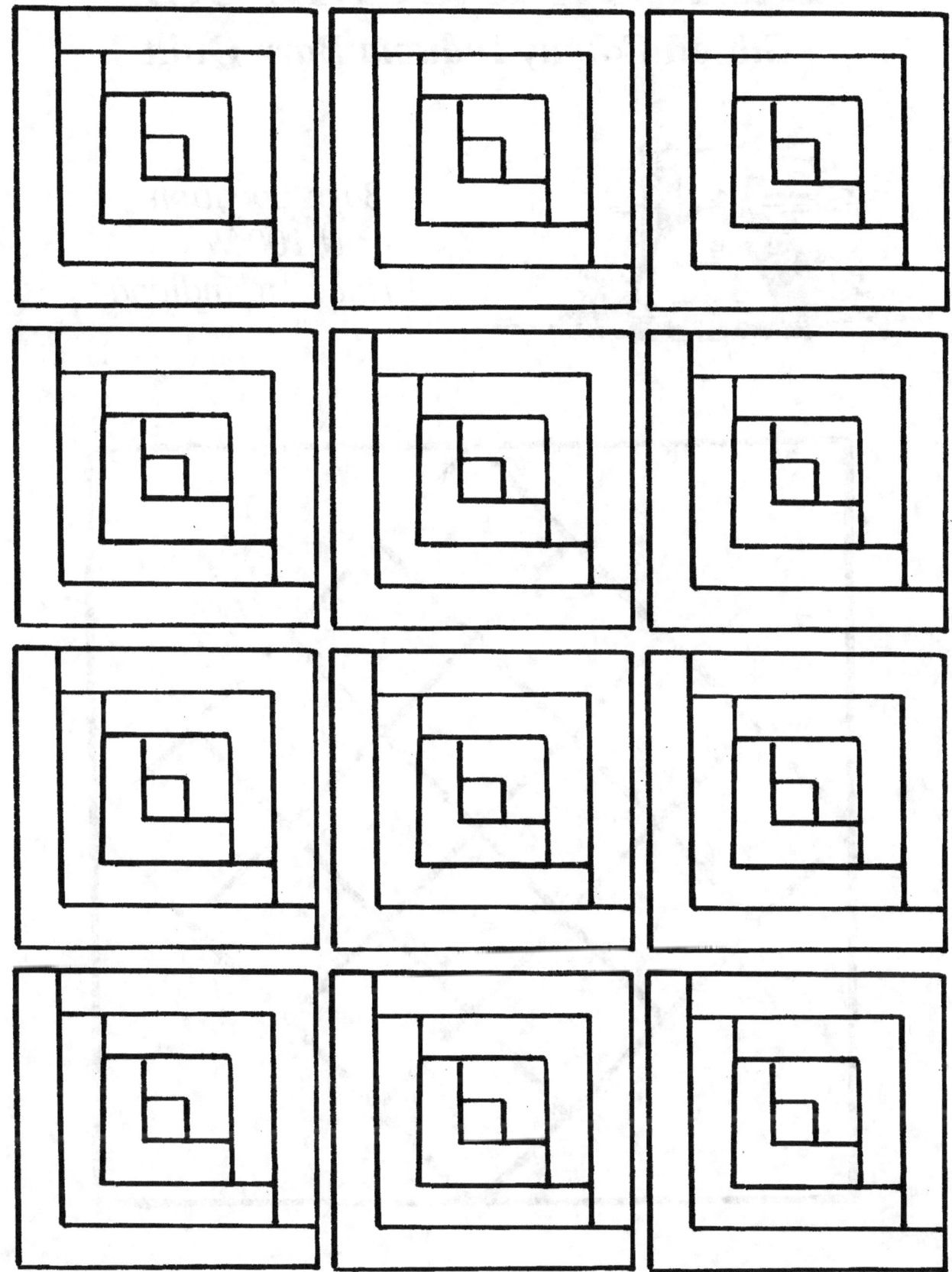

Barn Quilt Coffin Star
Gibson County Indiana Barn Quilt

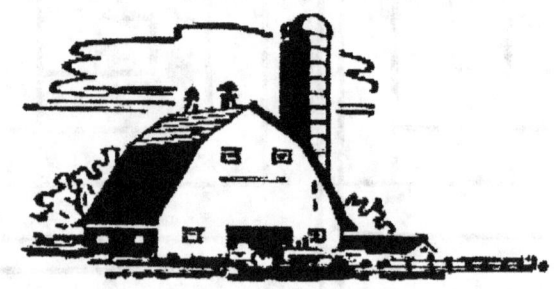

Barn Location
N 100 W
Princeton, Indiana

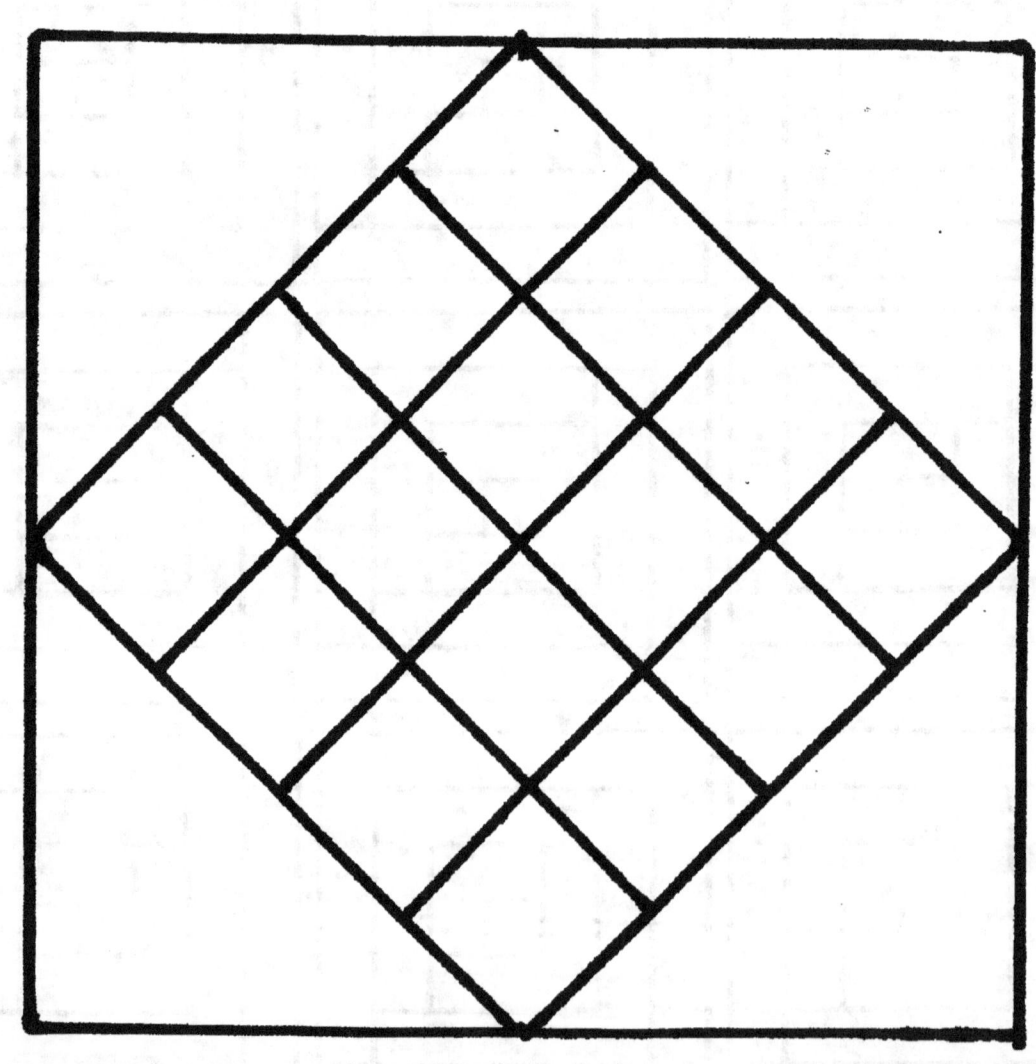

Gibson County Barn Quilt Coffin Star

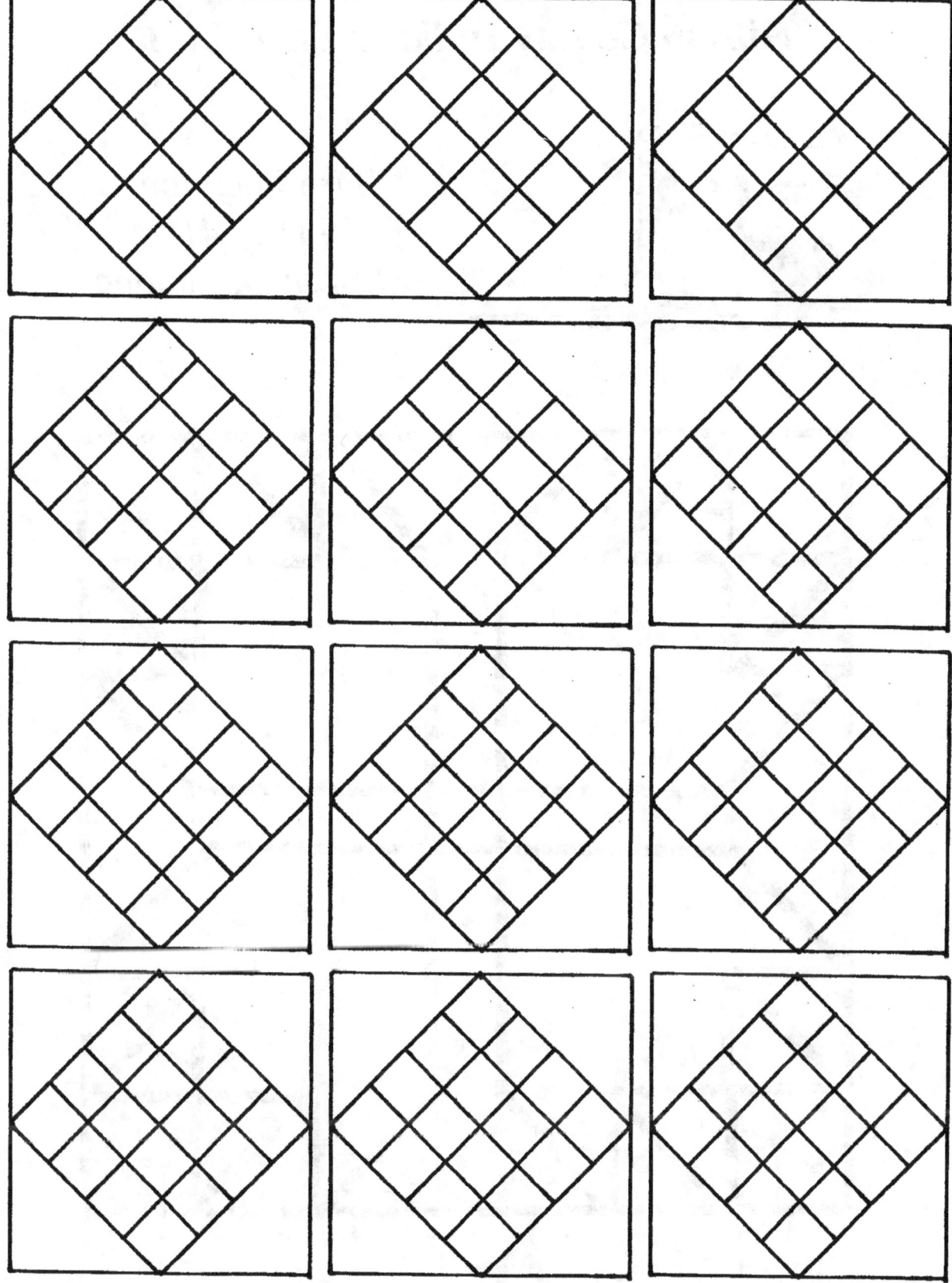

Barn Quilt Bear Paws
Gibson County Indiana Barn Quilt

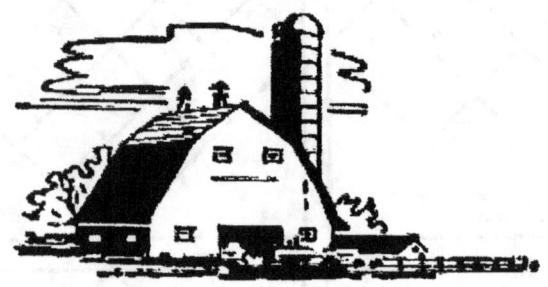

Barn Location
S Hwy 41
Ft Branch, Indiana

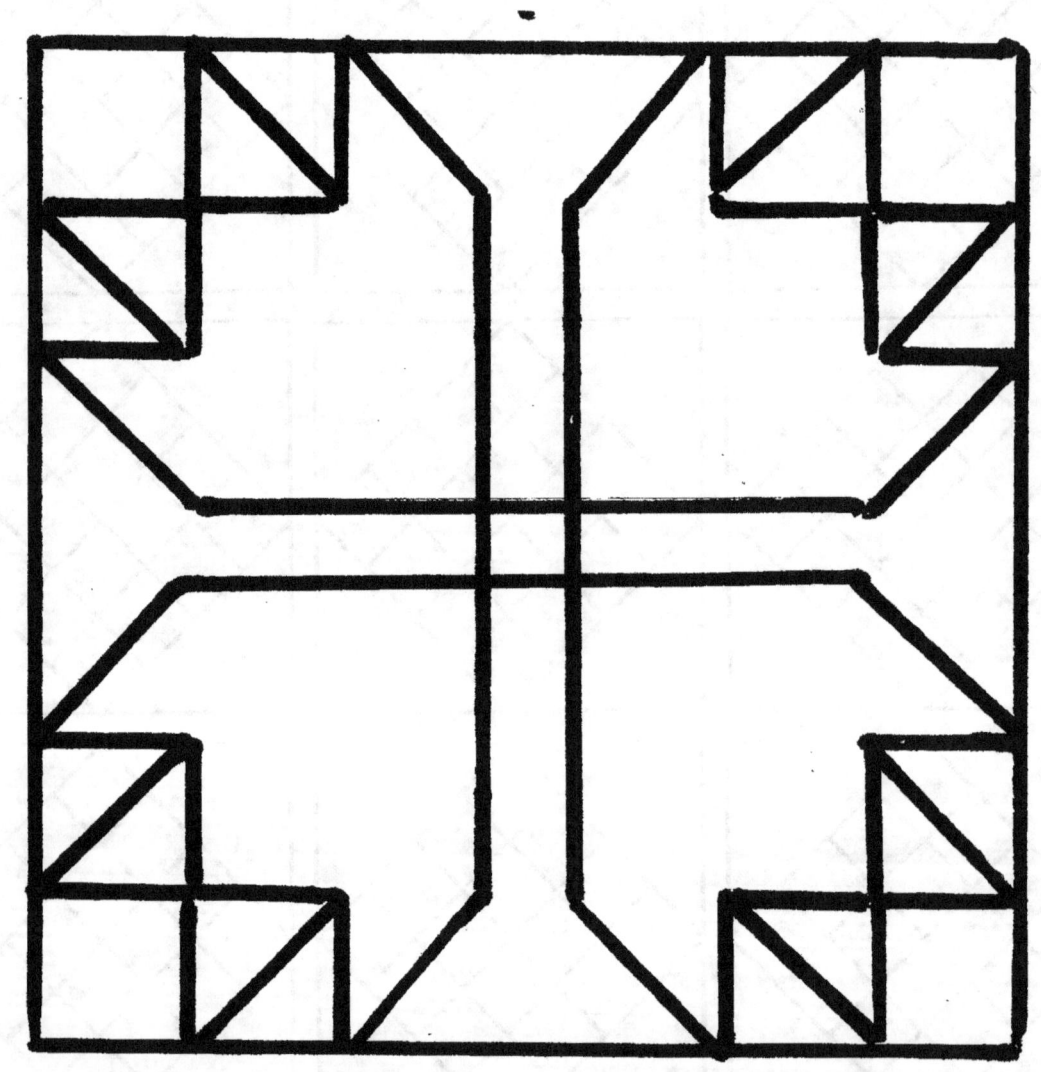

Gibson County Barn Quilt Bear Paws

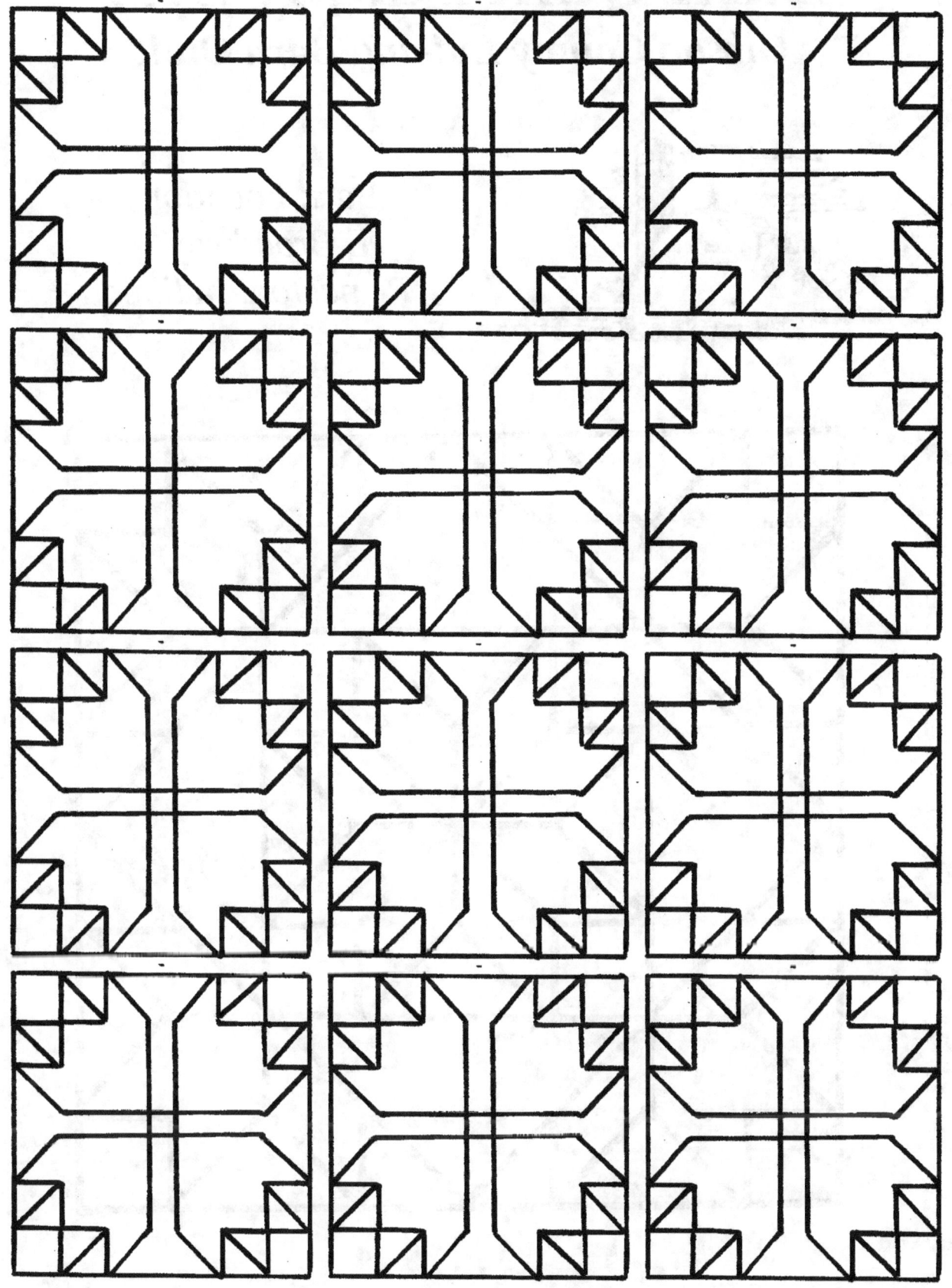

Barn Quilt Family Star
Gibson County Indiana Barn Quilt

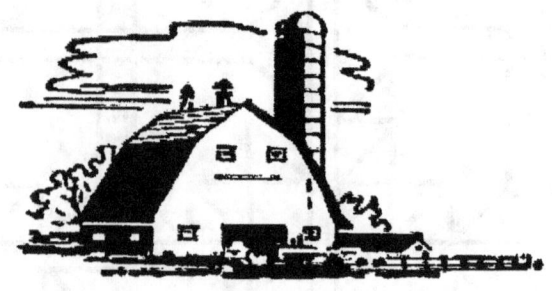

Barn Location
E Broadway
Princeton, Indiana

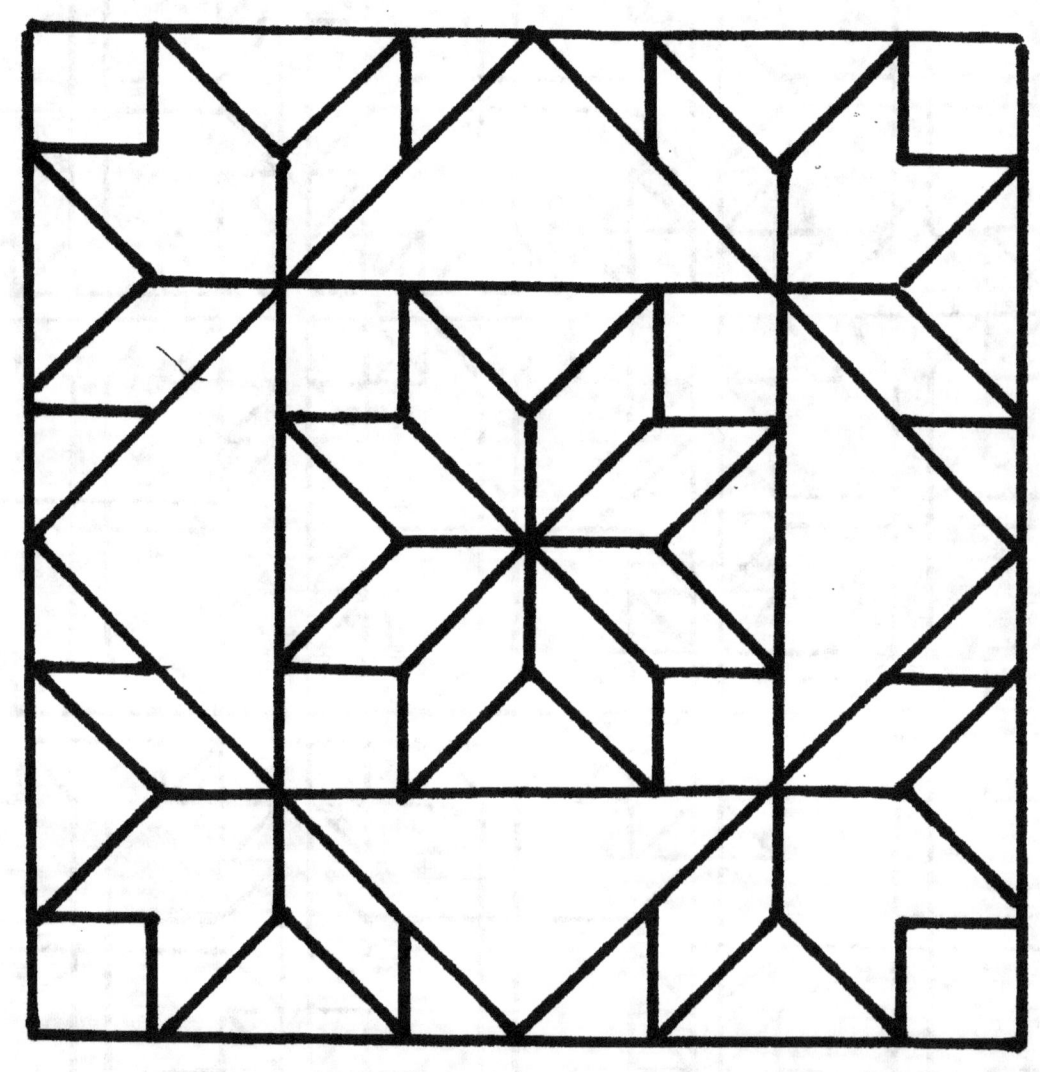

Gibson County Barn Quilt Family Star

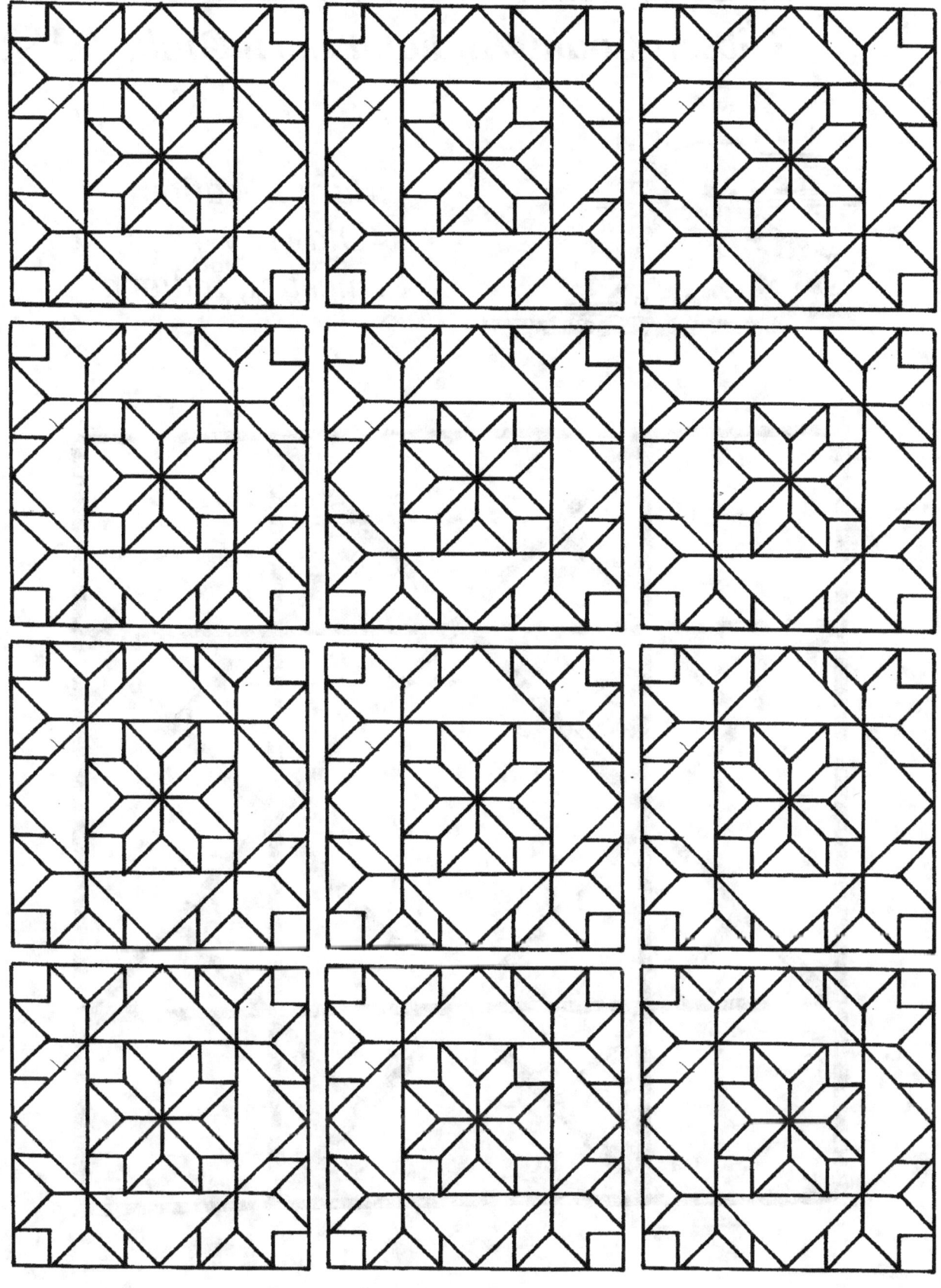

Barn Quilt Missouri Star
Gibson County Indiana Barn Quilt

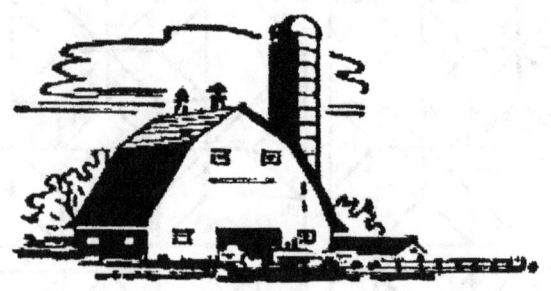

Barn Location
Old Hwy 41
Princeton, Indiana

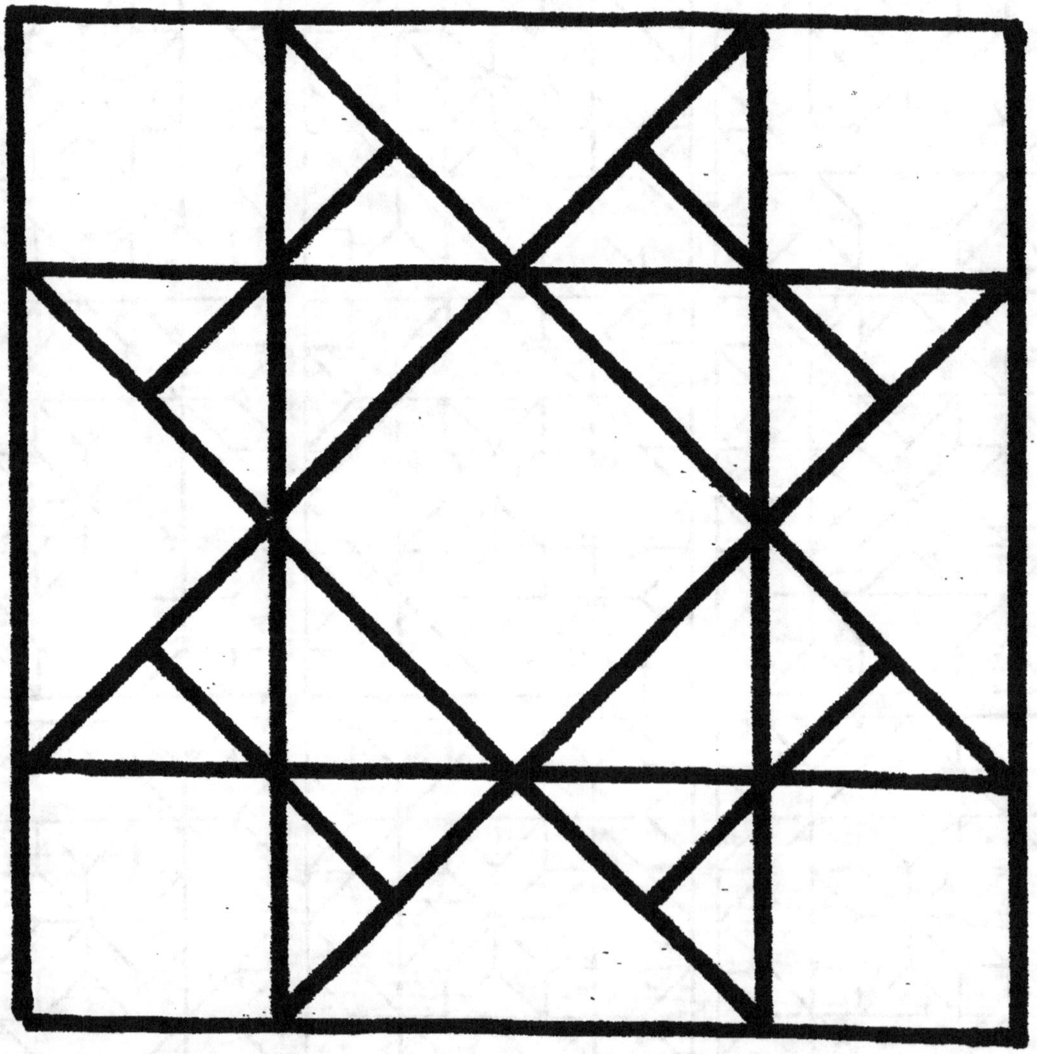

Gibson County Barn Quilt Missouri Star

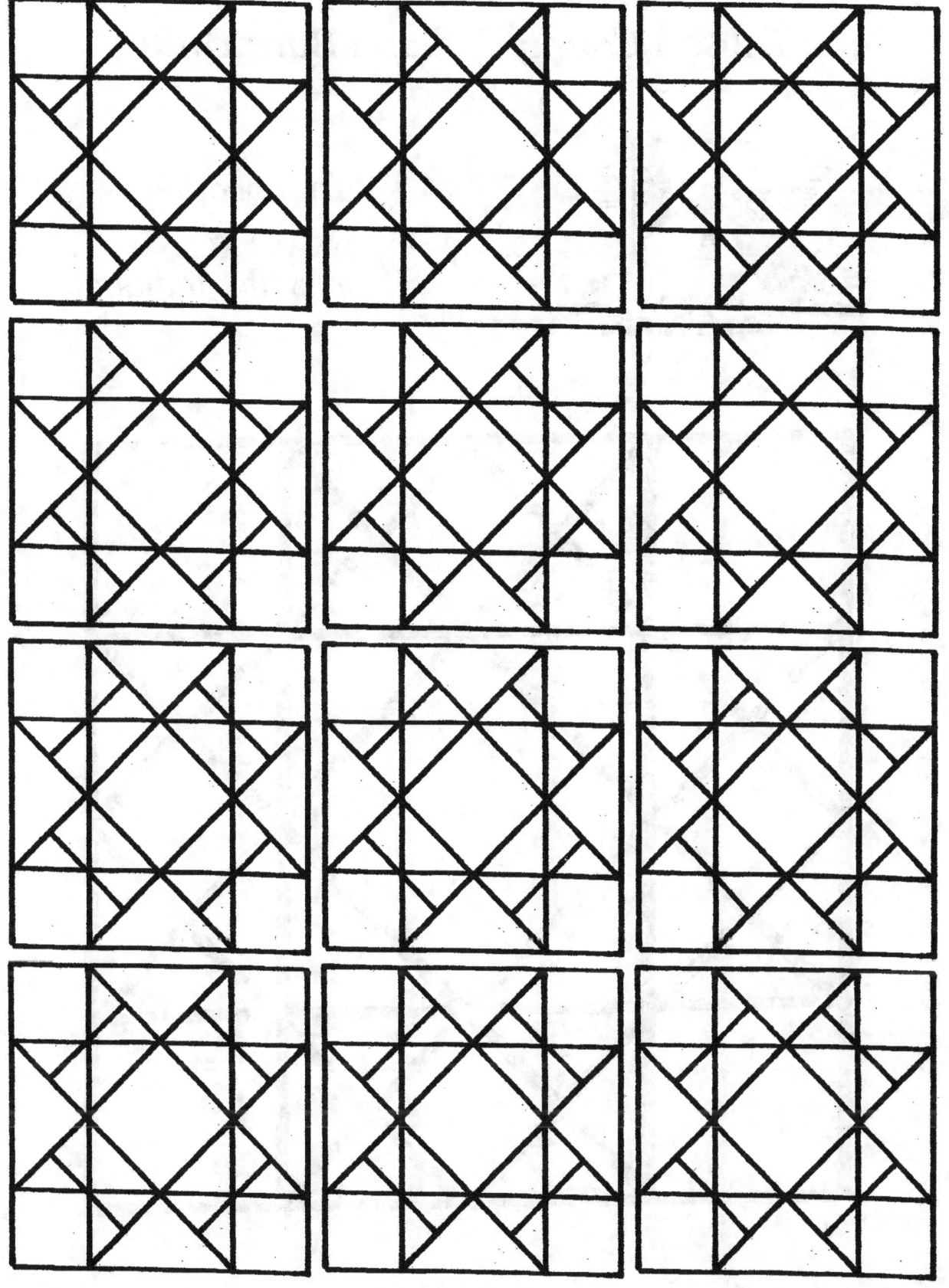

Barn Quilt Girl's Favorite
Gibson County Indiana Barn Quilt

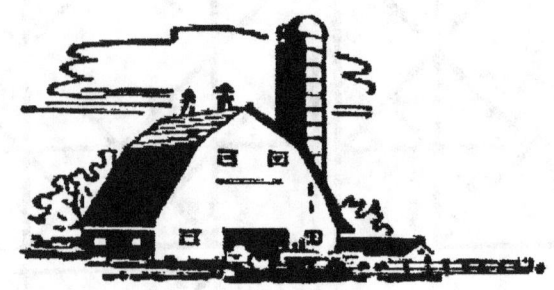

Barn Location
S 525 W
Owensville, Indiana

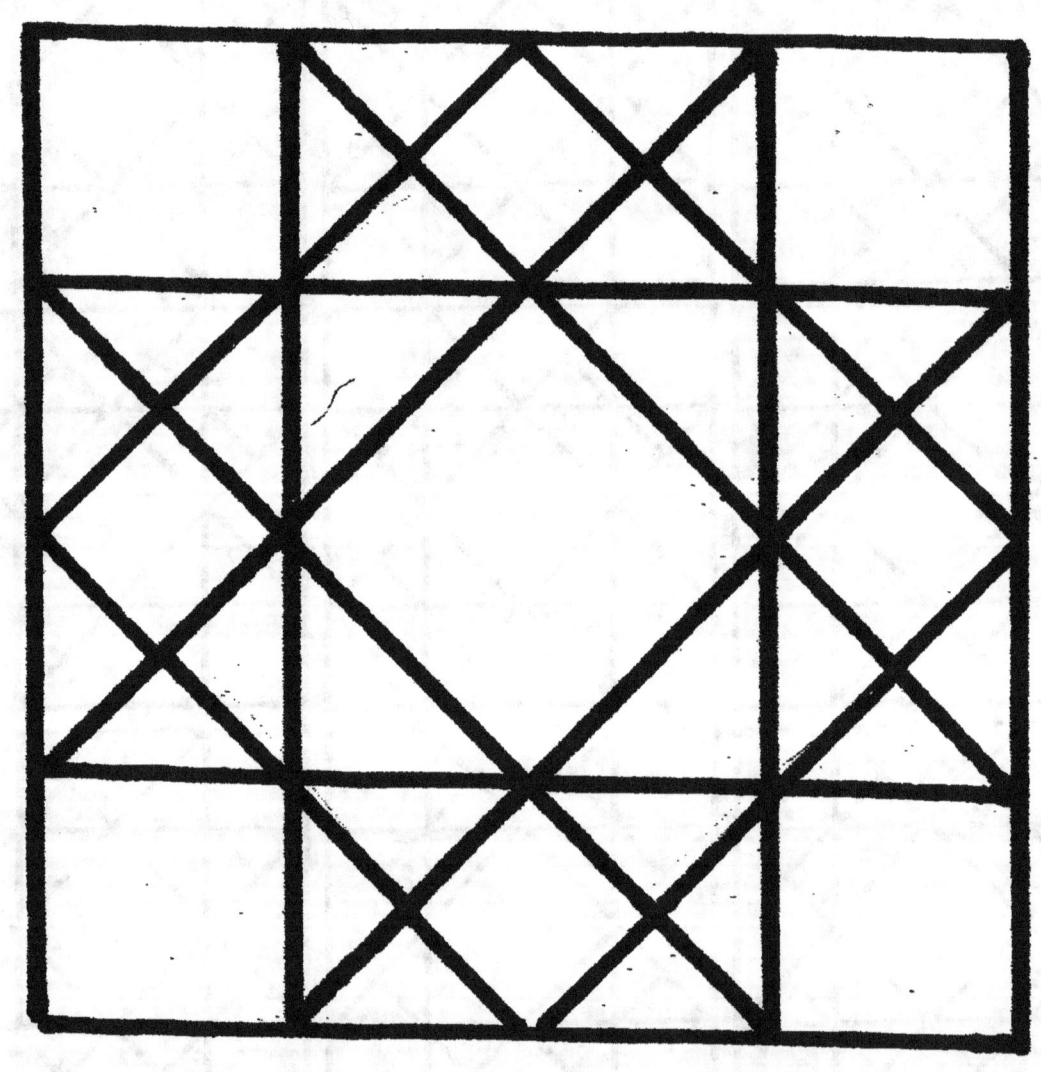

Gibson County Barn Quilt Girl's Favorite

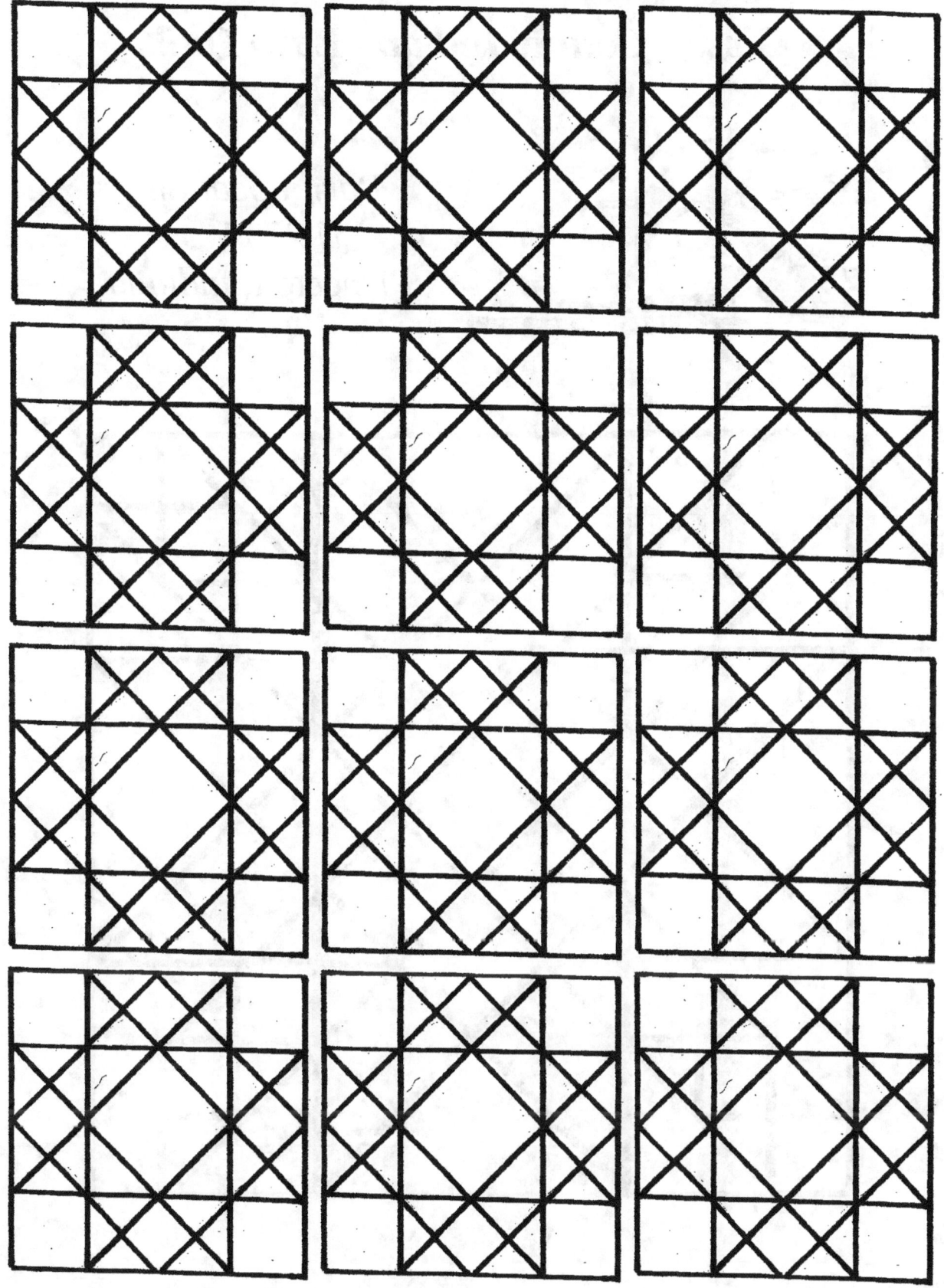

Barn Quilt Mexican Cross
Gibson County Indiana Barn Quilt

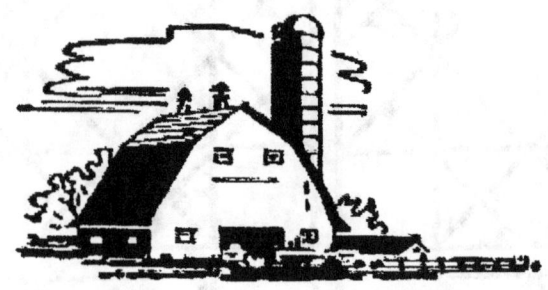

Barn Location
N 275 W
Princeton, Indiana

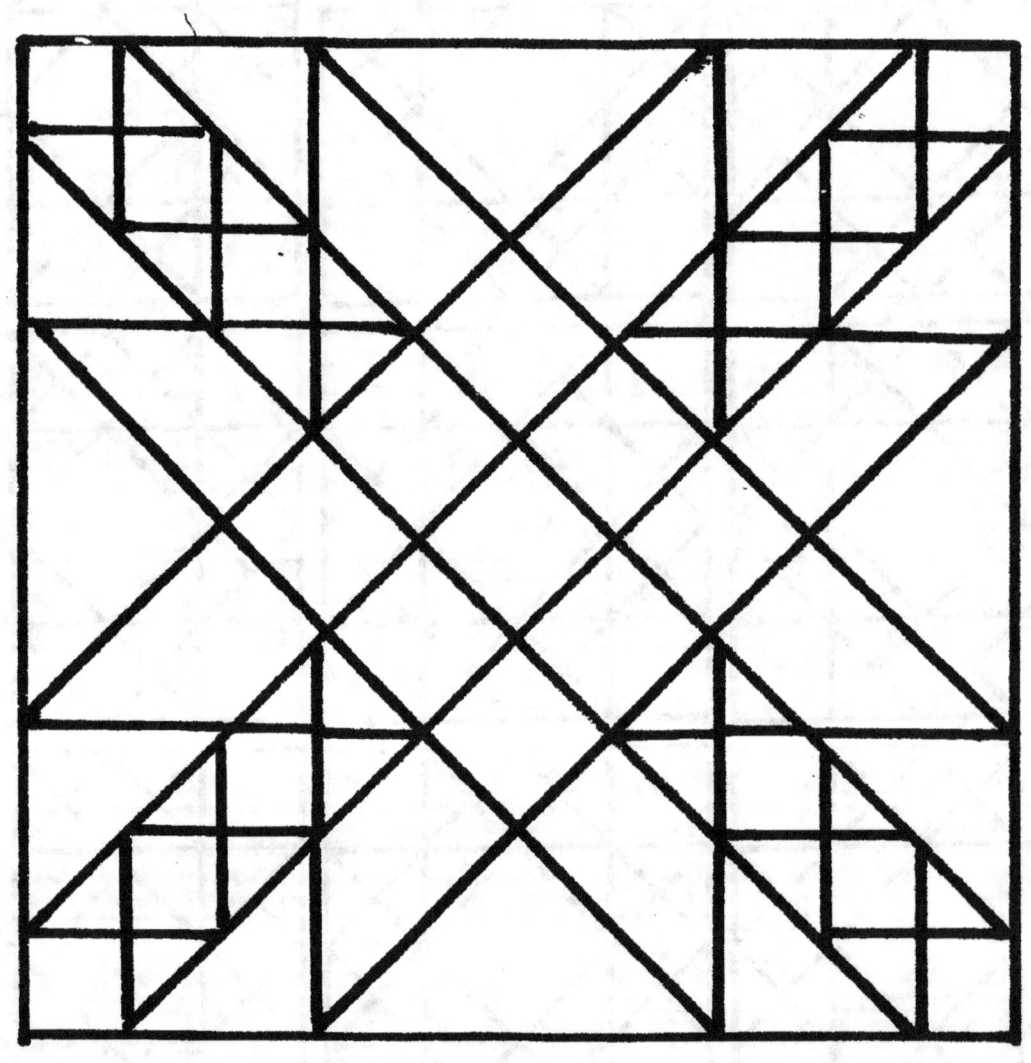

Gibson County Barn Quilt Mexican Cross

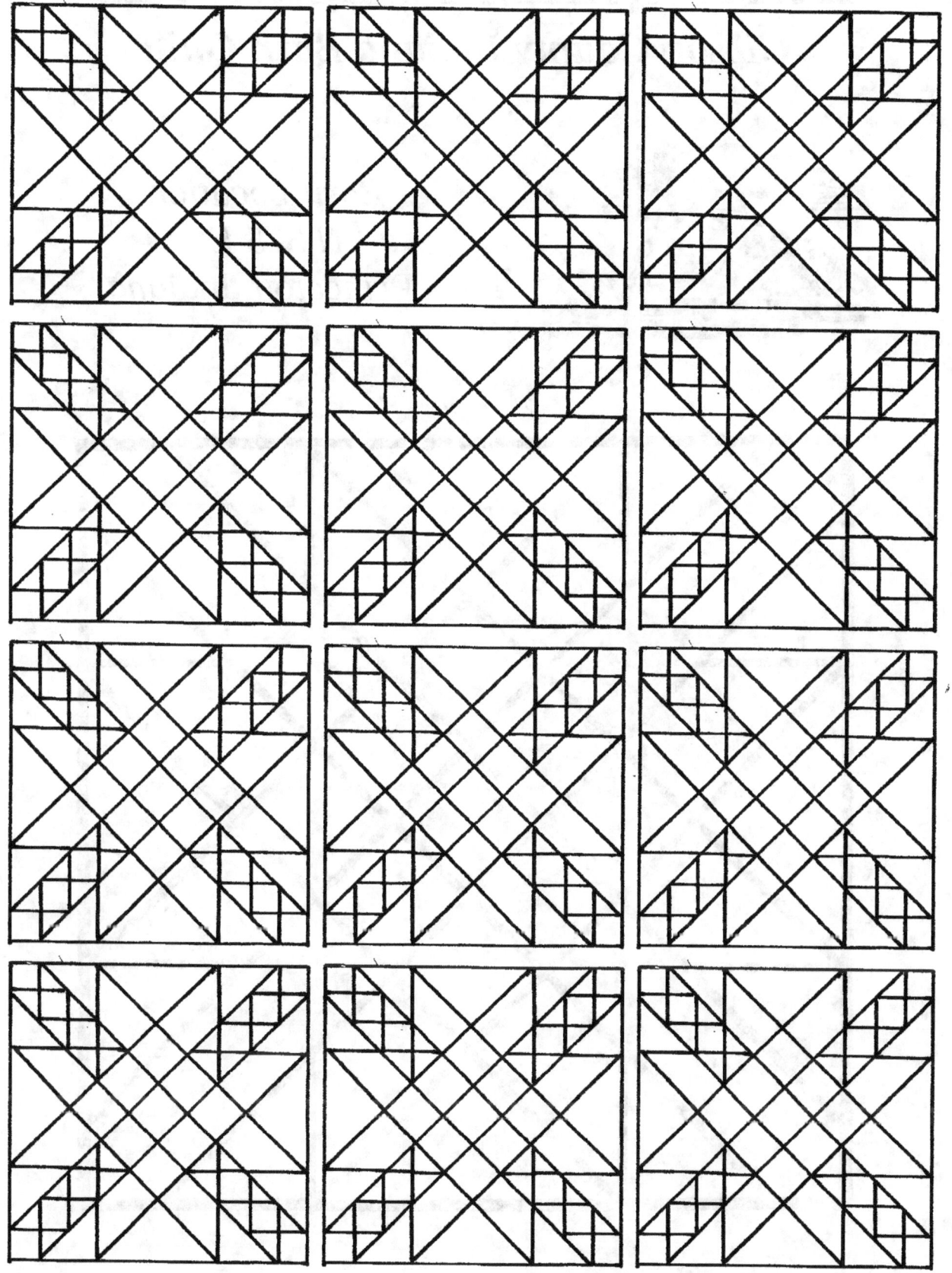

Barn Quilt Mexican Star
Gibson County Indiana Barn Quilt

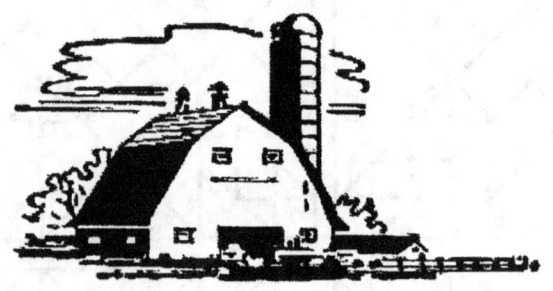

Barn Location
N 575 E
Princeton, Indiana

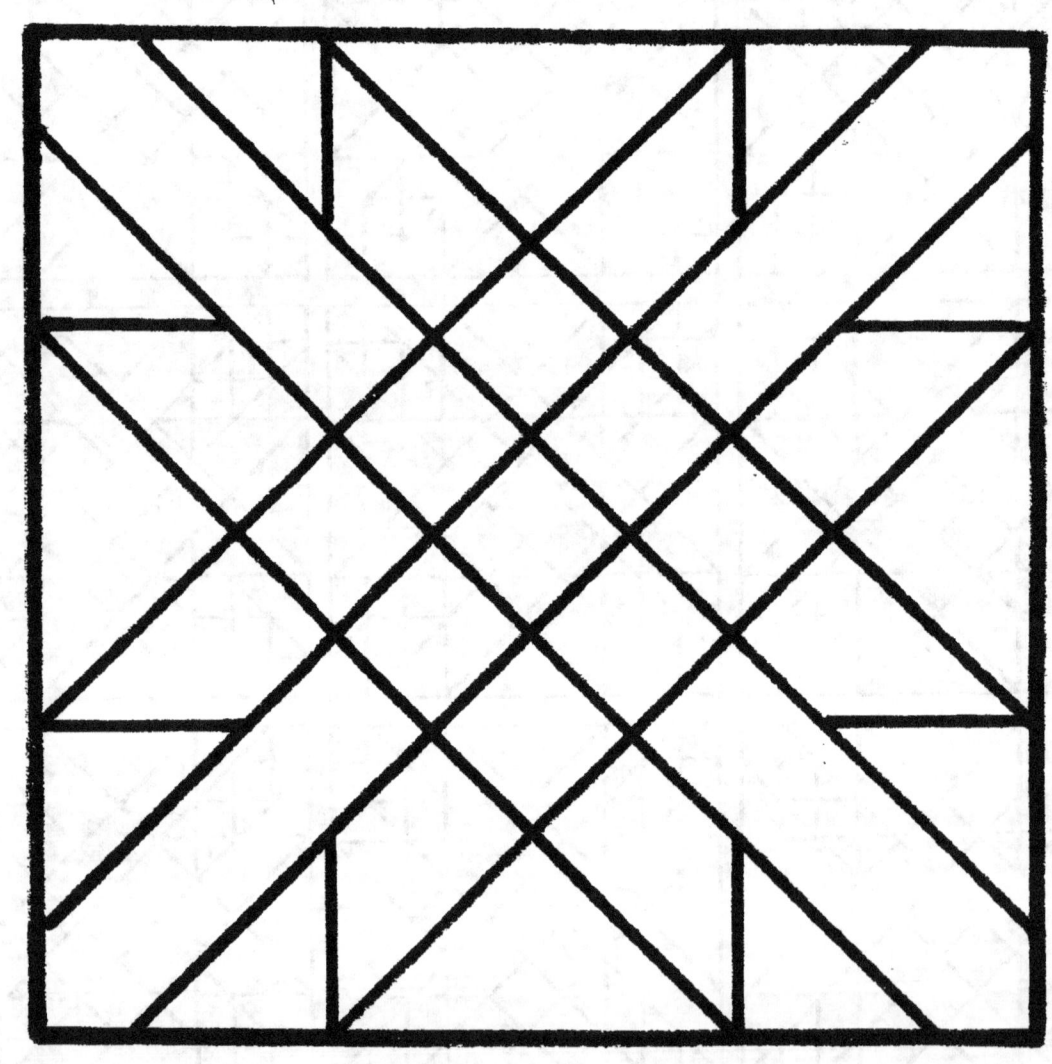

Gibson County Barn Quilt Mexican Star

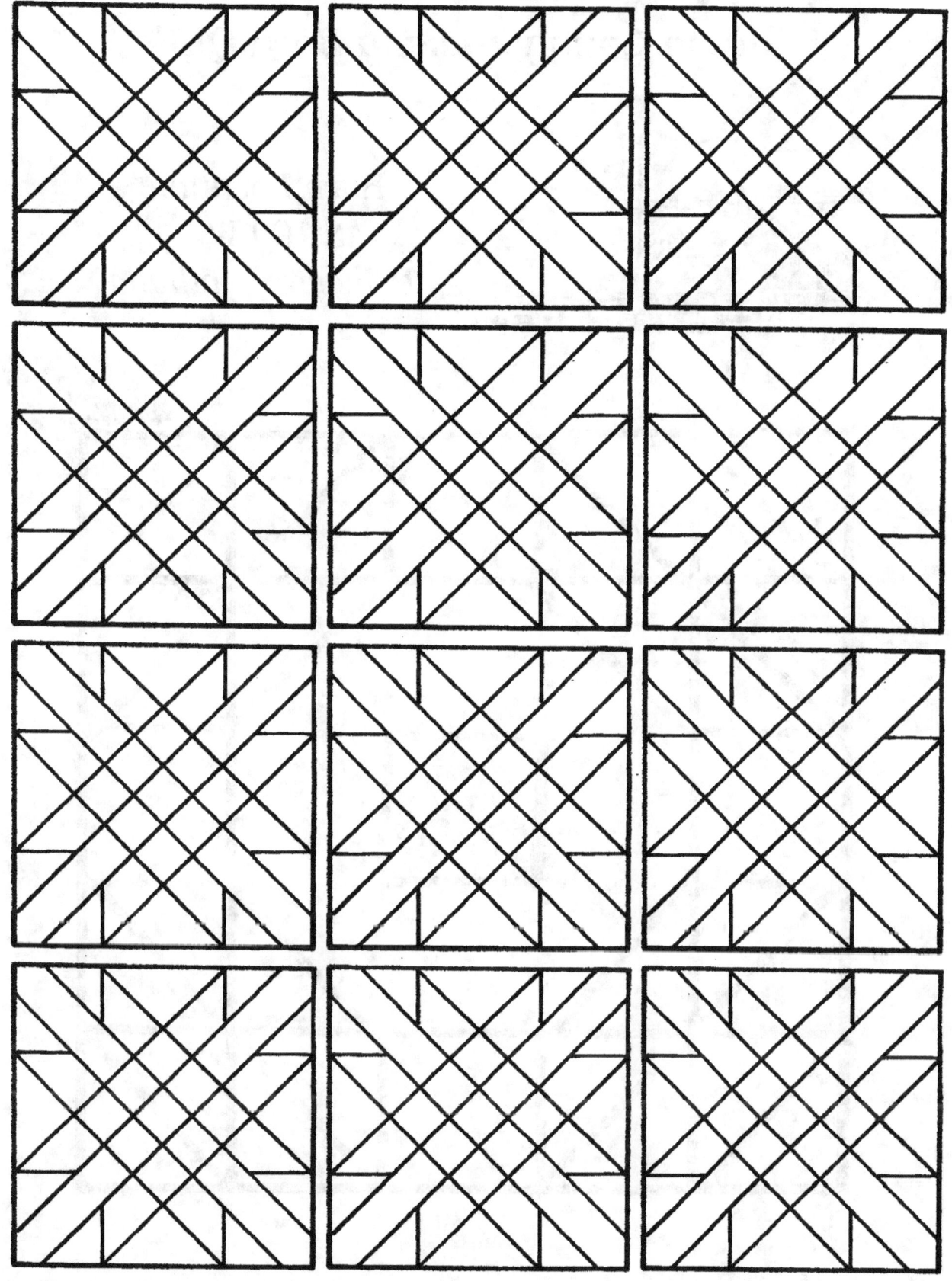

Barn Quilt Crown of Thorns
Gibson County Indiana Barn Quilt

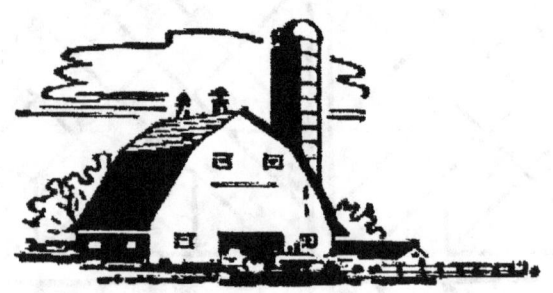

Barn Location
S 100 W
Princeton, Indiana

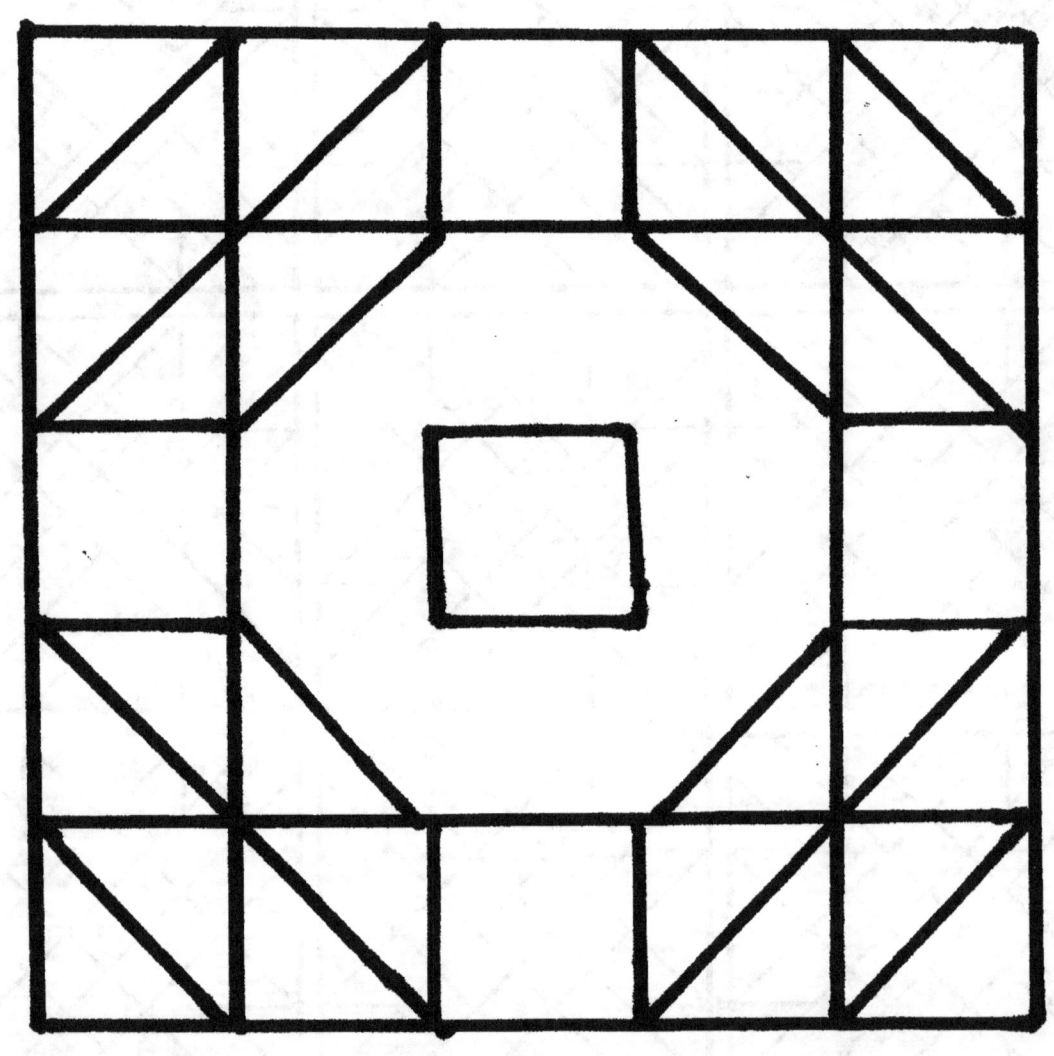

Gibson County Barn Quilt Crown of Thorns

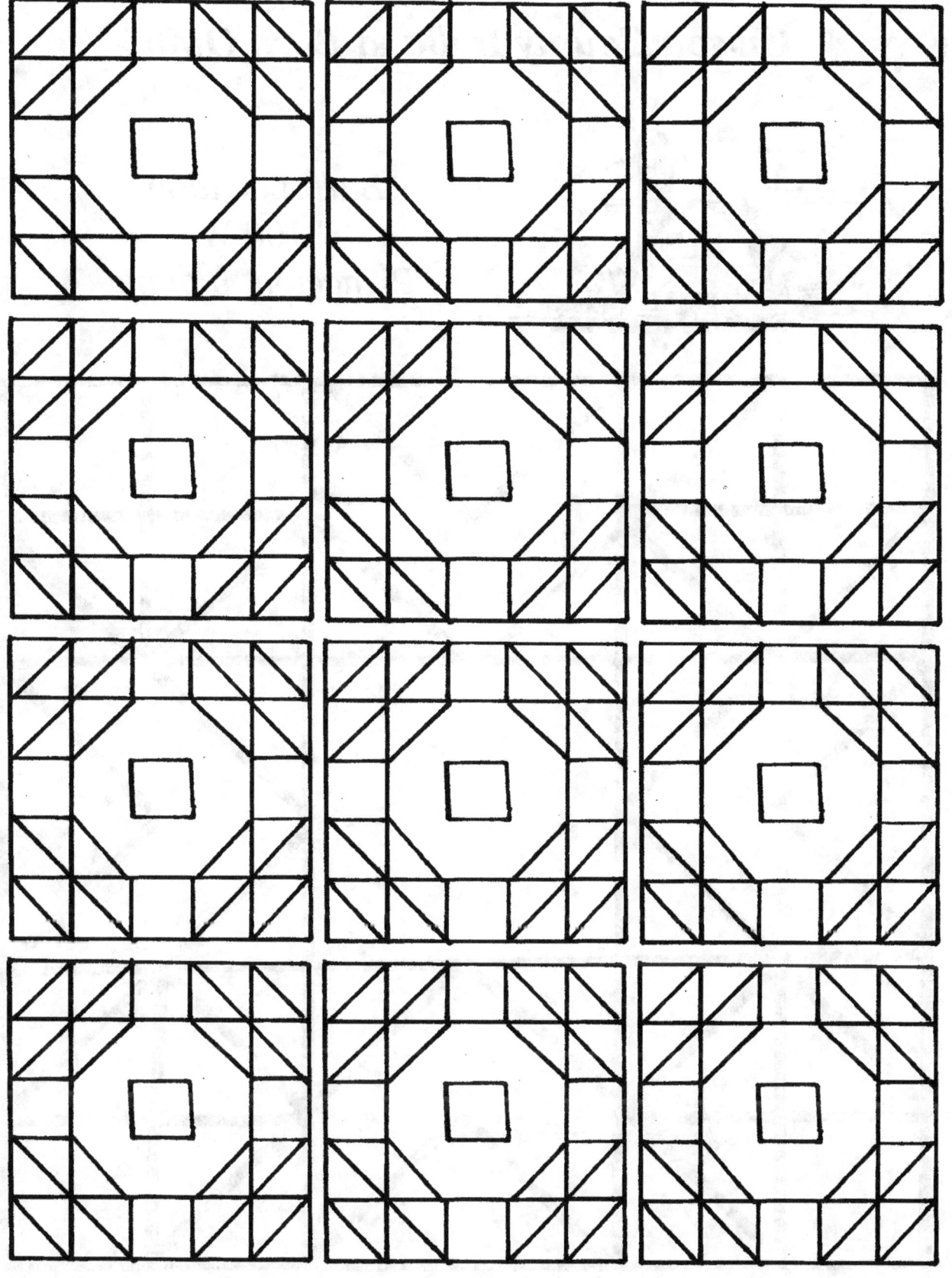

Barn Quilt Wyoming Valley
Gibson County Indiana Barn Quilt

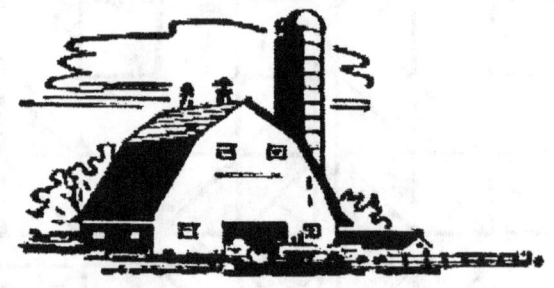

Barn Location
N 100 W
Princeton, Indiana

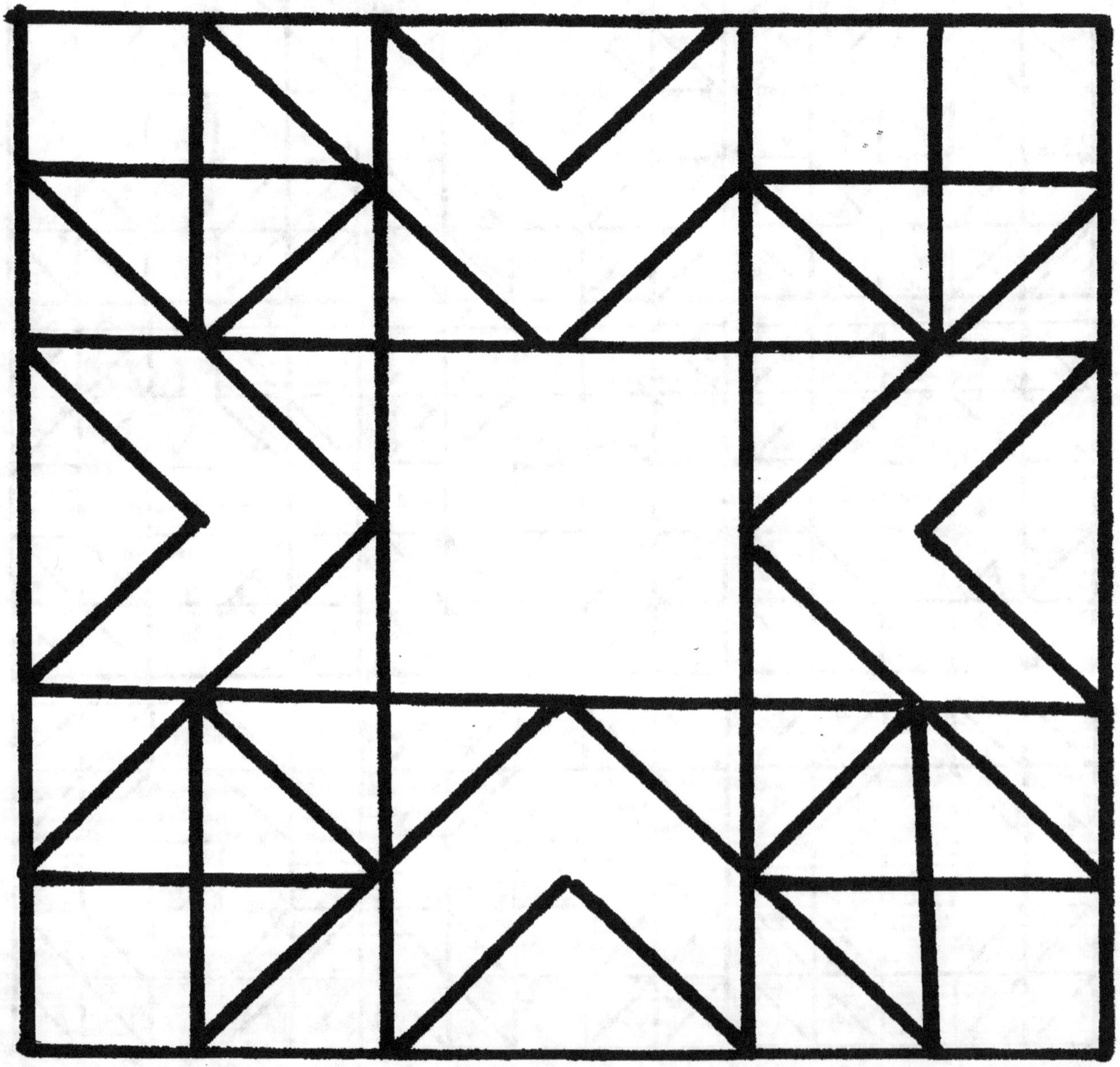

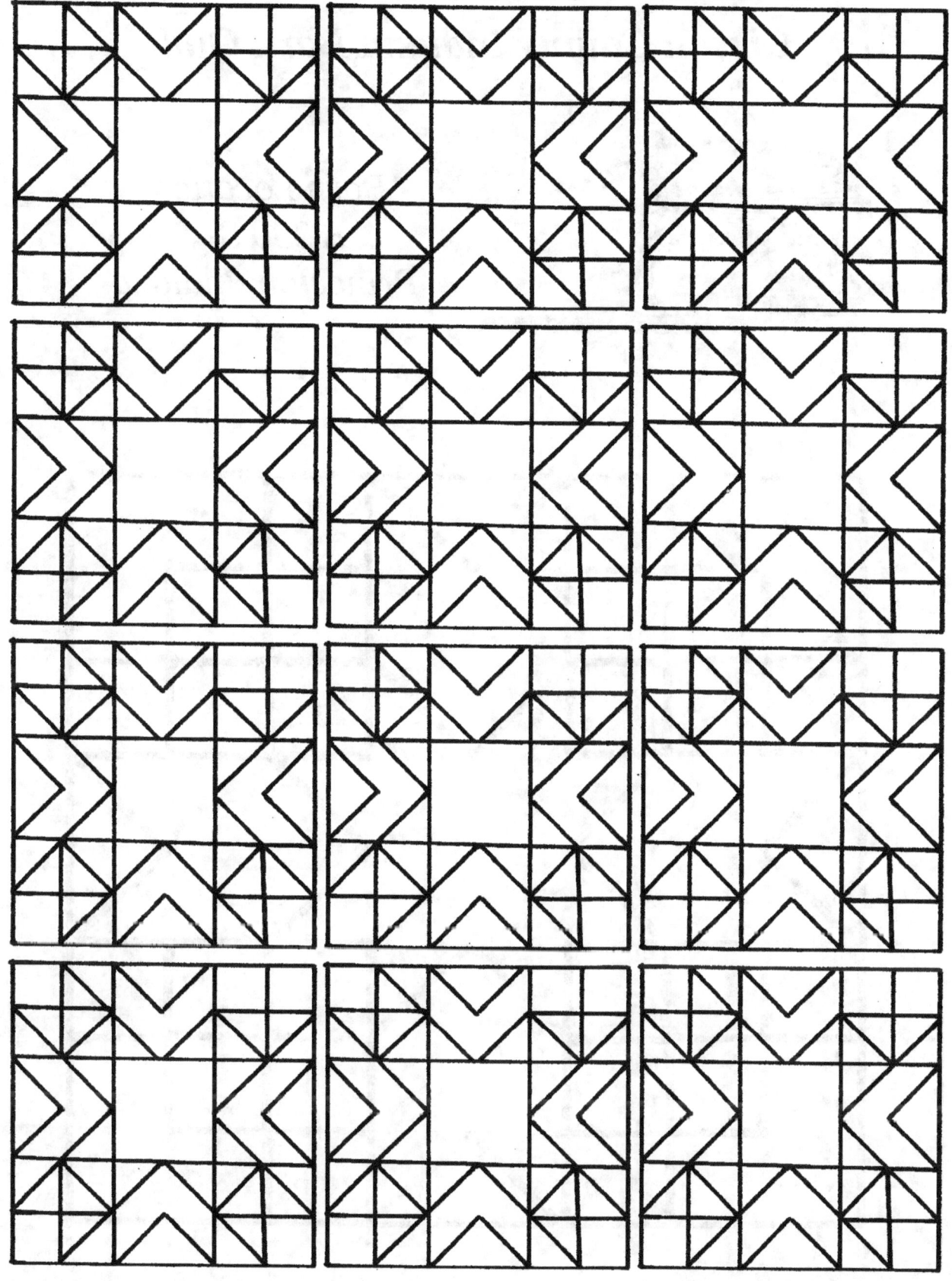

Barn Quilt Mayflower
Gibson County Indiana Barn Quilt

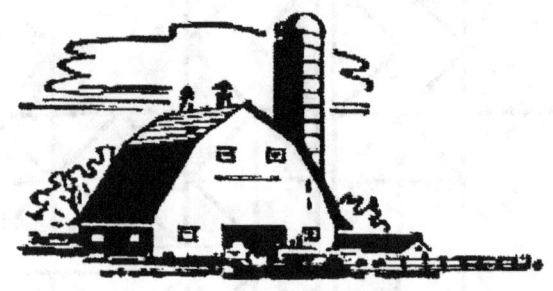

Barn Location
E 350 S
Princeton, Indiana

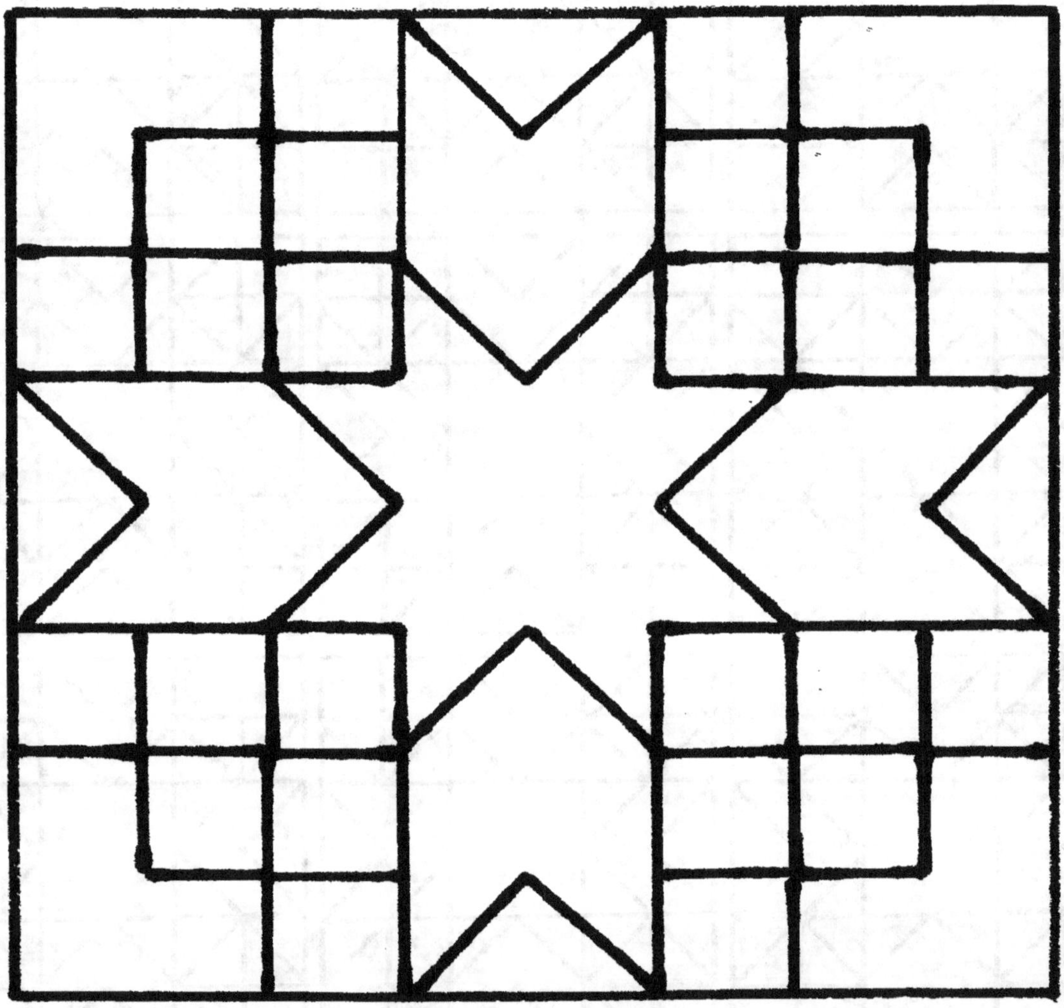

Gibson County Barn Quilt Mayflower

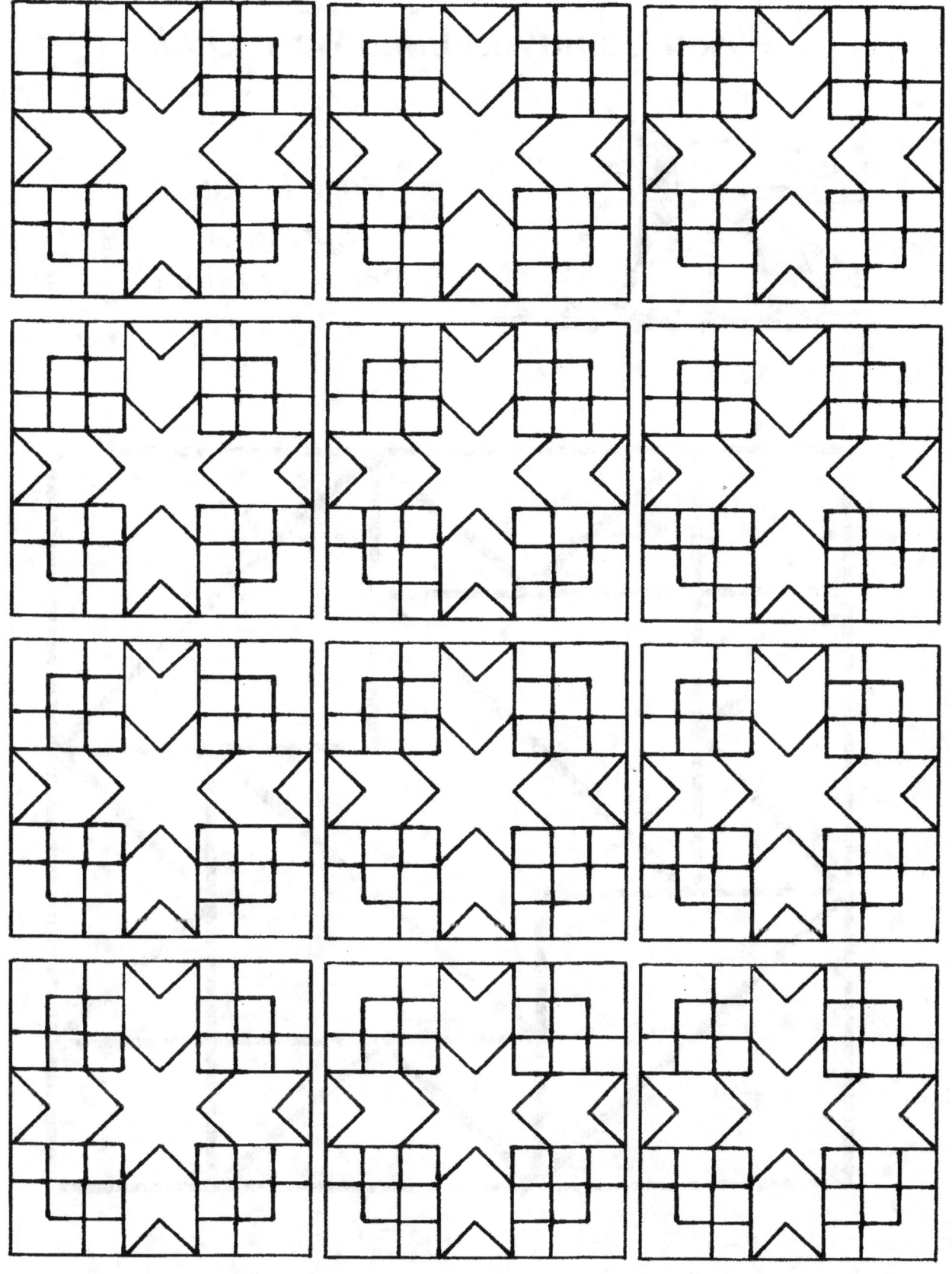

Barn Quilt Flying Geese
Gibson County Indiana Barn Quilt

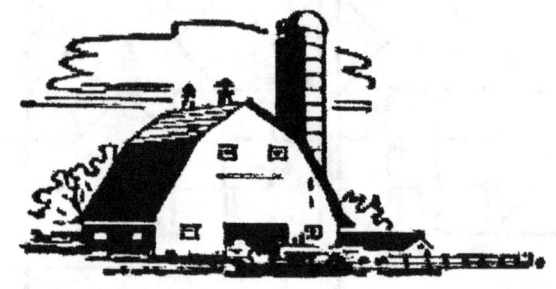

*Barn Location
Spring St
Patoka, Indiana*

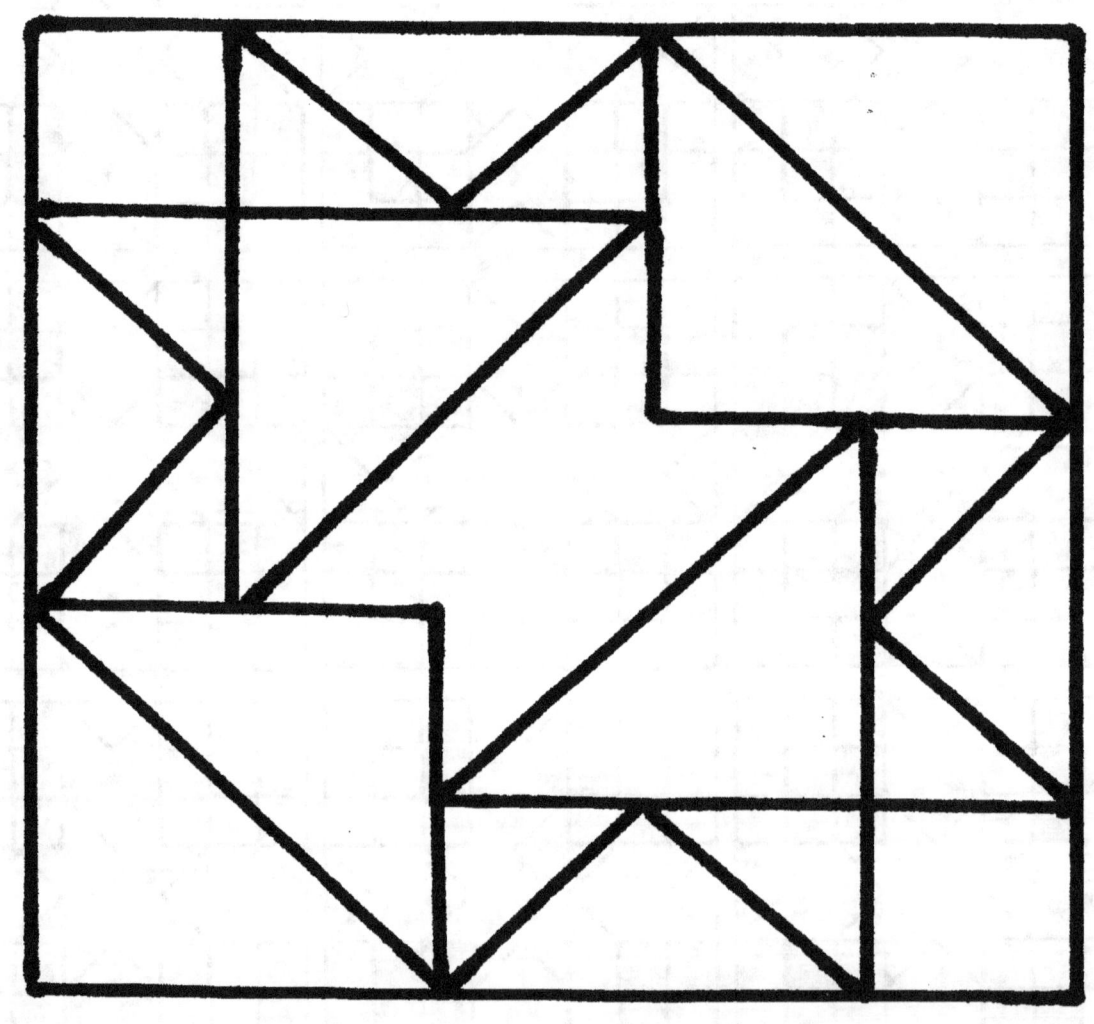

Gibson County Barn Quilt Flying Geese

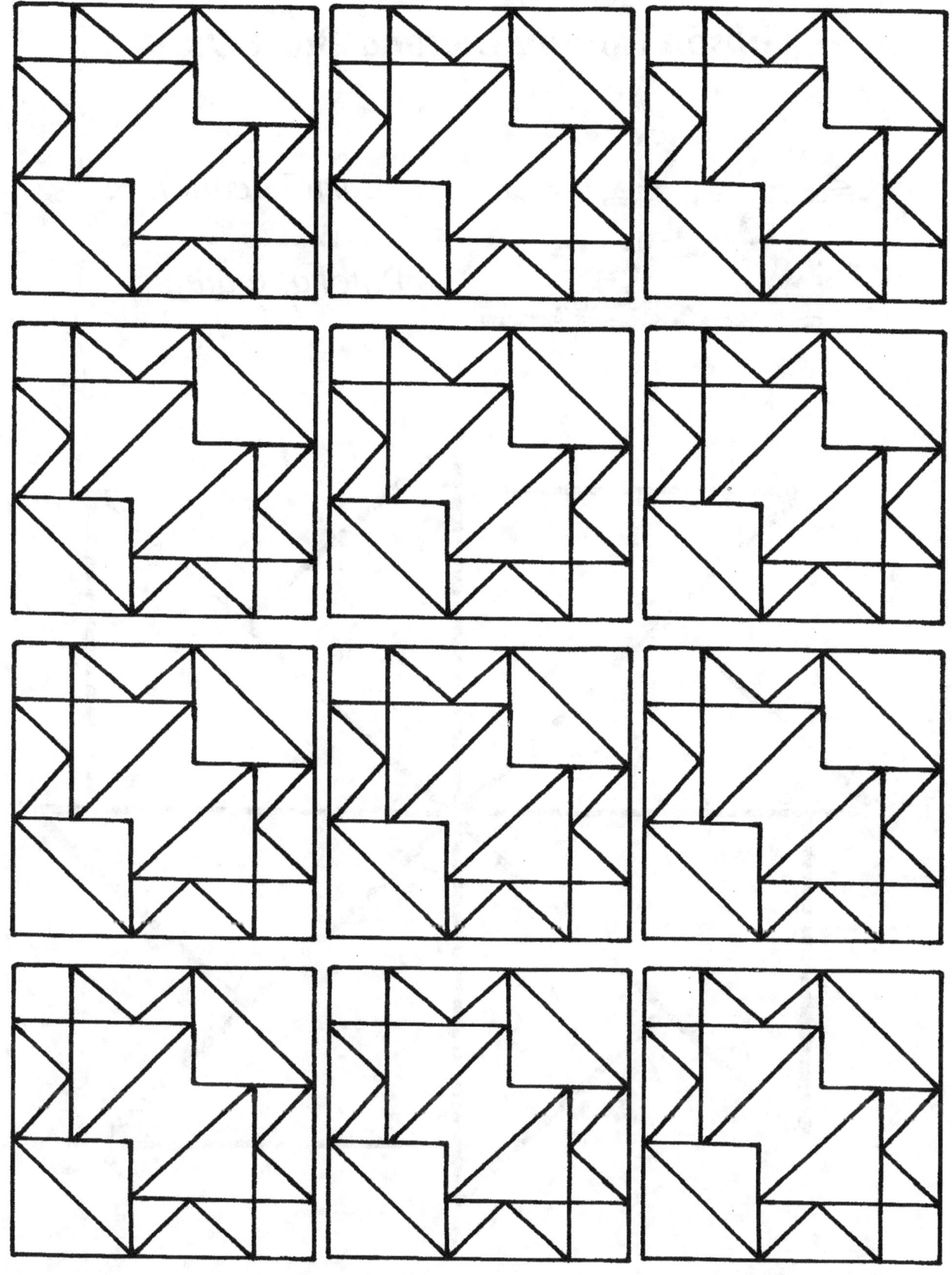

Barn Quilt Flying Kite
Gibson County Indiana Barn Quilt

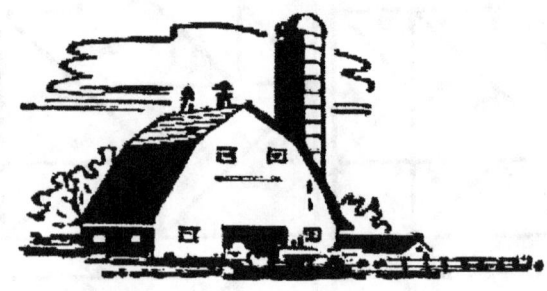

Barn Location
W 225 N
Patoka, Indiana

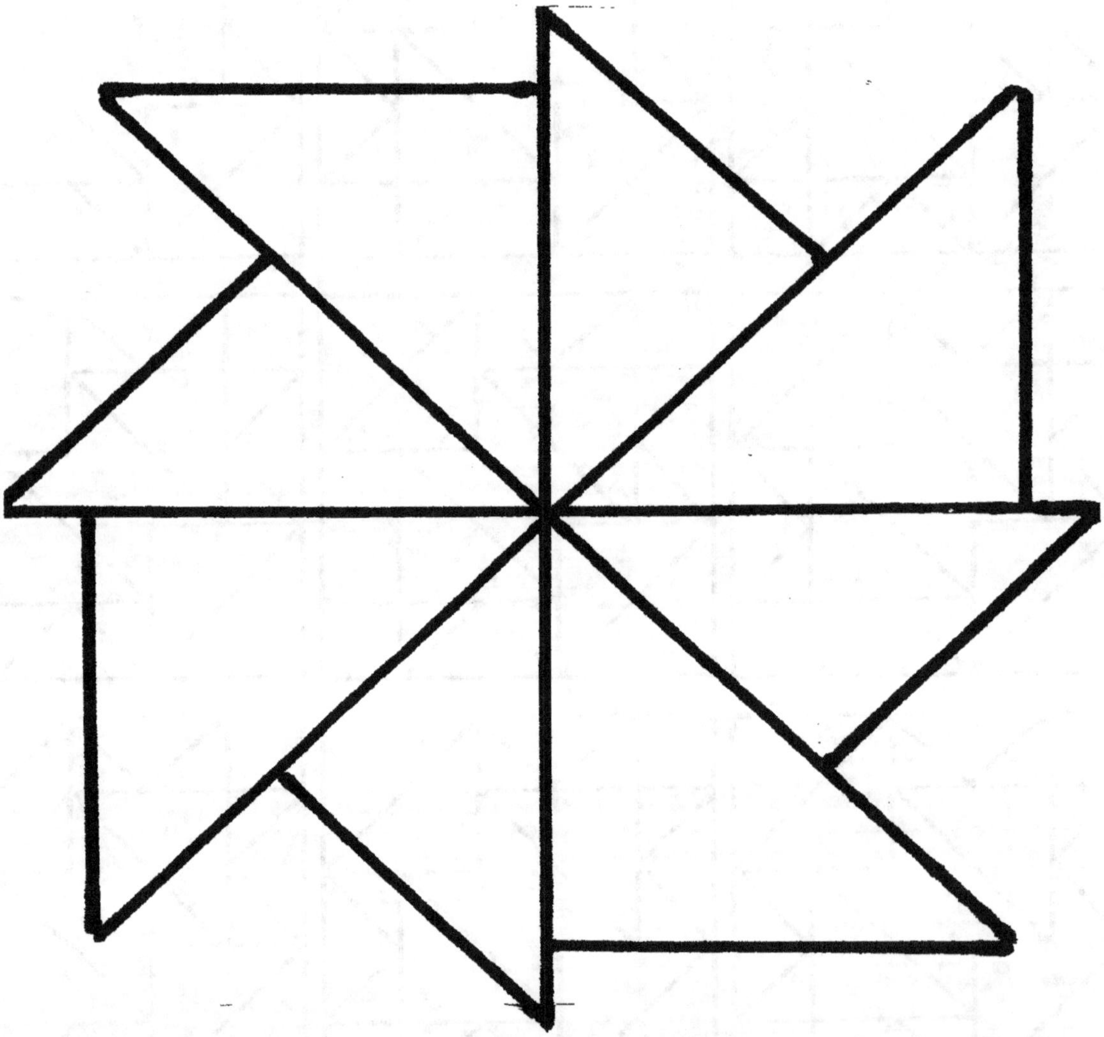

Gibson County Barn Quilt Flying Kite

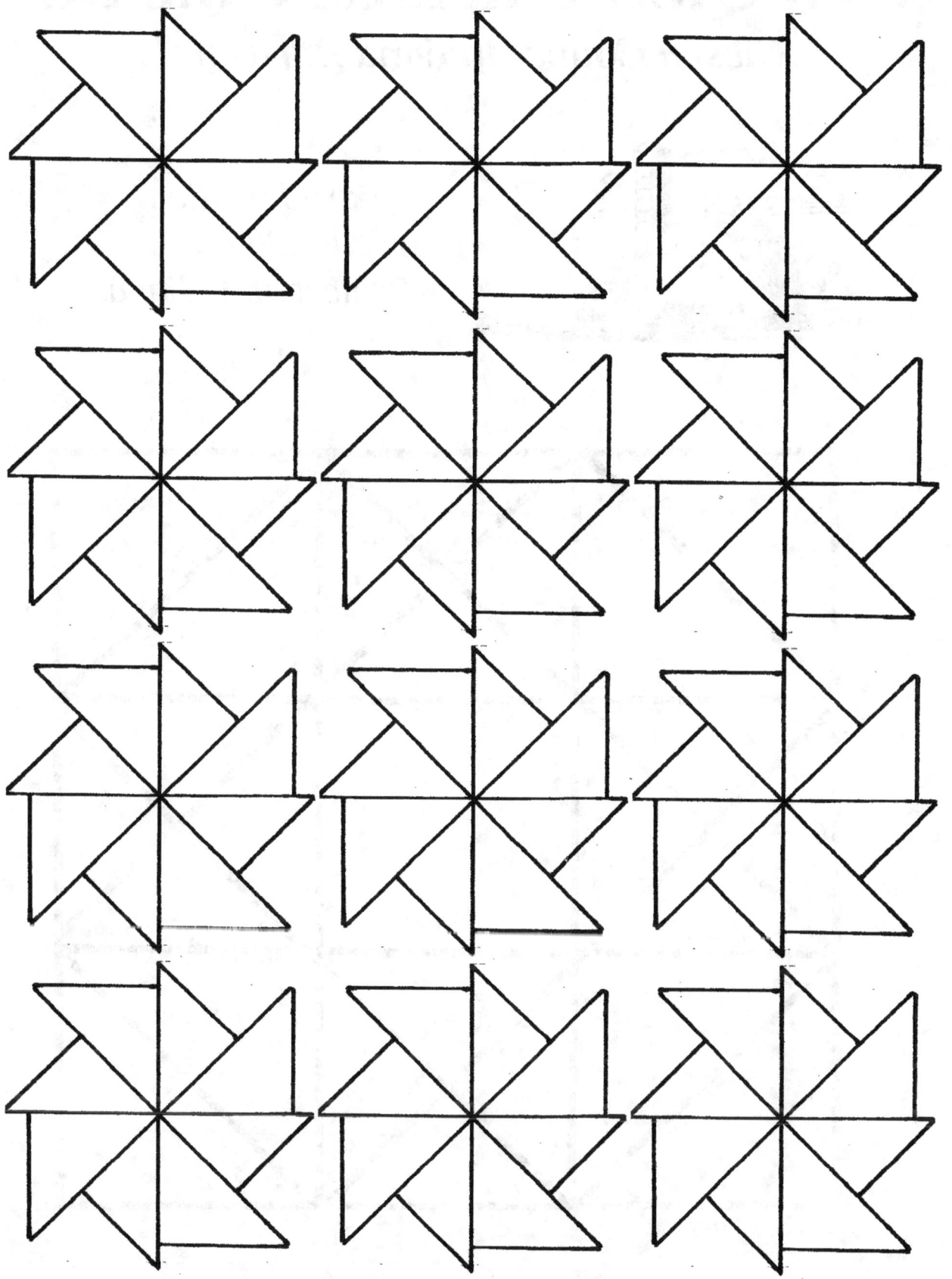

Barn Quilt Patriotic Ohio Star
Gibson County Indiana Barn Quilt

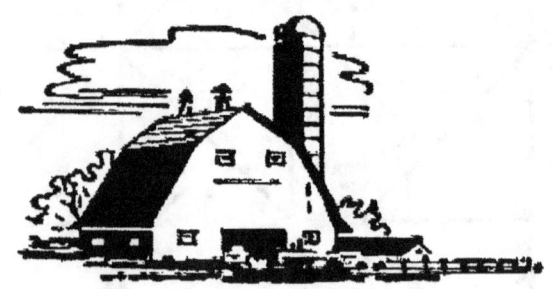

Barn Location
E 200 N
Princeton, Indiana

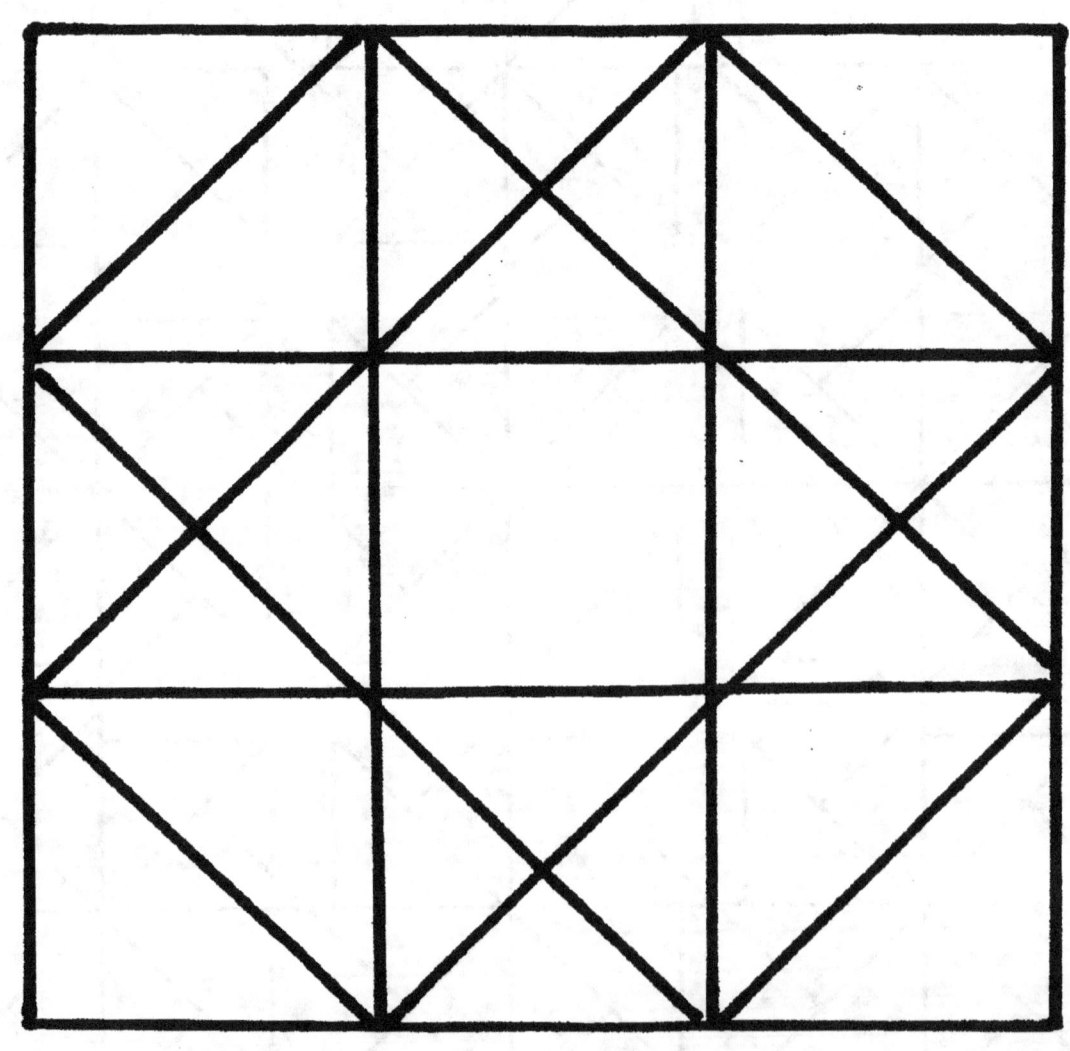

Gibson County Barn Quilt Patriotic Ohio Star

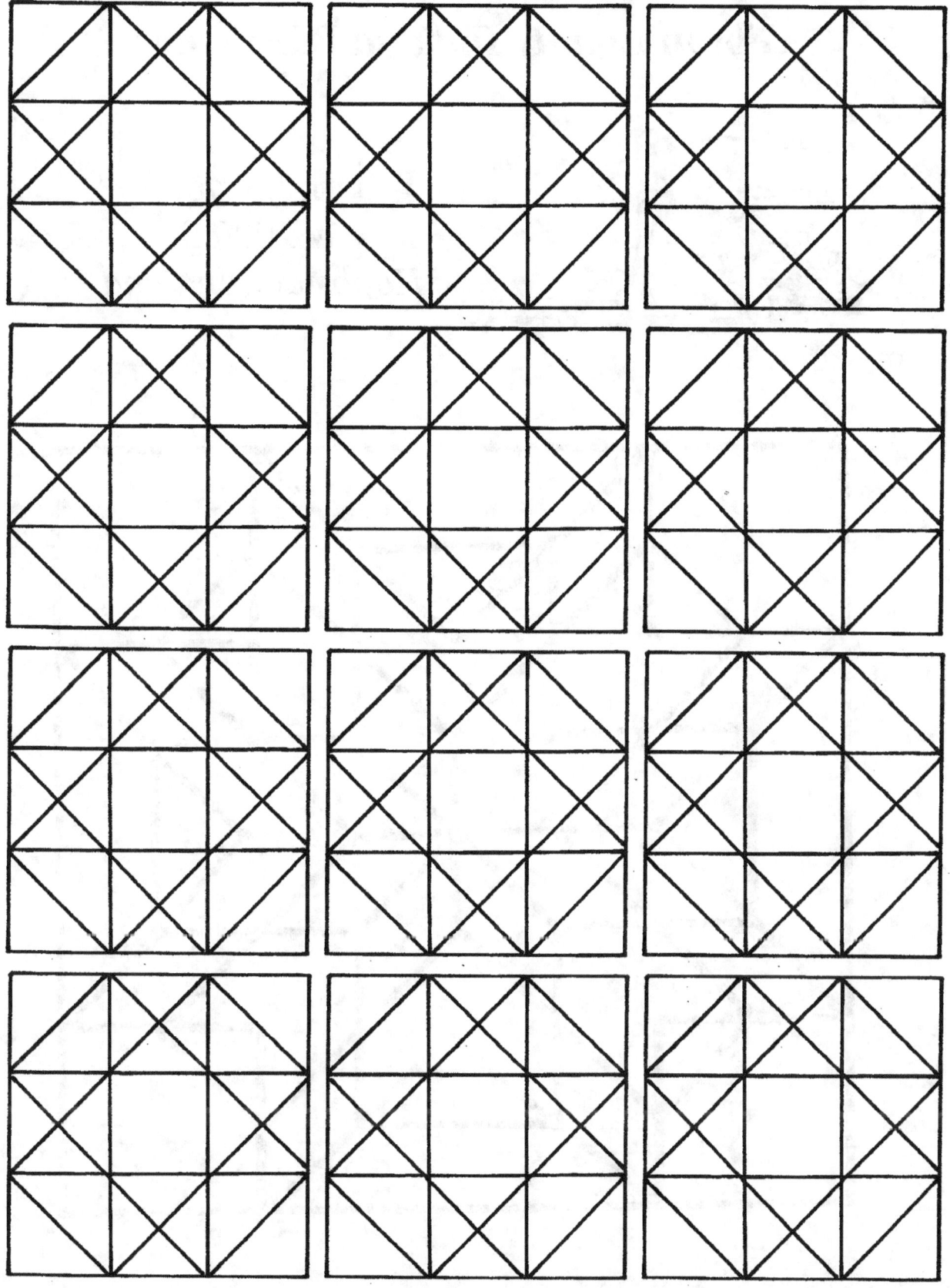

Barn Quilt Harvest Star
Gibson County Indiana Barn Quilt

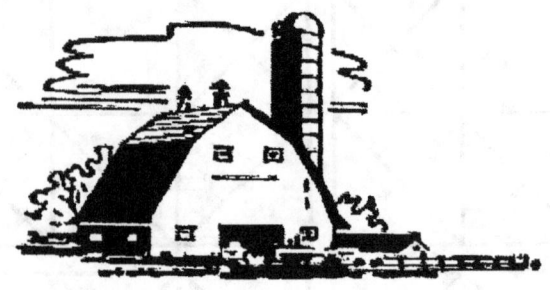

Barn Location
W 1000 S
Haubstadt, Indiana

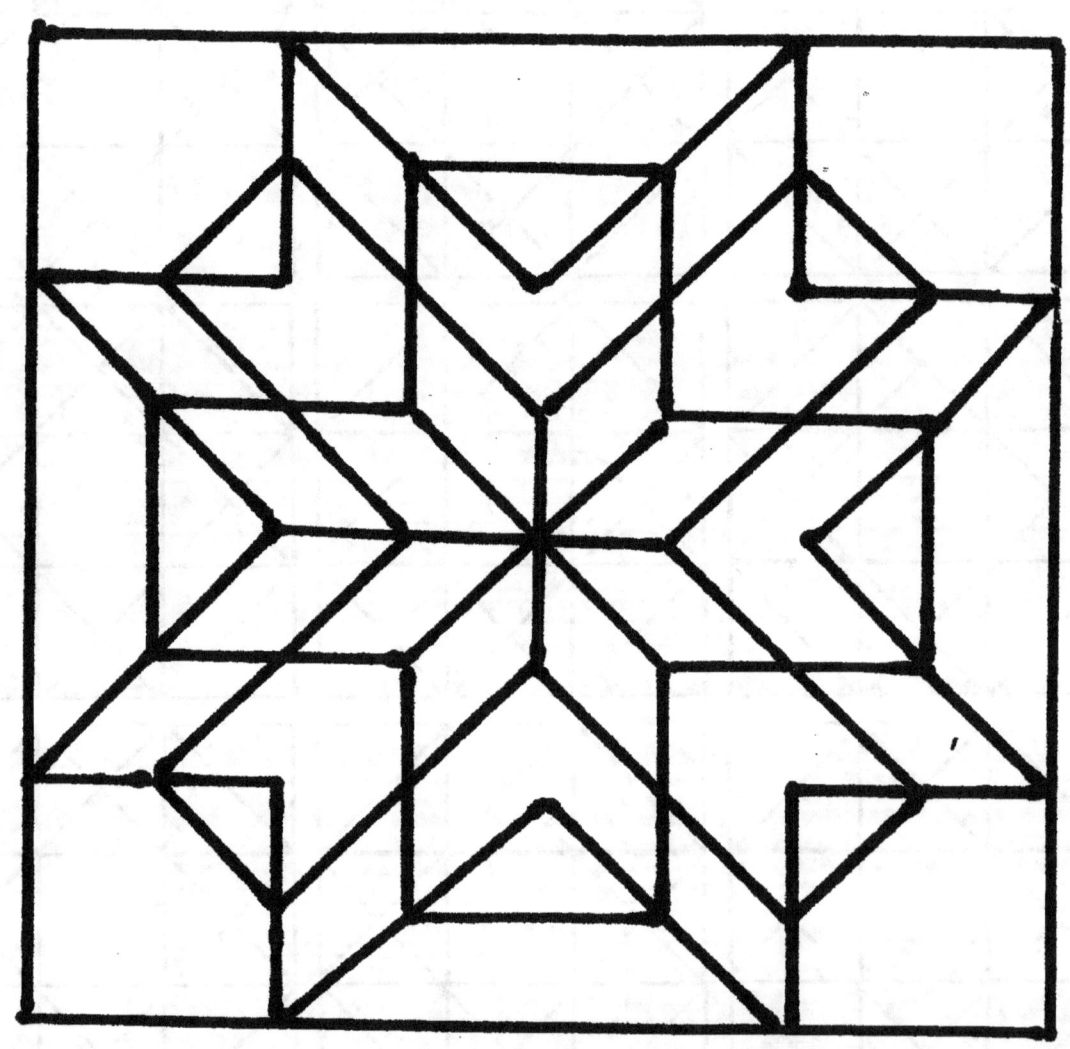

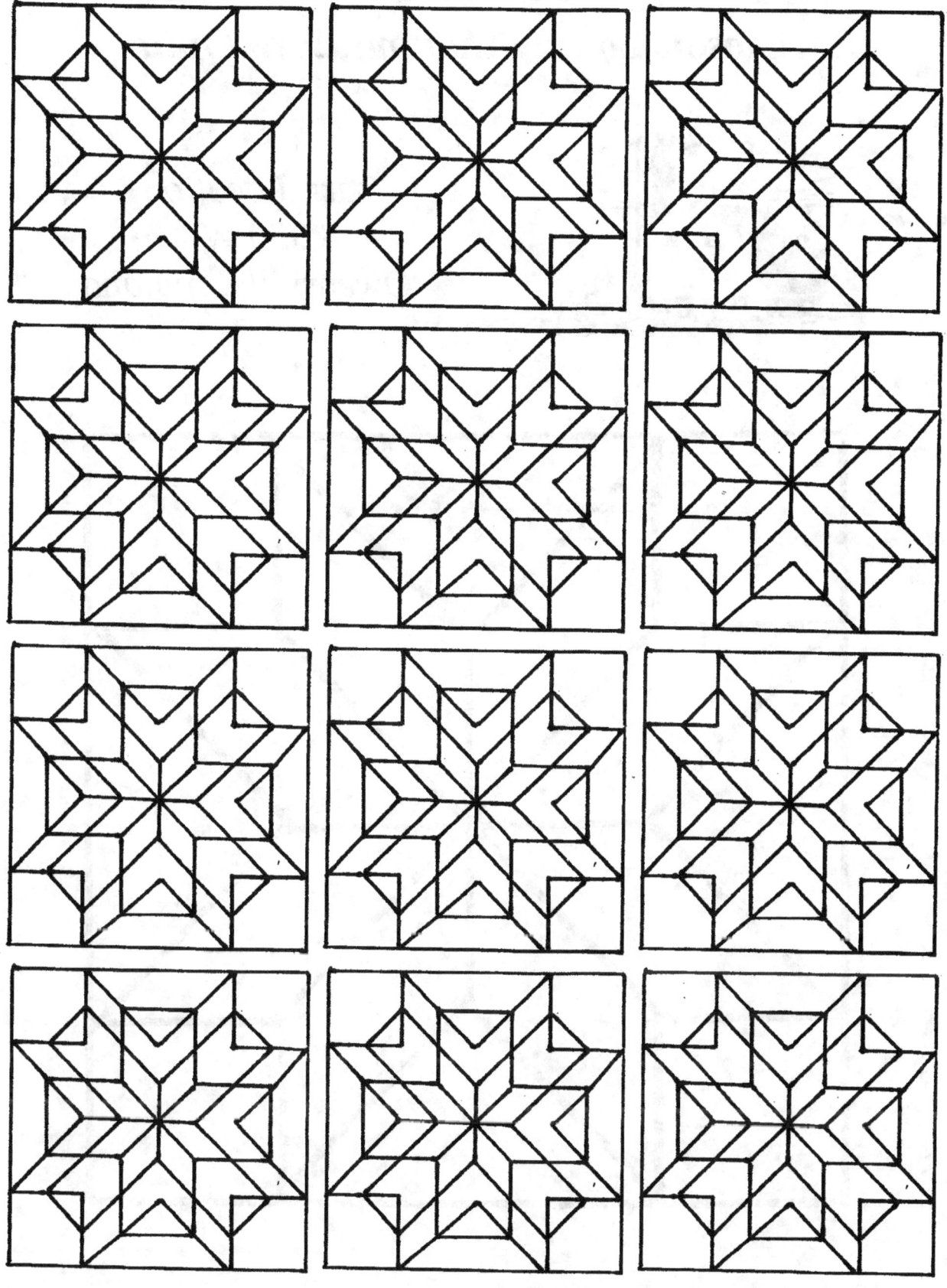

Barn Quilt LeMoyne Star

Gibson County Indiana Barn Quilt

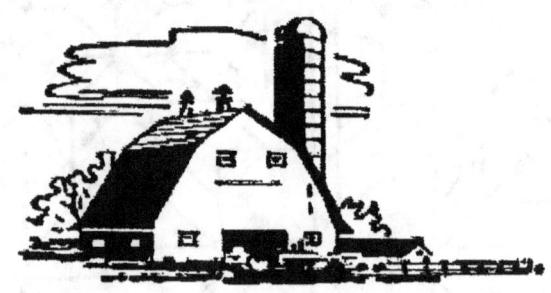

Barn Location
S 350 W
Owensville, Indiana

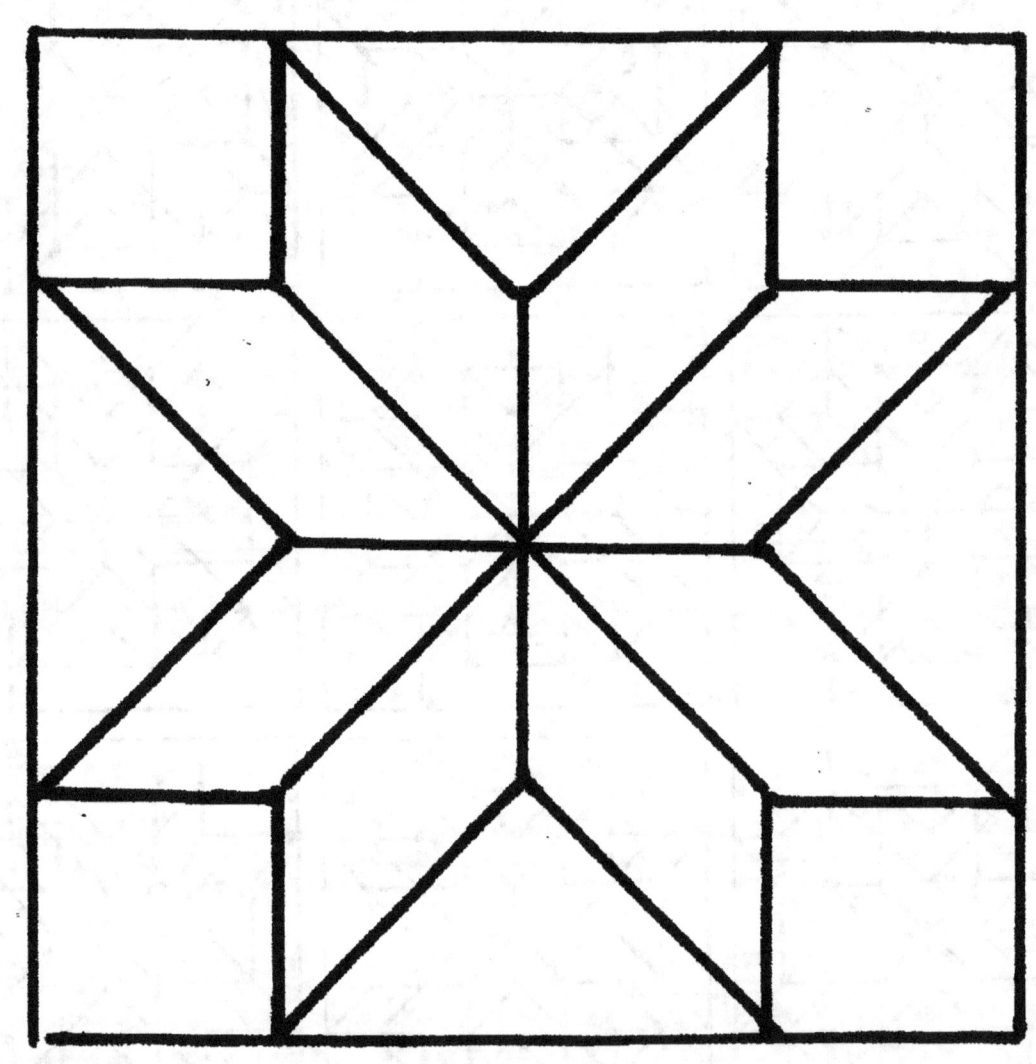

Gibson County Barn Quilt LeMoyne Star

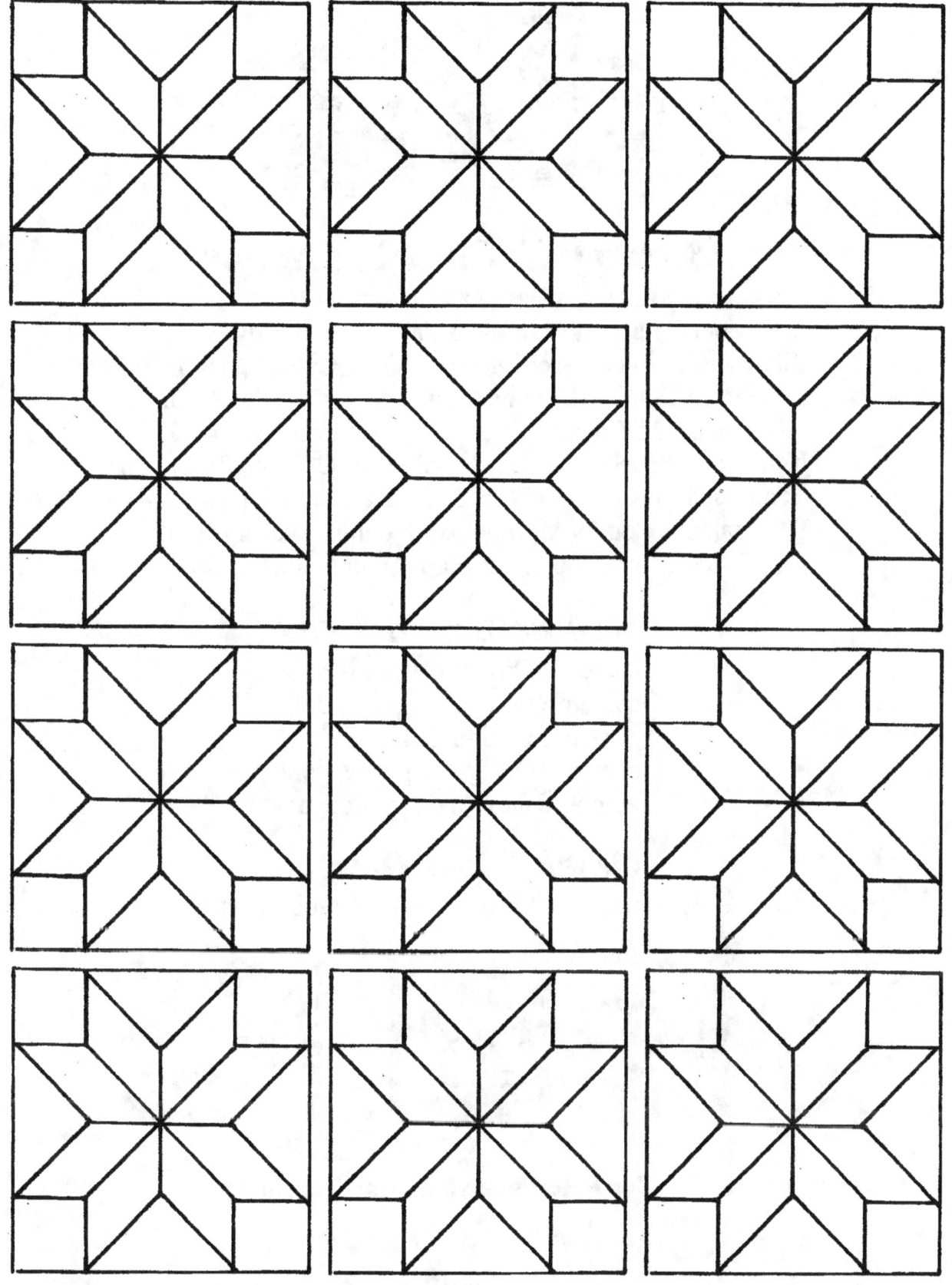

John Lettau Coloring Books

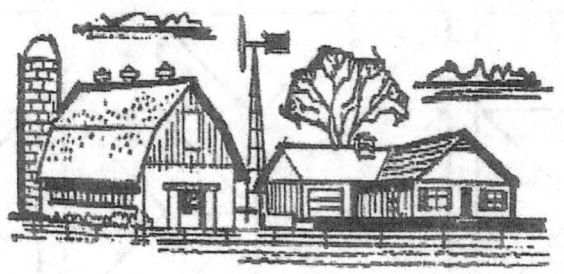

Barn Quilt Coloring Books

American Barn Quilt Coloring Book
Shawano County Wisconsin Barn Quilt Coloring Book One
Shawano County Wisconsin Barn Quilt Coloring Book Two
Green County Wisconsin Barn Quilt Coloring Book
Delaware County Iowa Barn Quilt Coloring Book
Tennessee Appalachian Barn Quilt Trail Coloring Book One
Tennessee Appalachian Barn Quilt Trail Coloring Book Two
Franklin County Vermont Barn Quilt Coloring Book
Lake County California Barn Quilt Coloring Book

Geometric Patterns

Geometric Design Coloring Book 1
Geometric Design Coloring Book 2
Geometric Design Coloring Book 3
Geometric Design Coloring Book 4
Geometric Design Coloring Book 5

Graph Paper Designs

Create Geometric Quilt Designs with Graph Paper Designs

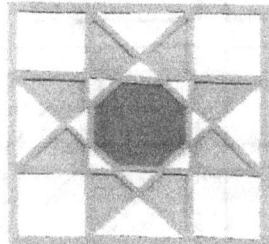 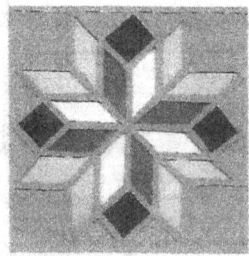 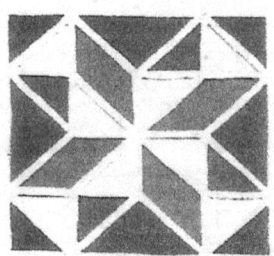

Color to Relieve Stress and Tension

Order...John H. Lettau at Amazon.com

READING & MATH BOOKS by JOHN H. LETTAU

1st Dimension	Grades 3-6
2nd Dimension	Grades 3-6
Primary Dimension	Grades 1-4
Aztec Math Primary Book One	Grades 1-3
Aztec Math Primary Book Two	Grades 1-3
Aztec Math Intermediate Book One	Grades 3-6
Aztec Math Intermediate Book Two	Grades 3-6
Aztec Math Jr. High Book One	Grades 5-8
Aztec Math Jr. High Book Two	Grades 5-8
Aztec Math Decimal Book	Grades 4-8
Aztec Math Fraction Book	Grades 4-8
Sum-Action Number Puzzle Book One	Grades 3-6
Sum-Action Number Puzzle Book Two	Grades 3-6
Sum-Action Number Puzzle Primary Book One	Grades 1-3
Sum-Action Number Puzzle Primary Book Two	Grades 1-3
Multiplication Number Puzzles	Grades 3-6
Geometric Design Puzzle Book One	Grades 3-6
Geometric Design Puzzle Book Two	Grades 3-6
Aztec Reading Primary Book One	Grades 1-3
Aztec Reading Primary Book Two	Grades 1-3
Math in Action	Grades 3-6
A-Maze-ing Number Puzzles	Grades 3-6
Graph Paper Designs	Grades 2-6
Pick-A-Dilly Papers	Grades 3-6
Awards for All Reasons	Grades 1-6
Time Marches On	Grades 1-3
Pennies, Nickels & Dimes	Grades 1-3
Super-Sum Activity Cards	Grades 3-6
Learning Center Game Boards	Grades 1-3
Aztec Design Coloring Book	Grades 1-6

www.ingramcontent.com/pod-product-compliance
Lightning Source LLC
Chambersburg PA
CBHW081738220526
45468CB00008B/2144